GENDER & SEXUALITY:
Perspectives on LGBT History and
Current Issues in a Changing World

GENDER & SEXUALITY:
Perspectives on LGBT History and
Current Issues in a Changing World

By

Jeremy T. Goldbach
University of Southern California

Matt Kailey
Metropolitan State College of Denver

Michael Phillips
Collin College

Carolyn Perry
Collin College

Abigail Press   Wheaton, IL 60189

Design and Production: Abigail Press
Typesetting: Abigail Press
Typeface: AGaramond
Cover Art: Sam Tolia

Gender & Sexuality: Perspectives on LGBT History and Current Issues in a Changing World

First Edition, 2015
Printed in the United States of America
Translation rights reserved by the authors
ISBN 1-890919-80-2
13 digit: 978-1-890919-80-1

Dedicated to Matt Kailey

His reasonable voice and tireless efforts
to make the world a kinder place

I don't remember being born and I'm not going to remember dying, so the thing that really matters is what I did with the life I was given in between those two events.

Matt Kailey

Contents in Brief

INTRODUCTION 1

CHAPTER ONE
    UNDERSTANDING SEXUALITY IN THE NINETEENTH CENTURY 5

CHAPTER TWO
    SEXUALITY IN THE TWENTIETH CENTURY 17

CHAPTER THREE
    THE BIRTH OF THE GAY CIVIL RIGHTS MOVEMENT....................................27

CHAPTER FOUR
    GAY PROTEST AND REBELLION IN THE 1960s AND 1970s.................................43

CHAPTER FIVE
    HIV 101...61

CHAPTER SIX
    SOCIOCULTURAL AND HISTORICAL IMPACT OF HIV/AIDS IN
    THE GAY COMMUNITY..73

CHAPTER SEVEN
    TRANSGENDER AND BEYOND..91

CHAPTER EIGHT
    TRANSGENDER ISSUES 111

CHAPTER NINE
    CREATING AN AMERICAN LGBT LITERARY TRADITION...................................133

CHAPTER TEN
    LGBT CHARACTERS AND CULTURE IN FILM AND TELEVISION 163

CHAPTER ELEVEN
    CONTEMPORARY EXPERIENCES OF LGBT PEOPLE: Health Disparities,
    Adolescence, and the Queer Movement 189

BIBLIOGRAPHY 198

INDEX 218

Contents

INTRODUCTION 1

CHAPTER ONE
UNDERSTANDING SEXUALITY IN THE NINETEENTH CENTURY.... 5
   Early Understanding of Homoeroticism and Transgenderism............... 6
     Psychology 6
     Sexology... 7
       Richard von Krafft-Ebing... 7
       Albert Moll 8
   Significant LGBT Activists & Writers of the Late Nineteenth Century . 9
       Havelock Ellis.. 9
       Karl-Maria Kertbeny (Benkert) 10
       Karl Heinrich Ulrichs 10
       Magnus Hirschfeld.. 12
       Oscar Wilde 12
       Edward Carpenter 13
       Henry James 14
       Walt Whitman 14

CHAPTER TWO
SEXUALITY IN THE TWENTIETH CENTURY 17
   The Impact of Freud... 17
     The 1920s and 1930s 19
       Henry Gerber and Early Civil Rights Efforts..................... 19
       The Study of Biological Links to Homosexuality................. 20
     The 1940s and 1950s... 20
       The Kinsey Reports... 20
       Increased Government Sponsored Research 22
   The Search for a "Cure" 22
   Toward Contemporary Perspectives of Sexual Orientation 25

CHAPTER THREE
THE BIRTH OF THE GAY CIVIL RIGHTS MOVEMENT 27
   Foundations Laid During the War 27

Growing Self-Awareness..29
Birth of the Gay Press...30
Barriers to Overcome: Post-War Sexism and Homophobia 31
    The Lavender Scare..33
Gay Political Activism in the 1950s 38
    Bringing Lesbianism Into the Open 40

CHAPTER FOUR
GAY PROTEST AND REBELLION IN THE 1960s AND 1970s.............43
    The Sexual Revolution and Gay Politics...........................45
    The Influence of Feminism on the Gay Rights Movement.............46
    Homophobia in the Media..47
    Living Dual Lives..48
    The Road to Stonewall..51
    The Stonewall Riots..53
    The 1970s: The First Rays of Acceptance 55
    The Inevitable Backlash..56
    Harvey Milk and His Legacy.......................................58

CHAPTER FIVE
HIV 101...61
    Scope of the Problem...61
        What is HIV?...62
        How is HIV Contracted?.......................................63
            What Are the Symptoms of Infection? 64
            How Does One Discover if They Have HIV? 65
        What is AIDS? 66
        Treatment of HIV 66
    The Historical Experience of HIV.................................68
    The Development of Public Policy on HIV 69
    Federal Funding for HIV Prevention and Treatment................69

CHAPTER SIX
SOCIOCULTURAL AND HISTORICAL IMPACT OF HIV/AIDS IN
THE GAY COMMUNITY 73
    Stigma, HIV, and Gay Culture 74
        Abstinence and Harm Reduction: Competing Models 76
        Some Thoughts on "Culture" and HIV Among Gay Men 78
        Cultural Concerns for HIV Risk 79
            Bathhouses 79
            Sex Parties..80

The Internet 81
Considerations for HIV Risk Practice 81
    Age 81
    Race 82
    HIV and Hispanic Men 83
    HIV and African-American Gay Men 84
    Substance Use 86
Implications for Future Policy, Research and Clinical Practice 87
    Policy 87
    Research 88
    Clinical Practice 89

CHAPTER SEVEN
TRANSGENDER AND BEYOND 91
    Rate Yourself 91
    I Know What That Means to Me 93
    Sex and Gender 93
    Transgender 95
    Transsexual 96
    Trans Man and Trans Woman, FTM and MTF 98
    Trans and Trans* 99
    Other Identities 99
    Never Give Up! 102
    One More Label! 103
    Who Put the T in LGBT? 103
    The Other Letters 109

CHAPTER EIGHT
TRANSGENDER ISSUES 111
    Medical and Mental Health Issues 112
    The DSM and "Gender Dysphoria" 112
    Standards of Care 114
    Medical Abuse of Trans People 116
    Intersexual Children and Sex Assignment Surgery 116
    Transitioning 117
    Health Risks 120
    The Challenges of Aging 120
    Legal Issues 121
    Transgender Employment Protections 121
    Insurance Coverage 123
    Access to Public Accommodations and Housing 124

Marriage Equality..125
Parental Rights 126
Hate Crimes..128
Social Issues...128
Interactions with the Cisgender World 128
Transitioning at Work 128
Living and Working with Transgender People 129
Etiquette with Transgender Individuals.................................130
A Troubled Alliance: Transphobia in the Gay Community 131

CHAPTER NINE
CREATING AN AMERICAN LGBT LITERARY TRADITION.............133
Prominent White Gay and Bisexual Writers 134
Walt Whitman 134
Edward Prime-Stevenson..135
Tennessee Williams..137
Gore Vidal 138
Allen Ginsberg...139
Edward Albee 140
Matt Crowley...141
Tony Kushner's Angels in America 142
Noteworthy White Lesbian Authors 145
Emily Dickinson...145
Gertrude Stein..146
Ann Bannon and the Rise of Lesbian Pulp.................................146
Patricia Highsmith 148
Susan Sontag's Critique of Camp 149
Rita Mae Brown..150
Voices of Color: Lesbian, Gay, and Bisexual 152
Countee Cullen, Langston Hughes, and the Harlem Renaissance........152
James Baldwin 154
John Rechy 155
Audre Lorde 156
Paula Gunn Allen...156
Gloria Anzaldúa...157
Transgender Literary Activism 158
Kate Bornstein...158
Matt Kailey...159
Max Wolf Valerio 160
Janet Mock..161

CHAPTER TEN
LGBT CHARACTERS AND CULTURE IN FILM AND TELEVISION . 163
    LGBT Characters in American Movies 163
        Gay, Lesbian, and Bisexual Significance in Early Film, 1895-1933 164
        The Censorship Era, 1908-1956 166
        Pansies and Mannish Women, 1934-1956 167
        Silly, "Sick," and "Criminal" Homosexual Characters in
            1940s, 1950s, and 1960s 168
        Elevated LGBT Characters in the 1970s, 1980s, and 1990s 171
        Characters in Early Twenty-first Century Movies 174
    LGBT Issues and Characters in Television............................... 177
        Homosexuality Issues on News Programs of the 1950s and 1960s...... 177
        Gay and Lesbian Characters in Television Drama of the 1960s........... 179
        Integration of Homosexual Characters, 1970-1990 179
        Mainstreaming LGBT Television in the Twenty-first Century 181
        LGBT Presence in Animated Series 182
        LGBT Characters in Television Comedies and Dramas 183
        LGBT Figures on Talk Shows and Reality Programs......................... 185

CHAPTER ELEVEN
CONTEMPORARY EXPERIENCES OF LGBT PEOPLE: Health
Disparities, Adolescence, and the Queer Movement................................. 189
    Important Historical Events of the Twenty-first Century 190
        Don't Ask, Don't Tell 190
        Hate Crimes Legislation 190
        What Exactly is a Hate Crime?.. 190
        Advancing Definitions of Gender 191
        Marriage Equality... 192
    Contemporary Behavioral Health Issues Facing LGBT People 193
        Mental Health & Substance Use Disparities 194
        A Framework for Understanding Disparities........................... 194
        Stress Theory... 194
        Sexual Minority Stress.. 195
    The Queer Movement 195
        Queer Theory... 196

BIBLIOGRAPHY 198

INDEX 218

INTRODUCTION

We welcome you to the first edition of *Gender and Sexuality: Perspectives on LGBT History and Current Issues in a Changing World*, exploring the arts, sciences, and history of lesbian, gay, bisexual and transgender (LGBT) individuals in the United States. We are very excited to have produced this book, one of the very first developed to help students, scholars, and generally interested people better understand the rich and unique history that has become what is today's LGBT civil rights movement.

This volume is intended for a variety of audiences. Historians will find our discussion of the nineteenth, twentieth and twenty-first century illuminating. From the early American understandings of homosexuality in the nineteenth century, through the AIDS epidemic of the 1980s, the book will provide for a concise but honest account of LGBT rights and liberties across nearly 200 years. The social sciences, including psychology and social work, will also find utility in this text. For example, we describe the cumulative importance of early sexologists such as Karl Heinrich Ulrichs and Havelock Ellis to the medicalization of homosexuality and the inclusion (and finally removal) of homosexuality as a mental illness from the *Diagnostic and Statistical Manual* (DSM) of the American Psychiatric Society. We also describe in detail the HIV/AIDS epidemic among gay men and the way in which historical stigma has impacted the behavioral health of LGBT individuals into the twenty-first century.

We also invite revolutionaries, civil rights activists, and queer theorists to consider our book for their classrooms, ensuring that the history of the LGBT community is accurately accounted. We focus several of the enclosed chapters on the birth of the gay rights movement, ranging from the first drag shows, the impact of World War II on the LGBT community, the sexual revolution of the 1960s, and the life and death of Harvey Milk. For scholars in the Arts and Letters, we include chapters on prominent gay writers, literature, movies, and television.

A fine group of scholars have authored *Gender and Sexuality: Perspectives on LGBT History and Current Issues in a Changing World*. Michael Phillips earned his Ph.D. in History from The University of Texas at Austin. His books on race in Dallas and Texas House Speakers demonstrate his strong interest and expertise in American government as well as race, class, and gender issues. He teaches at Collin College in Texas. Jeremy T. Goldbach earned his Ph. D. in Social Work from The University of Texas at Austin. His interests are substance abuse and HIV prevention in vulnerable youth, social justice and diversity. He is at the University of Southern California in the School of Social Work. Matt Kailey was a transsexual man and an award-winning author, blogger, teacher, and community leader, as well as a nationally recognized speaker and trainer on transgender issues. Matt taught gender and sexuality classes at Red Rocks Community College and Metropolitan State College of Denver. Finally, Carolyn Perry earned her Ph.D. in Humanities from The University of Texas at Dallas. She has studied film at Northwestern University in Chicago. She teaches at Collin College in Texas. As one can easily see, we were fortunate to draw on the multi-disciplinary knowledge and talent of a number of superb academic writers.

Lesbians, gays, bisexuals, and transgendered men and women have never been more visible, more in the public eye, held more powerful positions in politics, the media, and education, or experienced more rapid advances in civil rights and social acceptance than in the past few years of American history. There have never been more openly LGBT novelists, poets, essayists, directors, actors, painters and sculptors along with athletes, journalists, members of the clergy, and politicians, having such a profound effect on American culture, religion, and public policy. Recent events underscore how relevant this work is. Even the most committed LGBT activists two decades ago could not have imagined the political climate prevailing as of the writing of this text.

On June 26, 2015, the Supreme Court, on a 5-4 vote, overturned bans on same sex marriage in the landmark *Obergefell v. Hodges* decision, thus allowing for the first time such unions to take place in all 50 state and the District of Columbia. According to the Pew Research Center, in 2001, 57 percent of Americans stood against same-sex marriage, with 35 percent supporting it. By 2014, the numbers had almost completely flipped, with 52 percent supporting marriage equality and only 40 percent opposing it. According to the Gallup polling organization, the number of Americans who believe that gay and lesbian relationships are "morally acceptable" went up from 40 percent in 2001 to 58 percent in 2014 and those who find such relationships "morally wrong" declined from 53 percent to 38 percent in the same time period. The change in attitudes toward same-sex marriage has paralleled a greater overall acceptance of gay, lesbian, bisexual, and transgender men and women among the general public. In 2003, Americans were almost evenly split on whether same-sex couples should be allowed to adopt children, with 49 percent saying yes and 48 percent saying no. The number accepting gay and lesbian couples as adoptive parents rocketed in the next 11 years, with 63 percent approving in 2015 and only 35 percent opposing.

By 2011, Americans who told pollsters they could vote for an openly gay, lesbian or bisexual candidate for president outnumbered those who said they could not, by a 2-1 margin. In 2012, Kyrsten Sinema became the first open bisexual elected to the U.S. House, and Tammy Baldwin the first open lesbian elected to the United States Senate. California, Colorado, Oregon, and Rhode Island all have had gay

House speakers in their state legislatures, and major cities like Houston, Portland, Santa Fe, and Seattle have elected gay and lesbian mayors.

This book aims to explain this social transformation and, above all, we hope that this accurate account of the LGBT community is relevant, flexible, and may serve as a resource to help your students and friends address some of the most pressing social justice challenges we will face in the twenty-first century. We recognize that misinformation has led to much uncertainty over time, and this volume is intended to serve as an accurate reflection of this rich and vibrant history.

Jeremy T. Goldbach
Michael Phillips

Chapter 1

UNDERSTANDING SEXUALITY IN THE NINETEENTH CENTURY

In writing this volume, the authors contend with the impossibility of determining the exact right moment in time to begin a book on lesbian, gay, bisexual, and transgender (LGBT) history. Societal attitudes and expectations toward homosexuality and homosexual behaviors (by both men and women) have varied considerably over time and across cultures. One could start as far back as ancient Greece, where Socrates (469 B.C.–399 B.C.), among other scholars, has been speculated to have engaged in homosexual behavior, although same-sex attitudes and practices during this time did not have the same social stigma as they would later.

Even identifying where to begin in American history is difficult. Research has established that homosexuality and same-sex behavior existed among indigenous tribes prior to the European colonization. In early Native American communities, so-called "two spirited" individuals engaged in same-sex and gender non-conforming behavior. These people commonly reported feeling their body simultaneously manifested with both masculine and feminine spirits, and were sometimes seen as shamans, revered as having special powers and engaging in sexual experiences with other tribal members of the same sex.

We have chosen to begin in the nineteenth century, when psychology became one of the first academic disciplines to formally study homosexuality as a distinct human experience. Historian Harry Oosterhuis makes a compelling argument in his article "Sexual Mondernity in the Works of Richard von Krafft-Ebing and Albert Moll," suggesting that the modern notion of sexuality took place during this time, albeit through labeling homosexual behaviors as perverse. Yet, even beyond the pathologizing nature of psychology, social attitudes toward homosexuality became distinctly more hostile in the late 1800s. The Labouchere Amendment, a British law passed in 1885, for example, which included the criminalization of "acts of gross indecency with another male," was successfully used to imprison the famous playwright Oscar Wilde, described in further detail near the end of this chapter.

We shall commence by analyzing the early markings of sexuality as a science, focusing on our early understandings of homosexuality, homoeroticism, and transgenderism. Continuing with the emergence of sexology and the pertinent theorists, philosophers, and psychologists who shaped the thinking about LGBT individuals into the twentieth century, we will end with a discussion of gay phenomena and icons of the period who emerged during this important historical time of LGBT awakening.

EARLY UNDERSTANDING OF HOMOEROTICISM AND TRANSGENDERISM

Homosexuality, and those who identify as "homosexual," has been defined throughout history using primarily theological, legal, and medical models. In Western culture, homosexual behaviors were first seen simply as a sin. Then, as religion began to decline, homosexuality was seen next as a transgression against society, outside of social norms. In the nineteenth and early twentieth centuries, homosexual became known as a sickness of the body or mind. Although homosexual behavior has existed throughout history, scholarship on the topic written before the nineteenth century is sparse and the concept of identifying as "LGBT" unknown. As Michael Bronski writes in his book, *The Making of Gay Sensibility*,

> The evolution of a homosexual identity is necessary to the development of a homosexual culture. Although this sense of identity may have existed earlier, it was only after the formulation of the medical model, in the later part of the nineteenth century, that a distinct homosexual identity emerged. Before the nineteenth century, some have argued, there were homosexual acts, but no homosexuals. The new medical perception of sexuality in relation to the individual and not in relation to the moral or social order was the social change that allowed homosexual identity to "come out."

Psychology

The field of psychology was the first to identify homosexuality as both an orientation and a discrete phenomenon. Unfortunately, this categorization quickly led to pathology. While late into the twentieth century the American Psychiatric Association (APA) would determine that homosexuality was not a diagnosable illness, societal attitudes during this time took a more adversarial stance. Around 1870, however, the medical-psychiatric community began to move away from the belief that homosexuality and homosexual acts were simply an immoral and temporary deviation from the norm and began to consider that individuals may in fact be homosexual in a permanent way. Prior to the late twentieth century, psychology viewed homosexuality in terms of pathology and mental illness. As described in the next chapter, this classification came under intense scrutiny in the twentieth century as research had failed to produce an empirical basis to suggest homosexuality was a disorder or inherently caused concerns in biological, psychological or social well-being and functioning.

Sexology

The sexology movement, an interdisciplinary study of human sexuality and sexual behaviors, became the first area to consider homosexuality from a clinical perspective. Outside of public health-focused interests (such as prostitution or the prevention and treatment of venereal diseases), medicine was primarily interested in the relationship between sex and crime, including the incidence of rape, sodomy, and, to a lesser extent, child abuse.

The belief that something in the environment or during birth caused homosexuality was also a novel concept. Prior to this time, medicine had primarily assumed that mental health disorders resulted from engaging in deviant (or "unnatural") acts. The idea that these unnatural acts were the result of mental health disorders, rather than the other way around, was a new consideration and meant that the "condition" was worth studying. With this new thinking, psychiatrists and allied professionals began to argue that sexual offenders (and deviants) should be treated as patients rather than criminals in the legal system. In the last decades of the nineteenth century, psychiatrists began collecting, documenting, and classifying a wide range of sexual behaviors including uranism, inversion, homosexual (and heterosexual) activities, exhibitionism, fetishism, pedophilia, bestiality, sadism, and masochism.

Richard von Krafft-Ebing

The field of sexology was essentially born when the Austro-German psychiatrist Richard von Krafft-Ebing published *Psychopathia Sexualis* in 1886. Largely credited as the first establishment of sexology as a discipline, the volume was widely disseminated as a forensic and diagnostic reference manual for psychiatrists, physicians, and judges. *Psychopathia Sexualis* became the first book to describe homosexuality (alongside nearly 200 other conditions) from a clinical perspective, describing it as a deviant sex practice, caused by either "congenital or acquired inversion." (Used to describe homosexuality in the nineteenth century, the term "inversion," was based on the idea, regardless of outward appearances, that gay men were inwardly female, and gay women were inwardly male.) The first edition, largely written for lawyers, judges, and medical practitioners involved in forensic science, began an extensive process of naming and classifying nearly all sexuality not intended for procreation as deviant and perverse. In fact, this became a core tenet of early psychiatric thinking around sexual deviations. In short, psychological concerns were seen as a result of being disconnected from the reproductive purpose of sexuality and increasingly interested in the simple satisfaction of sexual experiences. Scholars would later include the importance of love (and marriage) in their assessment of sexual deviance, but these early perceptions of the "purpose" of sex led not only to an expansion in our understanding of sexuality as both a physical and psychological phenomenon but also to a definition of homosexuality as a disease that remained in place until late into the twentieth century.

Albert Moll

Another scholar whose early writings on homosexuality greatly influenced subsequent medical literature was Albert Moll, a German neurologist who achieved notoriety for treating sexual perversions. During the late-nineteenth century, Moll became a well-respected sexologist, authoring *Die Conträre Sexualempfindung* [*The Contrary Sexual Feeling*], the first known medical textbook to focus exclusively on homosexuality. He clearly regarded Krafft-Ebing as the preeminent scholar on the topic, inviting the famous psychiatrist to write the preface for the book.

As Harry Oosterhuis noted, Moll was as much a theorist of sexual deviation as he was a medical doctor. In his book, *Libido Sexualis*, Moll elaborated on one of the most sophisticated and well developed theories on sexuality long before Sigmund Freud wrote *Three Treatises on Sexual Theory* (1905) or the 1910 publication of Havelock Ellis's *Studies in the Psychology of Sex*. Further, these two early figures in sexology differed in their attitude toward homosexuality. Whereas Krafft-Ebing became more supportive of homosexuality as he aged, Moll became less so. In fact, the expanding perspective of Krafft-Ebing that sexuality included an important psychological component (such as compassion, love, partnership) appeared to soften his perceptions of the deviant nature of homosexuality. As he described in his last article published on homosexuality, Krafft-Ebing recognized that his earlier writings describing homosexuality as pathological and immoral were one-sided and that his own patients expressed a desire for understanding and empathy.

SIGNIFICANT LGBT ACTIVISTS AND WRITERS OF THE LATE NINETEENTH CENTURY

Havelock Ellis

While Krafft-Ebing and Moll were less positive toward advancing the integration and acceptance of LGBT people in the nineteenth century, a small but passionate number of European physicians, writers, and social activists strongly disagreed. Havelock Ellis, a British doctor and writer who primarily studied human sexuality, for example, argued that homosexuality was inborn and therefore could not be immoral. He asserted that the behavior was not a disease and that gay men and women quite often made significant contributions to their community and society at large. Ellis wrote his first textbook on homosexuality (*Sexual Inversion*) in 1897, and a score of publications on a variety of sexual practices including the experience of transgender persons would follow. *Sexual Inversion* became perhaps the earliest study of homosexuality without moral or ethical sanctions. The book is widely seen as the first objective medical literature on homosexual relationships. Although widely sold, a British judge banned the work on obscenity grounds. As Ellis describes in the forward to the second edition:

> Although it is scarcely four years since this book was published, it has a somewhat eventful history. It was favorably received by the medical press on its first publication in London and no attempt was made to bring it before the general public. A prosecution was, however, initiated by the police against a bookseller who sold the book, and the Recorder of London, sitting as a judge, finally decided that it was not a scientific work and ordered it destroyed. It was a deplorable decision from many points of view, though I need scarcely say that I was able to bear with equanimity the recorder's opinion of my book's scientific value; I have the satisfaction of knowing that [no one] has entitled to an authoritative opinion on the subject with which I deal pronounced adversely to my book, while, on the other hand, many have spoken in its favor.

Ellis's personal life was quite unconventional for the day. In his autobiography, *My Life*, Ellis shares his experiences while married to Edith Lees, an openly lesbian English writer. Even after their wedding, the two returned to their separate living circumstances, never cohabitating. He also noted his own sexual concerns with impotency, stating that his renown as an authority on sex was "a fact which sometimes amused one or two (though not all) of my intimate women friends."

Karl-Maria Kertbeny (Benkert)

Although Ellis later disowned his responsibility for its widespread use, the term *homosexual* is largely attributed to Ellis's writing. In reality, the earliest writings using the terms *heterosexual* and *homosexual* came from Karl-Maria Kertbeny (born Karl-Maria Benkert), though this was not known until the late 1980s. An Austrian-born Hungarian journalist, Kertbeny had written a number of anonymous pamphlets calling for the legal emancipation of homosexuals and the removal of penal codes making homosexual behavior illegal. Within these tracts, he first coined not only the term homosexual but also heterosexual, *monosexual* (to refer to masturbation), and *heterogen* (applying to sexual experiences with other genus, such as animals).

According to Kertbeny, homosexuality had a number of subtypes including Platonism (love of older men directed toward younger boys), mutual onanism (masturbation), tribadism (female homosexuality), and pygismus (consensual anal intercourse). Notably, Kertbeny writes that heterosexuality (or normal sexualism) was perhaps the most dangerous because of its "unfettered capacity for degeneracy" stating they are "equally likely to assault male but especially female minors who have not reached maturity; to indulge in incest; to engage in bestiality and the misuse of animals; and even to behave depravedly with corpses if their moral self-control does not control their lust." The connection of these early pamphlets to Kertbeny became available only after the extensive research of the German gay writer and activist Manfred Herzer in the late 1980s.

Karl Heinrich Ulrichs

Before Kertbeny invented the term homosexual, however, Karl Heinrich Ulrichs had been coining his own terminology in his writing on transgender individuals. A German writer, born in Aurich in 1825, Ulrichs described in a number of his writings how from a young age he preferred playing with and wearing girls' clothing, and even revealed his desire to be a girl. After graduating from Berlin University in 1848, he worked as a legal advisor for a district court until 1857 when he was fired for his perceived homosexuality.

Five years later, in 1862, Ulrichs told his family and friends that he was transgender and began publishing under a pseudonym Numa Numantius. At the time, he called himself an *Urning*, referencing Plato's Symposium in which he discusses two kinds of love, symbolized by manifestations of Aphrodite born as both male (Uranos) and female (Dione). Later, this term would become more generally known as *Uranian*, referring to a person of the "third sex." Initially, this expression only referred to men who believed that they had a female psyche, but it later became extended to cover gender-variant females as well. Of note, in the early twentieth century, Havelock Ellis also spent much of his professional life understanding the experience of transgender patients, recognizing it as separate and distinct from homosexuality, calling it *eonism.*

In 1867, Ulrichs became the first transgender individual to speak publicly against criminalizing homosexuality, becoming regularly engaged with the legal system. His writings became increasingly criminalized as well, banned in Saxony, Berlin, and later throughout Prussia. In a lengthy correspondence between Kertbeny and Ulrichs, the key factor lay not in determining whether same-sex attractions and homosexuality were innate or not, but the fact that people deserved the right to be left alone in their own intimate lives. This argument can be seen in Ulrichs's and Kertbeny's early works. In 1870, Ulrichs had published *Araxes: A Call to Free the Nature of the Urning from Penal Law* where he demanded transgender rights, boldly asserting at one point:

> The Urning, too, is a person. He, too, therefore, has inalienable rights. His sexual orientation is a right established by nature. Legislators have no right to veto nature; no right to persecute nature in the course of its work; no right to torture living creatures who are subject to those drives nature gave them.

Similarly, Kertbeny did not seek a biological foundation for civil liberties, as he writes in a 1868 letter to Ulrich:

> To prove the innate nature [of homosexuality] is not useful at all, especially not quickly, what's more it cuts both ways, let it be a very interesting riddle of nature from the anthropological point of view. The legislation does not examine whether his inclination is innate or not, it merely focuses on the personal and social dangers of it, on its relation to society. . . . Thus, we wouldn't win anything by proving innateness. Rather, we should convince our opponents that exactly according to their legal notions they do not have anything to do with this inclination, let it be innate or voluntary, because the state does not have the right to intervene in what is happening between two consenting people over 14, excluding publicity, not hurting the rights of any third party.

These early writings are strikingly similar to the modern-day debate over civil liberties for members of the LGBT community. The view that homosexuality was both inborn and unchangeable would later be considered the "medical model" of homosexuality. Both Kertbeny and Ulrichs argued against the dominant view of the time, claiming that men who committed "sodomy" did so out of wickedness. Gay men, Kertbeny theorized, were not even by their nature effeminate, as many of the great heroes of history were gay (elaborated on more extensively by Heinrich

Hössli in his 1836 volume *Eros Die Männerliebe der Griechen*). In addition to these efforts, Ulrichs is widely seen as the first person to publicly (and in writing) come out of the closet and speak to defend transgender rights, seek equal protection under the law for transgender individuals, and make strong demands for women's equal rights.

Magnus Hirschfeld

Near the end of the nineteenth century, German physician and sexologist Magnus Hirschfeld began writing sympathetically on the experiences of homosexuals, publishing his first piece, *Sappho and Socrates*, on gay men in 1896 under the pseudonym Th. Ramien. Soon thereafter, he founded the Scientific Humanitarian Committee, intending to defend the rights of homosexuals and specifically to repeal Paragraph 175—the section of the German penal code that criminalized homosexual behavior. Similar to the arguments of Kengeny and Ulrich, Hirschfeld argued that the law only encouraged blackmail of homosexuals and that the law unnecessarily invaded the private lives of citizens. Ultimately, the organization supported a petition to repeal the law but was unsuccessful until well into the twentieth century.

Hirschfeld was not unanimously loved by his colleagues. He was known for suggesting that homosexuals were like disabled people and also posited that male homosexuals were effeminate by nature (perhaps leading to his significant work on transvestism). Hirschfeld was considered the "Einstein of Sex," developing a system that included 64 possible types of sexual intermediaries ranging from masculine heterosexual male to the feminine homosexual male. He also was the first to coin the term *transvestite*, which later led to the terms *transgender* and *transsexual*. Early in the twentieth century (as discussed in more depth in Chapter 2), Hirschfeld founded the *Institut für Sexualwissenschaft* or the Institute for Sexual Research, which housed both a medical and observational facility, an extensive library of sexuality literature, and a Museum of Sex open to the public.

Oscar Wilde

The Irish writer and poet Oscar Fingal O'Flahertie Wills Wilde (commonly known as Oscar Wilde) was born in 1854 and became one of Europe's most popular playwrights in the late nineteenth century. Perhaps his most notable accomplishment, *The Picture of Dorian Gray*, was considered both a masterpiece and blasphemous. While the novel ultimately appeared in the *Lippincott Monthly Magazine* as a serial piece, the publisher required large portions of the work to be edited prior to its release. As English literature professor Nicholas Frankel has described, the original version included "a number of things an innocent woman would make exception to," including content alluding to both homosexuality and sexual experiences with two mistresses.

Oscar Wilde's personal story also included a number of experiences that led him to become a gay icon in the later twentieth century. Although married with two children (and three additional children out of wedlock), Wilde began an affair around 1891 with Lord Alfred Douglas, an English author and poet. By 1895, at the height of his success, Wilde found himself embroiled in a legal battle with the Marquess of Queensberry. The Marquess was the father of Lord Douglas, and while Wilde filed a case of prosecution for libel against him, the trial ultimately led to his own arrest for gross indecency with another man that led to his own two-year prison sentence. By 1898, he had been released from prison, moved to Paris, and ultimately died at the age of 46.

Edward Carpenter

In the midst of Oscar Wilde's legal and professional scandals, Edward Carpenter also emerged as an early leader in the promotion of LGBT rights. Instrumental in founding the Fabian Society in 1884 (a British socialist organization that contributed to the formation of the center-left Labour Party a decade and half later), Carpenter was an English socialist poet, philosopher, and activist best known for his writings portraying civilization as a "disease," his advocacy for sexual freedom, and the belief that homosexuals would ultimately be the cause of radical social change. Insisting that sexual pleasure in and of itself was natural is perhaps one of Carpenter's most notable contributions. Perhaps inspired by his lifelong "mixed-class" relationship with George Merrill (a working-class man who had no formal education), Carpenter argued in his novel *The Intermediate Sex* that same-sex love had the power to end social class systems, saying

> It is notable how often [gay men] of good position and breeding are drawn
> to rougher types, as of manual workers, and frequently very permanent
> alliances grow up in this way, which although not publicly acknowledged
> have a decided influence on social institutions, customs and political
> tendencies.

Although Carpenter lived with Merrill in an openly gay relationship for nearly thirty years, his philosophy on brotherhood and sex was not abstract. Carpenter had a number of affairs with men throughout the rest of his life, influencing the future works of writers and scholars into the twentieth century. As Rictor Norton (1998) writes in *My Dear Boy: Gay Love Letters through the Centuries*

Merrill served as a model for the gamekeeper in E. M. Forster's gay novel *Maurice*, which Forster acknowledged was a direct result of a visit to Carpenter, when Merrill "touched my backside—gently and just above the buttocks. I believe he touched most people's. . . . It seemed to go straight through the small of my back into my ideas, without involving my thoughts. If it really did this, it would have acted in accordance with Carpenter's yogified mysticism, and would prove that at that precise moment I had conceived."

Henry James

Another phenomenon that emerged in the late nineteenth century came to be known as the "Boston Marriage." This term described two women living together, independent of financial support from a man. The concept emerged from the novel *The Bostonians* (1886) by Henry James, who wrote about a long-term co-habitating relationship between women. The novel, originally published as a serial, followed the story of Basil Ramsom, a Mississippi conservative, and Ransom's cousin (Olive), a feminist in Boston, living with Verena Tarrant (the so-called Boston Marriage). Largely inspired by his sister Alice who lived in a similar real-world relationship, the book examines feminism and the larger role of women in society, with lesbian undertones. Unlike most of James's work, *The Bostonians* contends with a number of political themes including those of feminism and the role of women in the society of the nineteenth century. Although James is not explicit about the lesbian attraction between Olive and Verena (likely due to the conservatism of the time), its presence in the novel clearly impacted the reception of the novel in the general public. As Darrel Abel observed (1885) "The Bostonians resented its satire upon their intellectual and humanitarian aspirations [...] But probably most offensive to Boston propriety were the unmistakable indications of Lesbianism in the portrait of Olive Chancellor, which made it a violation of Boston decency and reticence." The "Boston Marriage" would continue to be a discussion among women authors in the twentieth century. As Lillian Faderman writes in her book, these women and those who chose nontraditional paths (such as having a career) often gravitated toward each other for support in a commonly disapproving society.

Walt Whitman

Whitman was an American poet known by post-Stonewall liberationists as "The Good Gay Poet." While Whitman was well loved by the progressive literary faction of the nineteenth century, his work was also met with adversity in publication. When Whitman published the 6th edition of his literary works, *Leaves of Grass*, the District Attorney of Boston wrote Whitman's publishers, stating, "we are of the opinion that this book is such a book as brings it within the provisions of the Public Statutes respecting obscene literature and suggest the propriety of withdrawing the same from circulation and suppressing the editions thereof."

The undercurrent of homoeroticism found in other author's works was quite direct in Whitman's writings. Whitman regularly used the word "adhesiveness" to describe affection and sexuality between men; to declare it openly would have been both a sin and a crime. Although he used the term "adhesiveness," it was clear to readers the homoerotic nature of his work. As he writes in *Song of Myself*, "there is that in me . . . I do not know what it is . . . but I know it is in me. I do not know it . . . it is without a name . . . it is a word unsaid, It is not in any dictionary or utterance or symbol." Walt Whitman is discussed in more detail in the Literary Tradition, Chapter Nine.

Before the late nineteenth century, outside of an interest in public health (the prevention of disease) and forensics, such as in the investigation of rape and sodomy, little was written or known about human sexuality that went beyond acts of procreation. Early scholars such as Krafft-Ebing and Moll suggested that any sexuality with a purpose outside of procreation was by its very nature deviant, with homosexuality being perhaps one of the most egregious violations. Although these early scholars were not promoters of homosexuality, they were the first to write, from a medical-psychiatric perspective, on the diversity that exists within sexuality.

From these early perspectives and documentations of sexuality, discourse was begun. As Bronski writes

[Then] sexuality was viewed as an intrinsic part of the personality structure. New trends in thinking promoted the idea of the individual as a social entity equally or more important than the larger social structures and conditions that shaped society and culture. [However], although identified and defined as outcast, the homosexual counterculture developed a positive gay identity. There are two characteristics in the early evolution of gay sensibility. The first was social criticism in reaction to the oppression and ostracism placed upon the homosexual by society. Political theorists like Edward Carpenter, scientists like Havelock Ellis, and writers like John Addington Symonds all criticized prevailing social norms from the perspective of outsiders. [Second], because of social and legal injunctions against homosexuality, many artists and writers could not be public about their sexuality and so their work was infused with a plethora of signs and codes that allowed the like-minded to identify one another.

Additionally, the scholarship of Ellis, Kertbeny, and Ulrichs contributed to the belief that homosexuality was both inborn and unchangeable and would later lead to the "medical model" of sexuality that gained popularity into the twentieth century. The writings of Ulrichs and Hirschfeld also gave voice to what would later become the transgender movement and provided early considerations for normalizing the transgender experience.

Finally, in spite of draconian laws against homosexuality, such as Paragrah 175 of the German penal code, the nineteenth century set the foundation for a number of significant advances on our understanding of sexuality in the twentieth century, including those of Sigmund Freud and Alfred Kinsey. It is perhaps due to the counterculture of homosexuality in response to these discriminatory experiences that homosexual writers and artists were able to create a distinct political, artistic, and social identity.

Chapter 2

SEXUALITY IN THE TWENTIETH CENTURY

In the previous chapter, we described how the prevailing sentiment during the nineteenth century considered same-sex sexual activity within the same context of "unnatural acts" as masturbation, fornication (intercourse outside of marriage), bestiality, and anal sex. As the world entered the twentieth century, however, our understanding of homosexuality (particularly from a psychological perspective) changed drastically, providing valuable information that would contribute to significant advances for LGBT people in both public policy and social spheres in the second half of the century.

THE IMPACT OF FREUD

Sigmund Freud, the famous doctor of medicine at the University of Vienna with special expertise in neuropathology, contributed significantly to the advancement in attitudes within the scientific community at the turn of the twentieth century. In creating the field of modern psychoanalysis, he became fascinated with both the male and female libido, sexual orientation, and such theoretical constructs as the Oedipus Complex. (The Oedipus Complex, named after a Greek mythological figure, refers to the sexual attraction (Freud said) that boys feel towards their mothers between ages three and six. He argued that healthy males outgrow this attraction.) Freud believed homosexuality was deterministic—a combination of both biology and psychological choice. Although he argued that homosexuality was likely a deviation from more natural "sexual libidinal drives," his writings indicate a strong sense that homosexuality was deeply rooted in a person's psyche and difficult or impossible to change.

17

In Freud's best-known work on homosexuality, *Three Essays on the Theory of Sexuality*, published in the early 1900s, he posited four primary theories about homosexuality. As Kenneth Lewes accounts in his 1988 book, *The Psychoanalytic Theory of Male Homosexuality*, Freud's theories centered around the idea that:

1) Homosexuality is the result of the Oedipus conflict in young boys who discover their mother is castrated and find intense anxiety. (Freud believed that around the age of three, boys become aware that females do not have penises and attribute this difference to castration, creating what the psychiatrist called "castration anxiety.") This anxiety causes the boy to reject the castrated mother in favor of a "woman with a penis" (i.e., masculine male who seeks feminine men)

2) The result of an inverted Oedipus complex is a boy who seeks the father's love and attention, thus taking on feminine characteristics themselves and seeking out the love of masculine men (i.e., feminine male who seeks masculine men)

3) Homosexuality is the result of an overbearing attachment to the mother where the child is less able to differentiate himself from the mother, and thus seeks objects to love in the same way that his mother loved him

4) Homosexuality could be the result of poor reaction formation, caused by jealousy of brothers and father and transformed into homosexual behaviors for safety. (According to Freudian theory, many people try to distance themselves from a trait or feelings that they find embarrassing or disgusting by adopting an exaggerated opposite behavior, a process Freud called reaction formation.)

Freud also proposed a number of intellectual ideas from his practice experiences that would later be taken up by scholars including Alfred Kinsey. For example, Freud believed that there was an element of bisexuality in all people, with every person having some component of masculine and feminine tendencies. Similar to Kinsey's work, which will be described later in this chapter, Freud believed that some people were simply more naturally inclined toward one or the other. While not believing that homosexuality was a sign of illness (he wrote that it was a naturally occurring event), Freud did not suggest it was not problematic. He held that later homosexuality could be the result of significant life events such as trauma early in life. Under "normal" circumstances, the homosexual tendencies found in all people would be subdued, while those who remained in psychological conflict would be unable to arrest their inclinations toward homosexuality. Freud was likely the first great thinker to determine that homosexuality was both innate and a part of all people's psychological being.

The 1920s and 1930s

Henry Gerber and Early Civil Rights Efforts

In 1924, the Society for Human Rights was established in Chicago, Illinois. Founded by Henry Gerber and inspired by Dr. Magnus Hirschfeld (discussed in Chapter 1), the Society became the first recognized gay rights organization in the United States. While in Germany, Gerber had become associated with the work of Hirschfeld on reforming the anti-homosexual laws that criminalized sodomy and sex between men. A German immigrant to Chicago, Gerber had good reason to be concerned about gay rights in the United States. Four years after moving to the U.S. in 1913, he was briefly placed in a mental institution for being a homosexual.

From 1920 to 1923, he served in the U.S. Army during the occupation of Germany. During his time in Germany, he was exposed to the rise of organized movements to secure civil rights for homosexuals. He also explored the gay communities of Berlin. After his return to Chicago, Gerber filed an application for recognition of the Society for Human Rights as a non-profit organization with the State of Illinois in the winter of 1924, outlining the group's goals as follows:

> [T]o promote and protect the interests of people who by reasons of mental and physical abnormalities are abused and hindered in the legal pursuit of happiness which is guaranteed them by the Declaration of Independence and to combat the public prejudices against them by dissemination of factors according to modern science among intellectuals of mature age. The Society stands only for law and order; it is in harmony with any and all general laws insofar as they protect the rights of others, and does in no manner recommend any acts in violation of present laws nor advocate any manner inimical to the public welfare.

The Society quickly became known in the Chicago area. Publishing its newsletter, *Friendship and Freedom*, as the first gay-interest publication in the U.S. was difficult given blanket laws on the publication of obscene content (under the federal Comstock Act). At the time, all content determined to be homosexual in nature was considered obscene (and remained so until 1958 when the Supreme Court ruled differently in the *One, Inc. v. Olesen* case). The newsletter only had two publications before the Society closed just a few months later in the summer of 1925 after several of its founding members were arrested (primarily on obscenity charges later dismissed).

Despite its short life, the Society for Human Rights is credited as the precursor to the modern gay civil rights movement that we know today. In fact, Gerber described a clear strategy for obtaining equal rights (or what he referred to as "homosexual emancipation") that included:

1) engagement in a series of lectures pointing out the attitude of society in relation to their own behavior and especially urging against the seduction of adolescents;

2) keeping the homophile (the society's term for "gay") world in touch with progress using an ongoing publication; and

3) win the confidence of legal authorities and legislators through education

These elements of strategy would later be utilized throughout the LGBT civil rights movement down to the present day.

The Study of Biological Links to Homosexuality

The medical community became increasingly interested in determining whether there was a causal link, which could be observed in individuals through biological testing. In 1929, psychiatrist and neurologist John F. W. Meagher wrote "indulgent male inverts [i.e., homosexuals] like pleasant artistic things, and nearly all of them are fond of music. They like praise and admiration, and are poor whistlers. Their favorite color is green . . . where most individuals prefer blue or red." From these observations, Meagher began to draw conclusions about a possible genetic link to homosexuality.

Although dominated by psychological studies throughout the later twentieth century, some biological studies did move forward. For instance, the German-born American psychiatrist Franz Kallman during the early 1950s conducted a study of twins, finding that dizygotic twins (those developed from two ova released from the ovary simultaneously and fertilized at the same time) were much less likely to have concordance of sexual orientation than their monozygotic counterparts (who had developed into separate fetuses from a single fertilized ovum that split during embryonic development). This finding, Kallman concluded, provided evidence that there was a connection between genealogy and homosexuality.

The 1940s and 1950s

The Kinsey Reports

Likely the most notable advancement during the 1940s for LGBT civil rights was the 1948 publication of the book *Sexual Behavior in the Human Male* by the American sexologist Alfred Kinsey. This work, later coupled with its counterpart *Sexual Behavior in the Human Female* published five years later, became famously known as the Kinsey Reports. Kinsey became one of the first American sexologists to provide a deeper exploration of sexuality that went beyond simply understanding people as either homosexual or heterosexual. The reports also gave some of the earliest academic support for women's sexual liberation.

As many authors have noted, Kinsey's research went well beyond traditional research methods to include such elements as observation and participation in sexual activities (at times involving co-workers). Nevertheless, he justified the work as being necessary to gain the trust of research participants and even encouraged researchers working in his lab to experiment sexually. Kinsey developed what is known as the Kinsey Scale, which is still used today (although with added complexity). Rather than assuming that an individual's sexuality was binary (that is, a person is either homosexual or heterosexual), the Kinsey Scale recognized that an individual may feel their sexuality on a 6-point scale, ranging from "exclusively homosexual" to "exclusively heterosexual."

Later, "x" was added as a seventh option, representing "no socio-sexual contact or relations." This more comprehensive understanding of human sexuality allowed for more flexibility and also served to depathologize homosexual behavior in adults. As Kinsey wrote in 1948:

"Males do not represent two discrete populations, heterosexual and homosexual [...] While emphasizing the continuity of the gradations between exclusively heterosexual and exclusively homosexual histories, it has seemed desirable to develop some sort of classification which could be based on the relative amounts of heterosexual and homosexual experience or response [...] An individual may be assigned a position on this scale, for each period in his life. [...] A seven-point scale comes nearer to showing the many gradations that actually exist."

Rating	Description
0	Exclusively heterosexual
1	Predominantly heterosexual, only incidentally homosexual
2	Predominantly heterosexual, but more than incidentally homosexual
3	Equally heterosexual and homosexual
4	Predominantly homosexual, but more than incidentally heterosexual
5	Predominantly homosexual, only incidentally heterosexual
6	Exclusively homosexual
X	No socio-sexual contacts or reactions

Kinsey's reports suggested that approximately 10 percent of men and 7 percent of women had been "more or less exclusively homosexual" at some point in their lives, although not necessarily at the time the measure was taken.

Increased Government Sponsored Research

During the 1950s, some governmental agencies, including the National Institutes of Health (NIH), began taking an interest in exploring whether homosexuality was indeed an illness. In 1951, Clellan Ford and Frank Beach published *Patterns of Sexual Behavior*, reporting that homosexuality was common across nearly all cultures and existed in most nonhuman species. In 1953, Evelyn Hooker was awarded a grant from the National Institute of Mental Health (NIMH) to examine the experiences of gay men in the United States. Her work, published in 1956, studied the outcomes of 30 homosexual men and 30 heterosexual men on a battery of psychological testing, finding that when not told in advance of the sexuality of the participant, trained psychologists could not find any major differences between the groups. In short, gay men found similar outcomes to their heterosexual peers, beginning to erode the perspective that homosexuality was a deficit that created poor health outcomes.

THE SEARCH FOR A "CURE"

The relationship that LGBT individuals have had with the psychological community, and, more specifically, the pathologizing of homosexuality by the psychological scientific community, is complicated. Although psychology was one of the first disciplines to study homosexuality, it also brought a high share of condemnation. Throughout most of the twentieth century, psychologists viewed homosexuality as a disease. While the 1950s saw the emergence of more research, the general consensus of the academic and practicing community was that homosexuality was an illness that could (and should) be treated.

The idea of "curing" homosexuality was also popularized in the 1940s though its roots can be found much earlier. In 1935, in Freud's published "Letter to an American Mother," he suggested that while homosexuality is "assuredly no advantage, it is nothing to be ashamed of," further stating "many highly respectable individuals of ancient and modern times have been homosexuals, several of the greatest men among them (Plato, Michelangelo, Leonardo Da Vinci)." Generally, while the letter empathizes with the mother, Freud indicated to her that treatment was unlikely to be successful.

Freud was not the only psychologist interested in defining, measuring, and addressing the needs of homosexual individuals. While he believed that homosexuality was caused by a sexual immaturity, others saw it as a clear pathology. In 1940, the Hungarian psychoanalyst Sandor Rado published "A Critical Examination of the Concept of Bisexuality," wherein he argued against Freud's idea that all people had some innate bisexuality, and reiterated a pathological model for understanding homosexuality. Rado believed homosexuality was a "phobic avoidance" of the opposite sex, nearly always caused by trauma in childhood. Nearly all of the leading psychoanalytic scholars of the twentieth century followed Rado's model, believing that heterosexuality was the only nonpathological outcome of human sexual development. In fact, this pathological approach to homosexuality was, in large part, the precipice of the idea that a "cure" may exist, and an aim of identifying what might predict homosexuality in adults.

These cures (commonly known under the umbrella of "conversion therapy" or "reparative therapy") became popularized even before the 1940s, with mainstream medical researchers in Germany implanting the testicles of corpses into the bodies of homosexual men, generally without their knowledge. In doing this, the theory suggested the boost in testosterone would cure the person's homosexuality. These techniques became quickly discredited, in favor of behaviorally focused therapies. In the 1950s and 1960s, men convicted of homosexual acts were commonly given electric shock therapy, hallucinogenic drugs, and subjected regularly to brainwashing techniques aimed at reducing their homosexual cravings. Often, men could choose to volunteer for these treatments in place of jail terms. Volunteers for the commonplace "aversion therapy" were shown pictures of naked men and then given a series of electric shocks. Then, as a form of relief, the men were shown naked women in pictures or films. The idea of this approach was to increase interest in women while reducing interest in men through strict behavioral therapy approaches.

With the inclusion of homosexuality in the first edition of the *Diagnostic and Statistical Manual of Mental Disorders* (DSM) in 1952, the idea of finding a cure was also institutionalized. The original DSM classified homosexuality as a "sociopathic personality disturbance," which was far from controversial at the time given that the vast majority of people believed this to be true. While the DSM-2, published in 1968, removed homosexuality as a sociopathic personality disturbance, it remained as a "sexual deviation" until 1973. Of note, many homophile groups had taken to accepting homosexuality as an illness because doing so allowed them to organize for empathy and treatment as a disability rather than as a religious sin. Their thought was that such an approach would lead toward more humanitarian approaches to working with homosexual individuals.

During the early 1970s, activists began to realize that accepting the medical view of homosexuality was no more helpful than the religious one, as having a disability still meant the reduction of many basic human rights and fair treatment before the law. With mounting research indicating that homosexuality was neither an illness nor an independent predictor of poor health outcomes, a group of LGBT activists began a number of highly confrontational actions to force the American Psychiatric Association (APA) to address this inaccurate medical assessment. Finally, in 1973, the APA formally met with members of LGBT activist organizations to discuss their concerns and to review a number of now available scientific studies on the health and well being of homosexuals. The committee later conducted further investigation and ultimately proposed homosexuality be removed from the DSM in late 1973.

Although initially approved, full acceptance that homosexuality was not an illness was not quickly endorsed. A referendum on the change was conducted in early 1974, requiring the voting of the full APA membership. Even then, only 58 percent of members voted to uphold the decision to remove the diagnosis from the DSM, illustrating the uncertainty of the field. Further, the revised DSM-2 removed homosexuality but added a diagnosis of Sexual Orientation Disturbance (SOD). Thus, individuals who felt no conflict about their sexual orientation would no longer be considered to have a mental illness. However, those who felt conflict about their sexual orientation would meet criteria for SOD and could continue to seek therapy.

In the 1980s, the DSM-3 was released, which further defined how homosexuality could still be a mental illness. Changed to ego-dystonic homosexuality (EDH), the problem of pathology remained. Those who argued for the diagnosis contended that some homosexual individuals may feel estranged and distressed about their sexual orientation, and that in order to continue research and practice with these people a diagnosis was necessary. Those who were against it suggested that an individual's subjective reporting that their illness was indeed an illness was not in line with best practices for classifying and diagnosing psychopathology. Further, activists claimed that while the name had changed, EDH would continue to perpetuate the common belief that homosexuality was an illness and that people who claimed a gay identity would require treatment. Finally, in 1987, EDH too was removed from the DSM, allowing psychology (and the allied fields that agreed with these changes) to focus on understanding and improving the human condition of homosexual people, rather than focusing on the ability to change it altogether.

Today, conversion therapy is only supported by religious organizations and has been publicly refuted by all major scientific organizations. The American Psychological Association, American Psychiatric Association, and the National Association of Social Workers have all clearly expressed their understanding that the evidence does not support the notion that homosexuality can be "cured." As Speaker Nancy Pelosi stated in 2011, "a growing scientific consensus accepts that sexual orientation is a characteristic that is immutable," and, given this knowledge, therapeutic interventions may "cause social harm by disseminating inaccurate views about sexual orientation." The APA has recognized further that the relationship between homosexuality and poor health outcomes is related most likely to stigma, and not simply the condition of sexual orientation. In 1992, the APA released a statement summing up this perspective as follows:

> Whereas homosexuality per se implies no impairment in judgement, stability, reliability, or general social or vocational capabilities, the American Psychiatric Association calls on all international health organizations and individual psychiatrists in other countries, to urge the repeal in their own country of legislation that penalized homosexual acts by consenting adults in private. And further the APA calls on these organizations and individuals to do all that is possible to decrease the stigma related to homosexuality wherever and whenever it may occur.

This deeper and more accurate understanding of sexuality has been critical in moving research away from exploring the "cause" of homosexuality and toward addressing the disparities that exist in stigmatized groups. In fact, research attempting to make specific genetic links to homosexuality have become highly uncommon: if homosexuality is not a condition that needs to be "cured," and we intend to promote social equality for LGBT individuals, then the origins of sexual identity become irrelevant to achieving this goal.

TOWARD CONTEMPORARY PERSPECTIVES OF SEXUAL ORIENTATION

During the early 1900s, sexual orientation was described in terms of psychology and behavior. As early as 1905, Freud began to publish on sexuality, identifying the defining characteristic of sexual orientation as the sex that an individual is compared with the sex to whom the individual is attracted. Also during this time, researchers began to recognize that gender roles, expression, and sexual behaviors were not parts of the same construct but multiple aspects of one's sexual identity. Many regard the work of Alfred Kinsey as the first attempt to identify sexuality beyond a simple binary concept (i.e., heterosexual *or* homosexual). This early work of Kinsey and his colleagues helped us to understand that *sexual behavior* is a continuum that may change over time.

More recently, however, a sophistication of defining sexual orientation has grown beyond this to include dimensions of *attraction* (i.e., who a person finds attractive), *romantic beliefs* (i.e., who a person is romantically interested in), and *identity* (i.e., how an individual self-identifies). Given this complexity, a number of definitions have emerged. In the early 1990s, sexual orientation was defined as "the direction of sexual feelings or behaviors toward individuals of the opposite sex, same sex, or combination of the two." In 2011, the APA defined sexual orientation as "the sex of those to whom one is sexually and romantically attracted."

Today, research and practice have evolved, attempting to embrace all of these dynamic constructs simultaneously. Research today finds that sexual orientation is more likely an enduring emotional, romantic, or sexual attraction or non-attraction to other people; sexual orientation is fluid and people use a variety of labels to describe their sexual orientation. However, this more sophisticated understanding will be discussed in more length in Chapter 11, which examines contemporary issues regarding LGBT rights.

The twentieth century began with a strong pathologization of LGBT people and an intense interest in understanding the causes of homosexuality. Nevertheless, scientific understanding would eventually advance to the point that homosexuality could no longer be considered an illness or disease. Rather, the focus moved away from understanding an underlying cause to better comprehending the stigma and discrimination associated with homosexuality and its impact on the mental and physical health of members of the gay, lesbian, and bisexual community.

Freud was ahead of his time when he hypothesized that sexuality was likely an immutable human trait. He was followed by a series of scholars and scientists who would attempt to show otherwise. The push for pathology ultimately resulted in a long and tumultuous relationship between the APA and gay civil rights movements. With their inspirational roots for organizing going as far back as the mid-1920s, these homophile groups after World War II would help to set the stage for the contemporary LGBT civil rights movements described in the ensuing chapters.

Chapter 3

THE BIRTH OF THE GAY
CIVIL RIGHTS MOVEMENT

The 1950s represented a time of paradox for the gay community in the United States. American cities, especially New York City and San Francisco, became magnets for gay American veterans of World War II and for youth seeking to escape the bigotry and conformity of small town and rural America. Gay neighborhoods became the heart of a lively and growing subculture. In these cities during the late 1940s and 1950s, the modern gay civil rights movement emerged, and the first homophile (pro-gay) organizations, such as the Mattachine Society, formed.

Yet, at the same time, a fierce backlash against gays accompanied the widespread fear of communism, a period that some historians have called the "lavender scare." Gay men and women were kicked out of their families, hounded from their jobs, hospitalized against their will, and, in some cases, driven to suicide. Thus, the postwar era represented a time of both mounting activism and intense oppression—a period when the first open political expressions of what would later be called "gay pride" began to take place while the LGBT community increasingly felt the strains of being marginalized by a paranoid and intolerant straight majority.

FOUNDATIONS LAID DURING THE WAR

For many gays and lesbians, the Second World War opened their eyes to a new reality. Released from the isolation of their small communities, those who served saw a wider world and dreamed of a better, happier life after the war. In spite of the fact that the Military Code of Justice dictated that gay soldiers, sailors, and marines were to be drummed out of the service with a dishonorable discharge, gay men and women served in all branches during World War II, often evading detection because military psychiatrists, given the job of initially screening out homosexuals, as well as fellow soldiers who were straight that served alongside them, relied on stereotypes of effeminate gay men and masculine lesbians. In any case, the number of Americans serving in the military rapidly expanded from 334,473 in 1939 to more than 12 million by the time the war ended in 1945. In the rush to fill the ranks, the military made little serious effort to investigate the sexual lives of recruits.

For gay and bisexual inductees, the military provided the first opportunity for a social life. As a 20-year-old gay draftee wrote a friend, life in the military provided freedom from parental and neighborly scrutiny. "You see, the Army is an utterly simplified existence for me," he relayed in a letter. "I have no one to answer to as long as I behave during the week and stay out of the way of the MPs [military police] on weekends. If I go home, how can I stay out all night or promote any serious affair? My parents would simply consider me something perverted and keep me in the house." Chuck Rowlands, a gay inductee, was surprised at the number of gay officers that he encountered in the United States Army. "My first assignment in the Army was in the induction station at Fort Snelling, which became known as the 'seduction station,'" he later said in an interview. "I found that all the people I had known in the gay bars in Minneapolis and St. Paul were officers who were running this seduction station. When recruits would be lined up by the thousands, as they would be each morning outside our windows, all of us would rush to the windows and look out and express great sorrow that all these beautiful boys were going to be killed or maimed or something in the war."

Gay men at leave in big cities or stationed there often turned to YMCA dormitories and public parks, along with the more traditional gathering places, such as bathhouses and gay bars, to find sexual and romantic partners and to connect with a larger community. "Certainly [the war] brought a lot more people from the hinterlands out into conditions where they weren't living in small towns, where they were freer, where they met other people and, male and female, got into close, same-sex relationships and developed friendships," said one serviceman, Jim Kepner. "On the nights out, groups of soldiers might go looking for women and end up finding each other."

After the war was over, a flood of veterans joined a gay migration to the cities that had begun in the early twentieth century. They wanted to return to the social scenes that they had discovered during the war. The cities already had established gay communities, though the size of these metropolises also allowed a person to become anonymous if they chose. These soldiers were changed by the war. Growing up hearing stereotypes of gay men as weak, effeminate, easily frightened, gay servicemen had fought bravely and sometimes witnessed other gay men display battlefield valor. The insults and ridicule, these men realized, were a lie and for some soldiers this meant an end to self-hatred and the sense of inferiority. Just as important, they also realized they were not alone. "The effect of World War II is really, truly profound," said George Buse, who said he joined the Marines in part to prove his masculinity. "[It] will never again be what it was before that war. Gay people began to recognize that there were others like themselves from other parts of the country. Even though they were totally 'closeted' then, at least there was a certain perception that we weren't geographically isolated." Just as African Americans served in World War II to win a double victory (what they called the "Double V") against not just the Germans and the Japanese but also against racism and discrimination in America, so too did battle-hardened gay veterans return home seeking a victory against homophobia.

GROWING SELF-AWARENESS

In the years immediately following World War II, gay people often knew as little about homosexuality as the larger straight community. Even as they wrestled with their own sexuality, gay men and women in small-town America felt shocked when they discovered that there were untold numbers of people like them. Billie Tallmij later became an early member and organizer of what was perhaps the first lesbian rights organization in America, the Daughters of Bilitis (DOB). Tallmij later recalled her bafflement when she started college in the late 1940s and received a letter from a friend back home. "I was seventeen, and in my first year of college in Kansas . . . a high school friend wrote me a letter from school and described how she [had] gotten involved with another girl," Tallmij said. "It blew me away. I could not accept that Joanna could have done this." Tallmij said that she went to the dean of women who turned this opportunity into a teaching moment. Rather than condemn the friend, she loaned Tallmij a number of books on homosexuality, including the 1928 lesbian romance novel *The Well of Loneliness* written by British author Radclyffe Hall. "*The Well* opened the door for a lot of people, including me," she said. "I read that book and found that I was coming home. I recognized myself in the characters, and I also recognized the emotions that were so beautifully written there. I was always a tomboy and I had crushes on girls. I tried things with boys, but they were simply not my cup of tea. I was uncomfortable. This was an answer that I had sought for a long time."

Other gay men and women became aware of homosexuality as an identity more directly. Edith Eyde, a woman who later wrote under the pseudonym "Lisa Ben" (a play on the word "lesbian'), in 1947 founded *Vice Versa*, one of the first lesbian magazines in the country. She told an interviewer how the more permissive atmosphere of Los Angeles allowed her to understand her identity and the larger gay community after she moved there in 1945 from her home on an apricot ranch in rural Northern California. She had fallen in love with a girl in her home town and had regularly hugged and kissed her but did not know how to describe her feelings. She remembered feeling crushed when she ran into the young woman years later and found out she had married and had given birth to a child.

Eyde moved to Los Angeles not sure of her identity or why she felt different. "I didn't know any gay people when I moved here," she said. "As a matter of fact, I didn't even know the word *lesbian*. I knew how I felt, but I didn't know how to go about finding someone else who was like me, and there was just no way to find out in those days." She moved into an apartment building where a number of other women lived, and she noticed something right away about her new neighbors. "I noticed that although there was plenty of talk, they never mentioned boys' names. I thought, *well, gee, that's refreshing to hear some people talk who aren't always talking about boyfriends and breakups . . .* I don't know what brought up the subject, but one of the girls turned to me and said, 'Are you gay?'" Unfamiliar with the term as it applied to sexuality, she said, "I try to be as happy as I can under the circumstances." The other women laughed and explained what they meant. The women invited her to a softball game, and she later went to a gay bar in Los Angeles called the If Club where she got to dance with another woman for the first time. It was her first experience with a larger gay community.

The lesbian bars and clubs often drew curious men who gawked at the gay patrons. Eyde said Los Angeles police also made a heavy presence at such spots. Police harassment and brutality raised her political consciousness. She witnessed police humiliate one young man at a gay bar, forcing him to physically prove his male identity in hopes of catching someone violating ordinances against cross dressing.

BIRTH OF THE GAY PRESS

Eyde had an undemanding office job as a secretary at RKO Studios in Hollywood. "You won't have a heck of a lot to do here" her boss said, "but I don't want you to knit or read a book. I want you always to look busy." She used the abundant down time to launch *Vice Versa*, which she labeled in the masthead, "America's Gayest Magazine." She gave the crudely produced mimeographed publication that name, she said, because gay men and women supposedly lived in opposition to what mainstream society approved. This was not the first gay-oriented periodical in America, but it quickly became one of the most influential and helped usher in an era of journalism aimed at a gay audience.

Beginning in June 1947, she would type up an issue, make five copies on the mimeograph machine and give the small number of copies to her friends, telling them: "When you get through with this, don't throw it away, pass it on to another gay gal." In this way, the early editions of *Vice Versa* reached a surprisingly large audience.

Eyde anonymously authored most of the articles, although occasionally someone else would write a story. *Vice Versa* reflected her diverse interests, including book and movie reviews. She wrote a review of *The Well of Loneliness*, even though it had been published almost two decades earlier because, as she said, "there were very few books around at that time that said anything about lesbians." She would also alert readers if possibly lesbian characters or scenes suggesting lesbianism appeared in movies. She carefully avoided including any sexually explicit material in the magazine to avoid legal problems. In the fourth issue, she declared that "gay gals" were a permanent fixture of American life and that the straight world had better get used to it: "Whether the unsympathetic majority approves or not, it looks as though the third sex [gay men and women] are here to stay."

Eyde produced nine issues of *Vice Versa* through February 1948 until another company bought RKO, instigated mass layoffs, and she lost her secretarial job. Her next position did not provide her the spare time to write and publish further issues, so *Vice Versa's* brief life ended. However, her work made gays all over Southern California and beyond aware of the city's emerging gay community, bolstered many readers' confidence, and, in the words of Rodger Streitmatter (an historian of the gay press), became a major influence on later gay periodicals. She continued her writing career for one such publication, *The Ladder,* which was published by the DOB. While writing for *The Ladder,* she began using her pen name. (Her original choice was "Ima Spinster," but the editors rejected it. "I thought that was funny, but they didn't," she said.)

BARRIERS TO OVERCOME: POST-WAR SEXISM AND HOMOPHOBIA

As gay men and women flocked to American cities after World War II and began achieving an independent identity, 1945 to 1960 marked an era of almost unprecedented backlash against the LGBT community. The gay African-American writer James Baldwin suggested in his 1949 essay "Preservation of Innocence: Studies for the New Morality" that the hatred of gay men was directly related to straight male society's contempt for women. "[O]ur current debasement of and our obsession with [the male homosexual] corresponds to the debasement of relations between the sexes." In part, this conclusion was based on the belief that because Western society valued masculinity more than femininity and gay men were seen by a homophobic society as having chosen an identity that rejected the rightful masculine role. It is not surprising, therefore, that the widespread oppression of gay men in particular accompanied a fierce backlash against women in the post-war United States.

During World War II, millions of women replaced men serving in the military in industrial jobs and played a key role in the manufacturing of the tanks, planes and guns that helped to win the war. The number of women working outside the home increased by 50 percent during the war years (1940-1945), climbing to 36.5 percent by the last year of the war. Women had never earned higher wages, enjoyed more financial independence, or been given more authority, but as millions of male soldiers returned home, they demanded a return to the status quo, with women in subservient roles. Employers targeted female workers for layoffs. The percentage of women earning wages outside the home fell to 30.8 percent by 1947. Among women who stayed in the workplace, many lost industrial jobs and returned to lower-wage, more conventional positions as secretaries.

Women faced layoffs, salary reductions, and ridicule in marketing, television, and the movies. An advertisement for Drummond sweaters featuring two mountain climbing men was blunt. "Men are better than women. Indoors, women are useful—even pleasant. On a mountain they are something of a drag." A print ad for Van Heusen ties showed a woman on her knees as she served a man breakfast in bed under the slogan, "Show her it's a man's world." Another commercial for Van Heusen shirts showed a series of pictures in which a man in a button-down shirt and tie spanks a woman, ravishes her, and gets adoringly hugged by her alongside the slogan, "It's daring, it's audacious, it's the bolder look in shirts." The message was clear: real men are controlling and violent when necessary, and they are here to be tough and dominate meek women. Gay men, assumed to be more like submissive females, could not possibly fill this role.

Several movies in the era depicted assertive women as causing a supposed rise in juvenile delinquency, homosexuality, and other alleged social ills. Movies such as *Rebel Without a Cause* (1955), *Psycho* (1960), and *The Manchurian Candidate* (1962) depicted children raised by domineering mothers with no strong male in the house as liable to become at best dysfunctional or feminine, and, at worst, homicidal monsters. For example, in *Rebel Without a Cause*, James Dean hangs out with a gang of misfits including a troubled boy nicknamed Plato (played by gay actor Sal Mineo) who obviously has a crush on Dean's character, Jim Stark. Raised by a domineering mother and a weak father, Stark ends up a juvenile delinquent. To drive home the dangers of men acting like women, Stark's father, played by Jim Backus, spends part of the film wearing a feminine kitchen apron and doing the dishes—women's work. Stark suggests life would be better if his dad acted like more of a traditional man, even if it meant a little domestic violence against his mother. At one point, Stark moans that his mother "eats [dad] alive and he takes it." Stark later insists, "if [dad] had guts to knock Mom cold once, then maybe she'd be happy and then she'd stop pickin' on him, because they make mush out of him." This cultural hostility towards women made gay men particularly vulnerable amid the paranoia and fear that accompanied the Cold War.

The Lavender Scare

The United States' ally of convenience against Nazi Germany in World War II, the Soviet Union quickly became an ideological enemy and global rival after the conflict ended. The Soviet Red Army occupied the eastern portion of Germany as well as most of Eastern Europe, establishing communist regimes under their control. Meanwhile, in Asia, the Korean peninsula lay divided, with a pro-Soviet communist dictatorship controlling North Korea and a pro-American capitalist regime controlling South Korea. Further, many Americans mistakenly believed that the Russians engineered Mao Zedong's successful communist revolution in mainland China in 1949.

Republican and Democratic politicians alike panicked at the advance of communism and incorrectly believed they were witnessing a repeat of history and that Soviet leader Josef Stalin, like Hitler before him, planned to conquer the world. This fear turned to hysteria when the Soviets detonated their first atomic bomb in August 1949, thus ending the American monopoly of that terrible weapon. The American political right, in particular, believed that the United States faced a bitter, twilight struggle between good and evil and that, unless communism was stopped, the world faced a dark future of totalitarian rule emanating from the Soviet capital of Moscow. The hunt for closeted communists in America started shortly after World War II but only intensified after the trial and execution of accused Soviet spies Julius and Ethel Rosenberg.

Senator Joseph McCarthy of Wisconsin and others on the far right charged that thousands of communists had infiltrated the executive branch of the federal government, the military, public schools and universities, and the film and infant television industries. Americans were hounded from their jobs on the flimsiest of evidence of communist sympathies during the so-called "Red Scare." At the same time, a "Lavender Scare" or "Gay Scare" also took place. (Because it was considered by some to be a flashy, feminine color, lavender came to be associated with gays by the 1950s. The gay community eventually embraced the color as a symbol of their community, and in the 1970s one gay rights group, in tribute to the radical African American Black Panthers organization, dubbed itself the Lavender Panthers.)

McCarthy and other right wingers argued that homosexuals were particularly vulnerable to blackmail by communists who supposedly threatened gays in important positions to reveal secret information to the Soviet Union. Government agencies, schools, and other employees fired suspected gays because they allegedly represented security risks. In any case, gay men in particular were accused of being weak and perverse, prone to cowardice, and susceptible to wicked ideas that would undermine the struggle against the Soviet Union.

In 1950, a State Department official announced that his office had fired 91 employees for suspected homosexuality. Republicans in Congress claimed that gays had infiltrated President Truman's administration. Meanwhile, Republican Party national chair Guy Gabrielson fired off a letter to thousands of party activists. He warned that "sexual perverts" were "perhaps as dangerous as actual communists" and urged the party to take action against them. In June 1950, the Senate authorized an investigation into "homosexuals and other moral perverts" holding government positions.

In December 1950, the government released a report, "Employment of Homosexuals and Other Sex Perverts in Government" that charged, "The lack of emotional stability which is found in most sex perverts and the weakness of their moral fiber makes them susceptible to the blandishments of foreign espionage agents . . . [and] easy prey to blackmailers." A purge of gay government workers ensued. Investigators warned the targets of the gay witch hunt that their lifestyles would be publicly revealed and they could face criminal prosecution if they did not provide names of other homosexuals working in federal agencies. By January 1955, about 8,000 federal employees lost their jobs because they were security risks, with 600 fired due to acts of "sex perversion."

One victim, a government scientist named Dr. Frank Kameny, noted that federal employees suspected of homosexuality did not have the right to face their accusers. "We have information that leads us to believe that you are a homosexual," he was told by an investigator in 1957, while the Harvard Ph.D. and astronomer was working at the U.S. Army Map Service. "Do you have any comment?" Kameny asked, "What's the information?" The government agent refused to offer him any details, saying, "We can't tell you, that might reveal our sources." Likewise, Kameny refused to offer specifics. ""Well, then, I can't give you an answer," he said. "You don't deserve an answer. And in any case, this isn't any of your business." Kameny's career was ruined. "By the end of the year, sort of as a Christmas present, I was out." Like many gays and men and women falsely accused of being gay, he was fired. The number of government employees fired during the "gay scare" increased by twelve times in the period between 1950 and 1953.

Shortly after being sworn in as president, Dwight Eisenhower issued an executive order barring any gay man or woman from working for the federal government. Even companies doing business with the government began screening employees for "homosexual tendencies."

A gay purge happened in the military, with annual discharges doubling through the 1950s. Soldiers, sailors, and marines could be terminated even if they were deemed only to have "homosexual tendencies." One woman in the military became a target of suspicion when a number of her friends in the service were investigated for their sexual orientation, and she said she faced constant harassment from authorities. "I was in the service during the McCarthy era, '51, 2, and 3," she told interviewers for the documentary *Before Stonewall*. "The OSI [Office of Special Investigations] started an investigation of me because some of the women I had been associated with were under investigation for homosexuality," she said. "There was no time of day when they wouldn't come and get me. I'm not easily intimidated but I was totally intimidated by these men. This had been going on for 10 or 11 months, and I knew I was at an emotional, physical, and mental breaking point. I knew it was either tell them now, or see myself in some hospital someplace."

Before they were removed from the ranks, soldiers accused of homosexuality often suffered physical and sexual abuse and found themselves confined in "queer stockades" until their branch processed the discharge papers. Gays kicked out of the service received "Undesirable Discharges," which was universally understood to mean that they had been removed from the ranks because of homosexuality. Other gays faced receiving a Section 8 discharge, meaning they had been deemed mentally ill. Such discharges haunted gay Americans, making it much more difficult to find work. Other military careers ended more tragically. One lesbian soldier, Pat Bond, recalled what happened at her base in Tokyo as five hundred were discharged. "They called up one of our kids—Helen," Bond said. "They got her up on the stand and told her that if she didn't give names of her friends they would tell her parents she was gay. She went up to her room on the sixth floor and jumped out and killed herself. She was twenty."

Ironically, two of the top figures promoting the Red Scare and its related Gay Scare were Roy Cohn, the closeted gay attorney for Senator Joseph McCarthy's Committee on Government Operations, and FBI director J. Edgar Hoover, who was widely rumored to be gay. Most gay men like Cohn, and possibly Hoover, stayed in the closet and a few tried to prove their heterosexuality by being publicly anti-gay. As early as 1937, Hoover had done all he could to stir the homophobic pot. "The present apathy of the public towards perverts, generally regarded as 'harmless,' should be changed to one of suspicious scrutiny," Hoover warned in a widely reprinted 1937 article for the *New York Herald Tribune*. "The harmless pervert of today can be and often is the loathsome mutilator and murderer of tomorrow . . . The ordinary offender [transformed] into a dangerous, predatory animal, preying upon society because he has been taught he can get away with it." Such rhetoric linking gay men in particular with child molestation and even murder would do much to inspire violence against gays in the twentieth and twenty-first centuries. Powerful motives kept men like Cohn and perhaps Hoover in the closet. The consequences of being known as gay reached far beyond the workplace.

The federal gay purge probably inspired increased harassment of homosexuals by local police departments, which increased raids on gay bars, bathhouses, and night clubs. Police frequently beat gay suspects. Washington, D.C., police arrested more than 1,000 suspected gays per year in the early 1950s, while other sweeps of gay hangouts frequently took place in Baltimore, Miami, New Orleans, and Dallas. Anti-gay sweeps reached epic levels in some communities. Los Angeles Police Chief William Parker, known to the city's gays and lesbians as "Wild Bill," in particular urged his officers to root out homosexuals. His detectives often parked outside of gay bars and nightclubs, wrote down the license plates of cars in parking lots, and when the automobile's owners were identified, officers visited their employers and told them they had been seen at a gay hangout. The victims of such stakeouts, especially teachers whose contracts included a "morals clause," and those working in the burgeoning aerospace industry who had security clearances, often lost their jobs.

Entrapment, in which undercover officers offered or requested oral sex or other acts from gay men in parks and the restrooms of gay businesses, destroyed many lives. Draconian California sodomy laws in the mid-twentieth century made such encounters with police a dangerous business. A person convicted of engaging in anal sex faced life imprisonment, while a conviction for an act of oral sex could mean as much as five years. Such laws were extremely difficult, however, to enforce. The real threat came from Section 674 of the California Penal Code, which prohibited "lewd and lascivious conduct." Under this statute, many unfortunate men responding to the come-ons of California police officers found themselves behind bars. Those charged with such offenses often became unemployed and received two-year probation with the stipulation that they would not associate with other known homosexuals. This became the fate of so many gay men that some mistakenly believed it was illegal in the state to take part in even private gatherings with other gay men.

During the 1950s, large numbers of parents more closely monitored their children's social behavior to discern whether their boys were properly "masculine" and their girls were appropriately "feminine." Children suspected of being gay sometimes were forced to go to psychiatrists or, if the parents' fears proved true, found themselves disowned. Marge Summit, who later became a bar owner in Chicago, experienced such heartbreak. "When we were growing up, most of our parents, when they found out we were gay, we were excommunicated from the family or we were just totally dropped. We weren't invited to a lot of family affairs. My mother tore up my brother's wedding invitation to me because she didn't want the 'queer' coming to the wedding. There were a lot of things like that happening to gay kids growing up in the Fifties." So pervasive became homophobia that men remained with wives they wanted to leave because of the fear they might be accused of being gay if they left to live on their own.

Some targets of the Lavender Scare committed suicide. One prominent politician committed suicide when the Washington, D.C. police vice squad arrested his son for soliciting sex with an undercover police officer in Lafayette Square. Roy Blick, the inspector of the D.C. police Morals Division, had overseen the arrests of numerous government employees in city parks as part of what the department called the "Pervert Elimination Campaign." Blick had told the United States Senate that there were 3,500 "perverts" working for the United States government though he later admitted to a reporter that the number was a "quick guess." On June 9, 1953, Blick's officers slapped handcuffs on Buddy Hunt, student body president at the Episcopal Theological School in Cambridge, Massachusetts. Young's father was Lester C. Hunt, a former governor of Wyoming and member of the U.S. House, who designed the bucking bronco featured on the state's car license plates and was currently serving as United States senator. Perhaps because of his father's prominence, the police initially dropped the charges against Buddy Hunt, but the story became a national scandal through the efforts of Senator McCarthy and his allies, Senators Herman Welker of Idaho and Style Bridges of New Hampshire, the chair of the Republican campaign committee, who smelled political blood. Republicans controlled the Senate by a single vote, 48-47. (One senator was an independent.) If Hunt, a Democrat, could be forced to resign, Wyoming's Republican Governor C.J. Rogers would pick his replacement and give the GOP a slightly more comfortable margin and allow an incumbent Republican to run for a full term.

Upon learning of the younger Hunt's arrest, Welker and Style called Blick to Welker's office and demanded to know why he had not filed charges against the young suspect. Blick said it was because Hunt had never been arrested before and because of his status as a seminary student. The senators asked Blick if Senator Hunt had bribed him. Blick said no, but under pressure from the lawmakers, the D.C. police re-filed charges against Buddy Hunt. A court convicted him of soliciting the undercover officer for "lewd and immoral purposes" and assessed a small fine. The Republican trio then turned their sights on the elder Hunt, launching a relentless campaign to force him to resign. Lester Hunt refused to back down and was leading in the polls as he ran for re-election the following spring, but McCarthy, Welker and Style refused to let up. They threatened to distribute 25,000 campaign fliers in Hunt's home state providing details on Buddy's arrest and conviction. The Eisenhower administration offered the Wyoming senator a job on the Federal Tariff Commission if he promised to end his campaign and never run for the Senate again.

Distraught and increasingly withdrawn, Hunt told his friend, political columnist Drew Pearson, that he would end his Senate campaign if his son's troubles became a campaign issue. Following a medical exam at the Bethesda Naval Station, Hunt wrote the Wyoming state Democratic Party chair a letter stating that he was withdrawing from his reelection campaign and would "never again be a candidate for elective office." On June 19, 1954, he entered the capitol building with a .22 caliber rifle, walked into his office, placed two photos of his children on the desk in front of him, sat down, and fatally shot himself.

GAY POLITICAL ACTIVISM IN THE 1950s

In the face of such fierce persecution, many gays understandably sought a low profile. Others, however, bravely risked all to roll back the Lavender Scare, to regain jobs, and to win human rights for their community. One writer realized that gays could not passively wait to be granted human rights by the straight majority but would have to fight for them. Edward Sagarin (who published under the pseudonym Donald Webster Cory) made this argument in his groundbreaking 1951 book *The Homosexual in America: A Subjective Approach*. Sagarin contended that gays represented a discriminated minority group due its civil rights and wrote, "there is no homosexual problem except that created by heterosexual society." Sagarin told his audience, "What the homosexual wants is freedom—not only freedom of expression, but also sexual freedom." A gay American had the right to use his body, he said, "so long as he does not use the force of violence, threat, or superior age, so long as he does not inflict bodily harm or disease upon another person; so long as the other person is of sound mind and agrees to the activity." Unless the gay man would "rise up and demand his rights" then "he will never get them, but until he gets those rights he cannot be expected to expose himself to the martyrdom that would come should he rise up and demand them."

Frank Kameny decided that he had nothing to lose by becoming an activist. As already noted, the astronomer lost his government job during the gay purge and was unable to get the government to reveal who identified him as a homosexual. After his dismissal, he experienced nothing but frustration seeking work and experienced hard financial times. He sued and fought a three-year legal battle to win back his government post, which ended unsuccessfully in 1960. He filed an appeal with the United States Supreme Court, but the High Court refused to hear his case. His perseverance, however, finally led the United States Civil Service Commission in 1975 to drop language added to its 25-year-old rules regarding the suitability of federal employees that allowed agencies to fire or refuse to hire people if they were found to engage in "sexual perversion."

Along the way, Kameny became a leader in the Mattachine Society. Though not the first gay civil rights group in the United States (the Society for Human Rights was briefly active in Chicago during the 1920s, and the Veterans Benevolent Association had appeared and quickly vanished in New York City during the 1940s), the Mattachine Society became the first organization to make a lasting impact. Henry Hay said that he formed the society in New York in 1950 as a response to the climate of fear that settled over the gay community after World War II. "The country, it seemed to me, was beginning to move towards fascism and McCarthyism; the Jews wouldn't be used as a scapegoat this time—the painful example of Germany was still too clear to us," Hay said later. ". . . It was obvious that McCarthy was setting up a pattern for a new scapegoat and it was going to be us—Gays. We had to organize, we had to move, we had to get started."

The British-born Hay in many ways embodied the fears of men like Joe McCarthy. Not only was he gay, Hay was also a communist who in the 1930s had been active in the Industrial Workers of the World, a radical group that sought to unite all working men and women in a struggle to replace capitalism with industrial democracy. Hay left the Communist Party because of its opposition to homosexuality, but he stayed in the closet, even marrying. Upon founding his new group, however, Hay decided he could no longer lie to himself and others, so he came out to his wife and his mother.

The Mattachine Society derived its name from the Italian word *mattachino*, which referred to a character who appeared in many Italian plays. Such characters were medieval court jesters who risked the wrath of kings by telling them dangerous truths. Masked musicians made up the Société Mattachine in Renaissance France. Hay thought that his new organization forced society to face the truth about homosexuality and that gays in the United States had been forced to wear a figurative mask to conceal their identities. The first chapter of the Mattachine Society formed in Los Angeles in 1950, with affiliates soon popping up in Boston, Philadelphia, Chicago, Denver, and Washington, D.C., the latter city the epicenter of the Lavender Scare. In its founding statement of principles, the group sought to consciously imitate other "minority" groups like "the Negro, the Mexican, and the Jewish people," in developing an "ethical homosexual society" and to campaign against "discriminatory and oppressive legislation" while assisting "our people who are victimized daily as part of our oppression."

The Society was unable to achieve some of the more ambitious goals that early members discussed, such as establishing retirement homes for elderly gays and shelters for gay youths who had been thrown out of their homes by their families. Education, however, became the organization's primary mission. The Society hosted discussion groups where members learned about their shared experiences, discussed the origins of homosexuality, learned about famous gays in history, and formed strategies on how to end homophobia. In Los Angeles, members met at the First Unitarian Church where gays and heterosexuals held relatively public the experiences and problems associated with being homosexual in an oppressive culture. Some members and curious visitors were so nervous that they brought along women to pose as their girlfriends. If anyone showed enthusiasm or interest at these gatherings, they were quietly invited to join. One early member, John Gruber, said that many who joined had lived lives of such self-hatred that much of the time was spent reiterating the message, "We are not ill. We are not insane."

The Los Angeles chapter launched a legal fight when local police entrapped one of its members, Dan Jennings. The Society held fundraisers, hired a skilled lawyer, and won an acquittal for Jennings even though he admitted he was gay.

The effect was electrifying for the gay community across the country. In 1952, the LA members also began to publish what became the first successful gay magazine, *One*, which circulated in cities across the country, purchased by over 5,000 readers, and passed hand-to-hand to many more. The name came from a line by the poet Thomas Carlyle who wrote, "A mystic bond of brotherhood makes all men one." The magazine often expressed views more radical than those held by most members of the Mattachine Society. At a time when many gays tried apologetically to accommodate straight society, the first issue of *One* included a poem by one member, Betty Perdue, called, "Proud and Unashamed." Seven months into the magazine's existence, postal authorities in Los Angeles, on orders from officials in Washington, D.C., seized copies of an issue on homosexual marriage on the grounds that the publication was obscene. The issue openly discussed rumors that FBI director J. Edgar Hoover was gay, which attracted the attention of the law enforcement agency. The groups sued but lost in the federal courts until the case reached the United States Supreme Court, which ruled in 1958 that the gay-oriented publication was not obscene, a groundbreaking decision

A more conservative leadership, led by Hal Call from San Francisco and Kenneth Burns of Los Angeles, took over by the mid-1950s. Radicals like Hay, who were described by conservatives in the group as a "disgrace to us all," quit or were eased out. Gays had enough problems, the conservatives charged, without facing charges that they were communists. As the group's California chapter put it, "Homosexuals are not seeking to overthrow or destroy any of society's existing institutions, laws or mores, but to be assimilated as constructive, valuable and responsible citizens." By declaring loyalty to society's laws, the group, in effect, was conceding the legitimacy of anti-sodomy statutes that made their sex lives illegal.

In general, the group preferred to use the word "homophile" to refer to itself, and its members sought to avoid the negative associations the psychiatric profession had attached to the word "homosexual." Group leaders also sought to ostracize and exclude men they regarded as "swishy," or effeminate. Mattachine members sought to convince straight society that gay men were as masculine as their heterosexual counterparts rather than to challenge the mainstream culture's concepts of masculinity and femininity or its sexism directly. An emphasis was adopting a respectable, middle-class persona. Those attending meetings were encouraged to wear business suits. Transgendered people were not welcome. The group began to fragment, with local chapters functioning independently and not agreeing on the organization's purpose, and membership declined.

Bringing Lesbianism Into the Open

Middle-class lesbians, according to authors Lillian Faderman and Stuart Timmons, avoided joining the Daughters of Bilitis for fear it would attract too much attention from a hostile majority. Lesbians from wealthier backgrounds, like many of their better-off gay male counterparts, preferred to maintain a low profile in order to keep their romantic and sexual lives hidden. One of the DOB's founders, Del Martin, complained that more affluent women "not only refused to support homophile groups but even 'damned [them] for bringing Lesbianism into the open, fearing that as the public became more aware, people might take a second look at them' . . . The more homosexuality was discussed in public, the more difficult it would become for two mature, unmarried women to pass as 'housemates.'"

Established in 1955 in San Francisco, the Daughters of Bilitis derived its name from the lesbian title character featured in an obscure cycle of poems by the late nineteenth and early twentieth century French writer Pierre Louÿs, *The Songs of Bilitis*. Martin, Phyllis Lyon, and other organizers picked the word "daughters" because they thought it would lend the group enhanced respectability, as enjoyed by the Daughters of the American Revolution. As the case with the Mattachine Society, however, the opaque name (perhaps intentionally) obscured more about the group's purpose than it revealed. The Daughters started as a social group, a club where lesbians could meet, socialize with, and learn about other lesbians. Meetings often took place in members' homes and often provided a place where members could safely dance. Soon, however, they began publishing a magazine, *The Ladder*, and hosting lectures and discussions. Similar to the Mattachine Society, they saw their primary function as not protesting injustice but educating the public in hopes of winning greater public tolerance for their members. Also, like the Mattachines, the DOB leadership urged its members outwardly to assimilate to heterosexual norms, with members encouraged to wear makeup and dresses or to wear only women's slacks if they chose to wear pants. The Mattachine Society and the Daughters of Bilitis sometimes worked together, but because of the latter's relatively scanty membership, the more established Mattachine Society often ignored the DOB. By 1959, the group had chapters in cities across the country, and in 1960 held its first national convention in the group's birthplace, San Francisco.

The DOB and the Mattachine Society shared one important flawed assumption. Both groups hoped that homophobia could be defeated by gentle, rational discourse. By accommodating straight society's ideas of proper masculine and feminine behavior and dress, by assuming that the freedom to choose one's romantic and sexual partners could be separated from the way in which society defined manhood and womanhood, these groups sold out a large percentage of their potential constituents who more deeply violated gender norms and suffered even greater discrimination and marginalization.

The accommodationist position taken by gay civil rights groups in the 1950s ultimately proved too passive to push back against the entrenched prejudices of heterosexual society. It depended in large part on the majority achieving enlightenment rather than on the LGBT community directly taking on its oppressors. Such an approach was doomed to failure. As African-American civil rights leader Martin Luther King, Jr., said of the black freedom struggle, "Freedom is never voluntarily given by the oppressor; it must be demanded by the oppressed."

Groups like the DOB and the Mattachine Society did help create a gay community and gave important encouragement to members, allowing the more vulnerable members to step away from a suffocating sense of isolation and self-hatred. Such early organizations created social networks on which later political activism could be built. Armed with the important research by scientists like Alfred Kinsey and Evelyn Hooker, they launched the first sustained assault on the idea that heterosexuality was a norm by which all should be measured, as well as the notion that homosexuality was a form of mental illness. In the 1960s, the Cold War eased from its paranoid peak in the 1950s, and the panic about gays as security risks slightly receded even as the LGBT community benefited from the rising feminist movement's assault on gender stereotypes. The gay community would learn as well from the black civil rights revolution and transition to a more confrontational and ultimately more successful gay rights crusade.

Chapter 4

GAY PROTEST AND REBELLION IN
THE 1960s AND 1970s

After the tumult and change of the 1960s and 1970s, it became common for people who had protested, marched, or immersed in the counterculture to describe themselves as having taken part in "the movement," as if all the revolutionary impulses of that decade were a single thing. Activists during those raucous years had many targets: racism and segregation, the Vietnam War and American imperialism, poverty, exploitation of migrant labor, sexism, and homophobia. The movements that organized to fight these evils often overlapped, and crusaders for one cause often joined the fray for other moral campaigns, but the so-called "movement" often fragmented over priorities and leadership.

African Americans often resented white attempts to control the civil rights agenda. Whites in large numbers abandoned the civil rights campaign after passage of the 1965 Voting Rights Act, focusing instead on protest against the Vietnam War. African Americans and Mexican Americans frequently kept each other at arm's length and sometimes became antagonists in their parallel fights for human dignity. Women often complained about sexism that they encountered within the civil rights and anti-war movements, leading some to make feminism their chief cause. Meanwhile, in the anti-war, civil rights, and labor movements, homophobia thrived.

There was no single protest movement during the 1960s, but, rather, a cluster of side-by-side struggles, the activists joined together by occasionally mutual interests in shifting coalitions. Protest movements differed on priorities. For instance, mainstream feminists in the early 1960s had little interest in battling for lesbian rights. Like women, gays would have to carry on their own separate liberation struggle.

At the same time, the gay rights movement learned and benefited from other activist causes. The anti-war movement questioned masculine violence and a culture where men were taught to suppress emotions and empathy, considering them traditional feminine traits. The feminist movement critiqued American society's definitions of "manhood" and "womanhood," the idea of male supremacy, and the economic and social roles assigned people based on gender. These initiatives gave gay men and women intellectual ammunition as they questioned their marginalization by straight society. African Americans who directly challenged racist segregation laws by demanding service at white-only lunch counters and riding in white-only seating on interstate buses, encouraged gay protestors to resist police harassment and violence. African Americans battling longstanding white supremacist ideology and embracing slogans like "Black Power" and "Black is beautiful," bolstered gays who now rejected the idea that their sexual orientation meant they were defective and worthless.

As early as 1951, Daniel Webster Cory, in his book *The Homosexual in America*, saw a clear connection between black civil rights and gay rights. "Our minority status is similar, in a variety of aspects, to that of national, religious, and other ethnic groups in the denial of civil liberties; in . . . discrimination; in the assignment of an inferior social position; in the exclusion from the mainstream of life and culture." The black civil rights movement opened doors for a full range of protestors during the 1960s and 1970s—pacifists, feminists, and gay human rights crusaders. The 1960s gay rights movement began to move sharply away from the accommodationist approach of earlier groups such as the Mattachine Society and the Daughters of Bilitis. During the 1950s and early 1960s, a major focus of the gay rights movement was to challenge stereotypes and to prove, as historian Bruce J. Schulman put it, "homosexual men were regular guys, professionals, working men." Promoting tolerance of sexual orientation took a back seat to changing the image of the gay community.

By the late 1960s, however, a new generation of gay activists wanted to move on from confronting stereotypes. Just as African-American activists in this era fought to include black history courses at public schools, and taught their children about black achievements in science, politics, literature, and the arts, gay activists moved from telling straight society that homosexual men and women, with the exception of their romantic and sexual partners, were just like their straight counterparts, to insisting that there was nothing wrong with men acting in a supposedly feminine way, or women being what society considered masculine or "butch." They moved beyond overcoming self-loathing to challenging narrow definitions of gender.

"Coming out" became an important part of what came to be known as "gay liberation" by the early 1970s. As long as gay people kept their sexual orientations secret from the outside world, as members of the Mattachine Society tended to, straight society would cling to the homophobic stereotype of gays and lesbians as sinister, unbalanced sexual predators. By coming out, gay soldiers, policemen, firefighters, doctors, lawyers, teachers, physicists, and philanthropists would demonstrate that not only was homosexuality compatible with mental health, but that gay people were as smart, stable, strong, brave, talented, loving, generous, and creative as the society at large. Gay people were not a problem, activists insisted. Anti-gay bigots were.

THE SEXUAL REVOLUTION AND GAY POLITICS

American culture seemed steeped in death to Sixties radicals, both straight and gay. By 1960, the world had lived for 15 years under the shadow of nuclear weapons. Realizing that they lived in a dangerous world in which all life could be annihilated many times over, young people questioned their parents' values system. Many youths also felt dismay at the hypocrisy of an American society that presented itself as a bastion of democracy and freedom, as opposed to the communist Soviet Union, while denying the most basic freedoms to African Americans. The Kinsey reports on male and female sexuality had revealed that a shockingly large number of American adults lied about their sexual behavior and violated the standards that they insisted their children should live by. Young people questioned so-called traditional values. The comedian Lenny Bruce lampooned a culture that celebrated bloodshed in books, movies, and television, but recoiled in horror at sex. Making fun of movie censors, he summarized their attitudes as, "Well, for kids to watch killing—Yes; but *shtupping* [a Yiddish slang word for having sex]—No! Because if they watch *shtup* pictures, they may do it some day."

The spread of the highway system, increasing prosperity for white middle-class Americans, and the ever-widening ownership of automobiles by young people also allowed teenagers and college-age adults more time free from the supervision of their parents and, consequently, more time for sex and sexual experimentation. Meanwhile, rock 'n' roll music, named after African-American slang for sex, encouraged more erotic and emotional dance moves and frequently featured sexually suggestive lyrics.

Adult magazines featuring photos of nude women such as *Playboy* reached a large male readership and spawned a chain of "Playboy Clubs" and, from 1959 to 1961, a late-night syndicated TV show called *Playboy Penthouse*. Under pressure from students, colleges began to drop rules that limited when men and women could visit each other in their dorm rooms and eventually ended regulations that prohibited off-campus cohabitation. A 1962 best-seller, Helen Gurley Brown's *Sex and the Single Girl*, said a girl should engage in sex anytime "her body wants to." Cumulatively, these more relaxed attitudes toward the human body would be termed the "Sexual Revolution." Although the culture remained for the most part fiercely homophobic, perhaps no group benefited from more permissive attitudes toward sex than the LGBT community. In the 1960s and 1970s Counterculture, the straight, monogamous, heterosexual married couple increasingly seemed less and less like a universal norm and more the product of a phony culture. This atmosphere created a friendlier culture in which a more assertive gay rights movement could thrive.

THE INFLUENCE OF FEMINISM
ON THE GAY RIGHTS MOVEMENT

After World War II, an unprecedented number of middle- and upper-class women earned college degrees but had nowhere to make use of their learning. Rather than careers, they found themselves stuck in low-wage jobs with little or no chance for promotion, or consigned to lives as stay-at-home mothers. During these years, Betty Friedan worked at women's magazines that told their readership that this was the proper and most noble role for females, but she found these suffocating limits maddening. She conducted an extensive survey of middle-class and affluent women similar to herself and concluded that American women had become victims of what she called the "feminine mystique," which glorified only women who played a traditionally subservient role to men. Friedan blamed the mystique for outbreaks of depression, anxiety, anger, and infantilization of adult women and their daughters. She summarized her findings in her 1963 best-seller, *The Feminine Mystique*, which sold more than a million copies.

The book would give rise to what would be called the "second wave feminism." (The first wave involved the struggle in the late nineteenth and early twentieth centuries by women to win the right to vote.) Second-wave feminists demanded greater access to higher education; the same access to jobs as men; equal pay for equal work; for the end of the "glass ceiling" that set a low upper limit for how high women could rise in business organizations; for husbands to share the same responsibility for childrearing and housework as their wives; for an end to discriminatory laws that, for instance, prevented women from opening bank accounts without a man's signature; for laws against domestic violence; and for an end to demeaning depictions of women in the popular culture.

Early 1960s feminists challenged what dominant men had always insisted was the natural role of women as subordinate "helpmates" to their spouses and the idea that men were born to lead and women to applaud and follow. They rejected the idea of masculinity being defined by aggression and cool detachment. These same assumptions had victimized not just women but gay men who fell short of the traditional masculine ideal. Like African Americans, the feminists of this era also provided a model for political activism to the later gay liberation movement. In the early 1960s, many women had been active in the civil rights movement and protests against the Vietnam War, but they found they were frequently victims of condescension by their male peers. Men discounted the ideas of their female comrades and made crude jokes about them. Men in protest organizations expected activist women to type letters for them and to make coffee. Female protestors at times found themselves the objects of intense sexual harassment.

Female activists realized that they would have to form their own civil rights group to be heard. In 1966, feminists established an organization named, at Betty Friedan's recommendation, the National Organization for Women (NOW). Made up overwhelmingly of white, straight, affluent female professionals, NOW focused (at least at first) on issues concerning female lawyers, government workers, and journalists. Like the NAACP, NOW primarily battled gender discrimination through lobbying Congress and state legislatures, and through litigation rather than through "direct action" protests. But early feminists had no interest in accepting open lesbians in their ranks and saw gay activism as a distraction, even as a threat to the women's movement. The battle against sexism was daunting enough without having to open a second front against deeply entrenched anti-gay hatred. Anti-feminists already stereotyped the women's movement as led by unnatural, sexually perverse man-haters, and the presence of lesbians in the movement, some feared, would only confirm the worst fears of their opponents.

Some straight feminists called lesbians "the lavender menace." One feminist, Abby Rockefeller, said in the late 1960s that lesbianism "muddles what is the real issue for women by making it appear that women really like sex as much as men— that they just don't like it with men." Straight feminists also assumed that, as in the dominant culture, one woman in a lesbian couple always played the "male" role and thus replicated the oppressive family structure feminists were supposed to reject. In any case, many gay women questioned why they needed to be part of a movement so focused on battling the sexism within heterosexual marriages. Gay men and women would obviously have to fight heterosexism not only in the larger society but within the movement as well.

HOMOPHOBIA IN THE MEDIA

The Lavender Scare of the 1950s and the 1960s gay activism drew the attention of the national media, which devoted increasing coverage to homosexuality, even if the tone of the stories remained intensely homophobic. For example, a 1964 photo essay in *Look* magazine opened with this dark description of gay night life, which portrayed homosexuals as an infestation:

> These brawny young men in their leather caps, shirts, jackets, and pants are practicing homosexuals, men who turn to other men for affection and sexual satisfaction. They are part of the 'gay world,' which is actually a sad and often sordid world . . . Homosexuality shears across the spectrum of

American life—the professions, the arts, business, and labor. It always has. But today, especially in big cities, homosexuals are discarding their furtive ways and openly admitting, even flaunting, their deviation. Homosexuals have their own drinking places, their special assignation streets, even their own organizations. And for every obvious homosexual, there are probably nine nearly impossible to detect. This social disorder, which society has tried to suppress, has forced itself into the public eye because it does present a problem—and parents are especially concerned.

That last line, by implication, drew on the ugly myth of gay men as especially prone to child molestation. The *Look* photo spread and its hostile tone was not unique in the early 1960s. *Time* magazine on January 21, 1966, ran a highly negative essay called "The Homosexual in America" that, in spite of the Kinsey reports, portrayed homosexuality as a mental disease suffered by a tiny minority of men (the article barely acknowledged the existence of lesbianism). The unidentified author said gay men were born of weak or absent fathers and domineering, mannish mothers. "For many a woman with a busy or absent husband, the presentable homosexual is in demand as an escort—witty, pretty, catty, and no problem to keep at arm's length . . ." the article declared. "The once widespread view that homosexuality is caused by heredity, or some derangement of hormones, has been generally discarded. The consensus is that it is caused psychically, through a disabling fear of the opposite sex." The author continued to ridicule the "pathetic pseudo marriages" of gay male couples before concluding, "Homosexuality is a pathetic little second-rate substitute for reality, a pitiable flight from life. As such, it deserves fairness, compassion, understanding, and, when possible, treatment. But it deserves no encouragement, no glamorization, no rationalization, no fake status as minority martyrdom, no sophistry about simple differences in taste—and above all, no pretense that it is anything but a pernicious sickness."

Like *Time*, CBS piled on anti-gay stereotypes in an hour-long news special on homosexuality aired in 1967. "The average homosexual, if there be such, is promiscuous," host Mike Wallace said. "He is not interested in, nor capable of, a lasting relationship like that of a heterosexual marriage." Meanwhile, on television entertainment programs, gays remained invisible, served as comic punchlines or played the role of villains on drama programs such as *Alfred Hitchcock Presents* or *Playhouse 90*. Press coverage of gays would remain hostile, almost without exception, throughout the 1960s.

LIVING DUAL LIVES

LGBT people often carried dual identities during the 1960s and the 1970s, building a thick wall of separation between their personal and their professional lives. The hyper-macho world of sports kept David Kopay in the closet. He played running back at the University of Washington in the early 1960s before signing with the National Football League's San Francisco 49ers in 1964. Though never achieving stardom, the determined Kopay served as a backup and special-teams player in a journeyman career that took him from the 49ers to stints in Detroit, Washington, New Orleans, and Green Bay. Special-teams players, who race down the field and collide with other players at top speeds during kickoffs, experience some of the hardest hits in football. Kopay earned the nickname "Radar," he said, because during kickoffs, "I could always find somebody to hit."

During his football career, Kopay did not discuss his sexuality, but he said that he privately felt compelled to play football in order to prove something about the toughness of gay men and because he felt camaraderie that he did not experience elsewhere based on his ability. "I loved being part of a team, part of a family," he said. "There was acceptance there purely based on what I could do. As long as I was able to play, I never minded being relegated to the special teams or 'suicide squads' . . . Recently, I've come to the conclusion that a lot of my extra drive came from the same forces that brought black athletes out of the ghettoes to the forefront of professional sports. They were out to prove—among other things—that they were not inferior because of their race. I was out to prove that I was in no way less a man because I was homosexual." He had a romantic relationship with teammate Jerry Smith while playing for Washington. (Smith later died of AIDS.)

Kopay played in the NFL until 1972, but never voluntarily came out of the closet during his career. Rumors, however, spread. He later said that African-American players who heard about his hidden identity were usually the most understanding players in the locker room. Kopay blames his reputation as a gay man for his inability to get a job coaching special teams at his alma mater and in the pros. Finally, he revealed his private life in a 1977 book, *The David Kopay Story*. Only four other former NFL players came out as gay after their careers since Kopay's revelation, although in 2014 a University of Missouri defensive end, Michael Sam, became the first collegiate player to come out of the closet. He was drafted by an NFL team, the St. Louis Rams, though he was cut before the regular season began.

College presumably would be a more open-minded place, but gay students in the early 1960s found that they were no more welcome there than in the larger world. Karla Jay recalled a time, when she was a freshman at Barnard College, when she was told about two women who had been expelled from the school the previous year. The two women had been spotted having sex in their dorm room by a male voyeur who was spying through their window with a pair of binoculars. The "Peeping Tom" reported them and was allowed to stay in school while his victims were expelled. Karla Jay later recalled that after hearing the story she "realized for the first time that there was something wrong with being a lesbian" and that she "had better cover up." As part of this concealment, she dated a man who she later decided was probably also gay.

Balancing personal integrity, keeping a job, and experiencing romance was particularly challenging for the writer Audre Lorde and Maua Adele Ajanaku, an African-American lesbian couple. The two said that New York's lesbian bars provided some of the few safe places where they could find relationships, but most such establishments were filled almost entirely with white women. Such bars could be unfriendly to African Americans. "The bouncers ostensibly were there to keep the johns [men who run prostitution rings] out, but because I was black, I was also undesirable," said Ajanaku. "I knew that someday this was going to have to be my strength and my power, but I also knew that, hey, we're all supposed to be the same." Lorde agreed that anti-black prejudice was often strong in the LGBT community. "In the Fifties, if you were different, you were just as suspicious within the gay community as you were in America [as a whole.] You have to remember that gay girls (that's what we were called then), were a reflection of what was going on around us."

In the 1960s, Lorde said, her gay identity became less of a focus because of the African-American civil rights struggle. "In the Sixties, my identity as a gay girl became less so, because I was involved in the civil rights movement, and I was married, having kids," she said. "My consciousness of myself as a lesbian was there, but at that particular moment, I was involved in living another life . . . The civil rights movement didn't develop as a conflict for me in terms of being gay . . . Even down in the Village [the Greenwich Village neighborhood of New York City], I was also in college. I was a closet student, I was a closet politico, I was involved in progressive movements, but—it was not cool to be a homosexual there. The saying then was it made us vulnerable to the FBI, but it was really homophobia. What you had to present to the world was a front that was impeccable, and perfect according to how they defined it. To take the position that, hey, I'm who I am, I don't want to hide—it was the refusal to hide that became questionable and revolutionary."

Craig Rodwell lived such a revolutionary life. After graduating from high school in Chicago, he briefly studied ballet in Boston before moving to New York City in 1958. Upon his arrival, he made little effort to conceal his gay identity. Angered at what he saw as the timidity of groups like the Mattachine Society, Rodwell preferred the company of open homosexuals to the middle class, accommodationist gays who belonged to such groups. He frequently experienced police brutality. In Greenwich Village, gays learned they had no freedom to just hang out. Cops would push billyclubs into their ribs and snarl, "Keep moving, faggot, keep moving." One night, while he cruised for a date, three undercover police officers jumped on him and wrestled him to the ground. Police dragged him to precinct headquarters and threw him into an interrogation room even though no one told him why he had been arrested. He demanded to know on what charges he was being held, which prompted a severe beating. Afterward, he was forced to appear at the local FBI office to prove that he had properly registered for the draft.

Such brutal experiences radicalized Rodwell by his late teens and early twenties. He sometimes spent nights "going wrecking"—strolling down the streets with other gay friends and deliberately antagonizing the straight people they encountered. The friends would sometimes ride the subway lines and form a chorus line, singing in falsetto, "We are the Village queens/We always wear blue jeans/We wear our head in curls/Because we think we're girls." It would not be long until Rodwell had another unpleasant encounter with the police. Local cops had long abused an ordinance banning "suggestive" swimwear at a beach in Riis Park in Queens, a popular gay hangout. Officers frequently harassed gay men and arrested them because they had supposedly violated the code. One day, the police stopped Rodwell who responded to being verbally accosted by yelling back. Once again, Rodwell was hauled to a police station, where he was asked the same short set of questions over and over again. Telling the officers he had already answered them, Rodwell then refused to speak, prompting yet another beating. He was charged with resisting arrest and rioting. The judge tried to give him fatherly advice and dismissed the original charges but grew suddenly angry when he finally realized the defendant was gay. Another beating, this time in the jailhouse, awaited Rodwell, who was eventually sent to what was then called the "Queen Tank." He spent most of his three-day sentence teaching ballet to gay street hustlers. (Rodwell later proposed and helped to organize the first gay pride parade held in New York City.)

There would be many Rodwells in New York, growing ever angrier at their terrible treatment by the police, particularly after a 1966 crackdown on "undesirables" in Times Square and Washington Square Park ordered by Mayor John Lindsay (normally a liberal politician) who wanted to prove his tough, law-and-order credentials. The resentment of many young gays at chronic oppression, and their frustration with the slow pace of the gay civil rights movement would finally explode one summer night in New York City in 1969 in an uprising that would prove the most galvanizing single event in American LGBT history.

THE ROAD TO STONEWALL

It is not surprising that the first gay rights protest centered on the military draft. On September 19, 1964, twelve members of the Homophile League of New York staged a protest outside of the Whitehall Induction Center because, they said, the U.S. Army violated its own policy about keeping draft records confidential when conscripts were rejected because of homosexuality. Employers were able to find this information and often refused to hire gay applicants as a result. Later, similar groups staged quiet, polite demonstrations in Washington, D.C., Philadelphia, and Los Angeles. By the mid-1960s, gay protestors held signs that read, "BILL OF RIGHTS FOR HOMOSEXUALS" or "15,000,000 HOMOSEXUAL AMERICANS ASK FOR EQUALITY, OPPORTUNITY, DIGNITY."

Police harassment of gay bars and their patrons became an important political cause in the gay community at the dawn of the 1960s. In 1959, San Francisco Mayor George Christopher faced the accusation from a challenger that he had allowed the West Coast city to become "the national headquarters of the organized homosexuals in the United States." Christopher, a supporter of black civil rights, won re-election but still fended off the charge that he was too lenient on gays by cracking down on gay entertainment establishments. Christopher's war on gay bars faced an obstacle because in the 1950s the California Supreme Court had ruled that a liquor license could not be revoked simply because a bar drew a primarily gay clientele. Courts insisted the state Alcohol Beverages Control Department (ABC) had to prove crimes had taken place on the premises. San Francisco police, with the encouragement of the ABC, filled gay bars with undercover officers who entrapped bar patrons, encouraging them to solicit sex, then slapping the handcuffs on them when they responded positively. Arrests and revocation of liquor licenses climbed sharply in 1960 and 1961.

Amid this campaign, a local gay entertainer, José Sarria, reacted by unsuccessfully running for a spot on the San Francisco Board of Supervisors. It would be more than a decade until another gay candidate, Harvey Milk, won a seat on the board, but Sarria established a groundbreaking example. Because the two established gay civil rights groups in the city, the Mattachine Society and the Daughters of Bilitis, were at this point too divided to respond to this police crackdown, the bar owners themselves filled the void. Forming the Tavern Guild in 1962, the new association began publishing a handbook on legal rights, provided arrested patrons legal funds, and conducted a voter registration drive, perhaps the first organized political effort aimed at electing candidates friendlier to the gay community.

One bar owner, Bill Plath, went a step further and established the Society for Individual Rights, which functioned as both a political and a social organization, sponsoring parties and health clinics as well as educating members about local candidates. The group worked closely with the Council on Religion and the Homosexual (CRH), a group run by local liberal Protestant ministers, which represented one of the first Christian outreach groups aimed specifically at gays in the country. The CRH took on many causes, including persuading city officials to lessen police abuse of gay men and women. One of the most important moments for the group, and for gay activism in the early 1960s, came when the CRH and another local group, the Society for Individual Rights (SIR), scheduled a New Year's Eve dance on the night of December 31, 1964, at a rundown venue, California Hall. City officials pressured the groups to cancel the event, but they refused and between 200-250 partiers showed up. Police flooded the street in front of California Hall with squad cars, shining klieg lights (bright carbon-arc lights that were often used in filmmaking and by the military to spot enemy planes at night) in people's faces, photographing and filming them as they entered the building, and periodically entering the hall to check and recheck closets for no obvious reasons. When a straight volunteer at the event, Nancy May, told the police to get a warrant when they announced they were going to "inspect" the dance hall, a raid began. Officers hauled May and three lawyers representing the CRH into squad cars for supposedly obstructing police officers. Ministers in the CRH held a press conference the following day in which they accused San Francisco police of intimidation, and one clergyman compared the force to the Gestapo, Nazi Germany's secret police force. Represented by lawyers with the American Civil Liberties Union, the defendants were acquitted before the defense even presented its case when the judge informed the jury that prosecutors had failed to prove the charges and directed a "not guilty" verdict.

The CRH also held a candidates' forum in 1965 in which local candidates answered questions of interest to gay voters but were never able to mobilize effectively a "gay vote" that could significantly influence city policies. Even though the number of gay voters in San Francisco climbed significantly in the 1960s, they remained an ineffective political bloc. Local elections at the time were held on an at-large basis, meaning candidates ran citywide, effectively diluting the collective impact of gays on election results. A tone had been set, however, that would intensify as the decade progressed. In 1965, gay protestors rallied in front of the Pentagon, the U.S. Capitol, and the White House to highlight federal policies that discriminated against gays. Umbrella groups, such as the East Coast Homophile Organizations (ECHO) and the North American Conference of Homophile Organizations (NACHO), helped organize smaller gay civil rights organizations across the country. A national conference sponsored by NACHO in 1968 adopted the slogan "Gay Is Good" in the 1960s. NACHO issued a five-point statement that insisted, in part, on an end to federal laws denying security clearances or visas, citizenship to foreigners, or jobs at the federal, state or local level based on sexual orientation. "Private consensual sexual acts between persons over the age of consent shall not be an offense," the platform said. So-called homophile organizations proliferated, beginning with the first formal campus gay organization at Columbia University in 1967, followed by other organizations at Cornell, New York University, and Stanford. Gay demonstrators were not yet a common sight, but that would soon change.

THE STONEWALL RIOTS

On June 27, 1969, New York City police conducted a raid on the Stonewall Inn, on Christopher Street, in the heart of the metropolis' gay community. "The 'Stonewall' catered to a young and largely nonwhite clientele, including many drag queens," historian Bruce J. Schulman wrote. Police were used to arresting and beating up gay people without encountering resistance. On this night, something different happened. Trouble started when police directed cross-dressers to female officers who, according to standard procedures up to that night, were supposed to take them to the women's room for confirmation of their gender. A cross dresser refused to comply, then a lesbian began to struggle against arresting officers when officers began touching her breasts.

As Lucian Truscott of *The Village Voice* newspaper reported in a condescending tone the following day, "The scene became explosive. Limp wrists were forgotten. Beer cans and bottles were heaved at the windows and a rain of coins descended on the cops." News of the uprising spread through the city, prompting as many as 1,000 protestors to arrive on the scene. Gay men, who for years had been clubbed and kicked by police, fought uniformed officers and painted graffiti on buildings along Christopher Street that proclaimed, "Gay Power!" Angry gays lit fires in trash cans, smashed windows, and started calling officers "pigs." The police department dispatched a riot squad to quell the disturbance, but demonstrations continued in New York for days, spreading past Christopher Street. As a form of protest, some gays began kissing and fondling each other in public.

Within a short time, gay men in New York established the Gay Liberation Front, consciously using the model of radical African-American groups like the Black Panthers. Similar groups formed all over the country in the wake of Stonewall, not only calling for acceptance of homosexuals but also demanding political power for gays. By 1973, more than 800 gay and lesbian civil rights, mutual support, and social organizations had formed across the United States, seeking to end the isolation and loneliness felt by many gays by encouraging those in the movement to publicly "come out." Declaring once-hidden sexual identities had a cascading effect, a drama played out in countless families, workplaces, and at public demonstrations across the nation. Gay bars had long been gathering spots for the community, but after Stonewall, restaurants, legal clinics, newspapers, churches and synagogues aimed at the gay public sprang up in cities across America.

The process of coming out often had the desired effect. As more and more gays stepped forward, they provided a real human face to what had been for many straights a grotesque, threatening caricature. Many straights discovered in the coming years that children, uncles, aunts, friends, colleagues, neighbors, celebrities, and even husbands and wives that they loved and admired were gay. As society saw more and more examples of openly gay people living successful lives, it became harder to defend the idea that homosexuality represented a mental illness.

Gay rights advocates won one of their most significant political victories in 1974. Until that year, the American Psychiatric Association defined homosexuality as a mental illness in its *Diagnostic and Statistical Manual of Mental Disorders* (DSM). The stigma that gays were mentally sick had not led to empathy on the part of straights, but instead encouraged job and housing discrimination and even violence as gay men often faced usually baseless charges that they were sexual predators. Activists demanded the profession provide objective scientific evidence that gays were less well-adjusted than heterosexuals, or drop the damaging designation. In 1974, the APA voted to drop homosexuality from the diagnostic manual. This decision had a positive ripple effect. The following year, the United States Civil Service Commission dropped its ban on the hiring of gay employees. City governments in Boston, Detroit, Houston, Los Angeles, San Francisco and Washington, D.C., followed suit and opened employment to gay men and women. Meanwhile, Dr. George Weinberg, a Manhattan psychotherapist, in the late 1960s coined the term "homophobia" to describe the fear of gay men and women, a pathological condition that, unlike homosexuality, was a real mental disease.

THE 1970s:
THE FIRST RAYS OF ACCEPTANCE

More than a decade of organizing and the energizing effect of Stonewall meant that the LGBT community would no longer greet hostile portrayals of their community in the mass media with silence. One popular ABC television drama, *Marcus Welby, M.D.*, featured two episodes that smeared gay men, prompting a fierce response from the LGBT community. In spite of the actions of the APA earlier that year, a 1974 episode of the show depicted homosexuality as a treatable disease. In one episode, Dr. Welby (played by TV icon Robert Young who in the 1950s starred in the situation comedy *Father Knows Best*) encourages a gay man to resist his gay urges. In another episode, a gay male teacher rapes a junior high student. Notified that the episode was going to air, the National Gay Task Force organized a letter-writing campaign that persuaded four advertisers to drop spots from the episode, the first time major companies responded to pressure from gay consumers. Some affiliates said they would not air the program, prompting the network to add a voice-over at the beginning of the show that specified the differences between homosexuals and child molesters. Around the same time, NBC responded to protestors and dropped an upcoming episode of *Police Woman* because it included a negative portrayal of lesbians.

Meanwhile, post-Stonewall, some of the first positive images of gays appeared in the mass media. In 1972, Hal Holbrook played a gay man who had separated from his wife and son after coming out and moving in with his lover and had to explain his new relationship to his child. The show included no scenes of love or intimacy being expressed between the two lovers, but it also included no demeaning clichés about gay men. Holbrook depicted his character with dignity and strength. The top-rated TV situation comedy *All in the Family* challenged the idea that gay men were effeminate, with an ex-football player in one episode revealing his homosexuality. Another 1970s sitcom, *Soap*, featured the first ongoing gay character (played by comedian Billy Crystal).

The gay subculture had for decades, without open acknowledgment, strongly influenced American music and Broadway theater. The disco music craze in the late 1970s, with roots in both black and gay culture, made the connection more explicit. One group, the Village People, featured performers dressed as masculine archetypes (a Native American in feathered headdress, a policeman, a cowboy, and so on.) The act enjoyed a string of novelty hits beginning in 1977, including "Macho Man" and "Y.M.C.A." (an inside joke within the gay community because YMCAs had, for much of the twentieth century, served as meeting places for men to make sexual hookups).

The larger society, however, lagged behind popular culture. Vietnam veteran and Purple Heart recipient Technical Sergeant Leonard Matlovich of the United States Air Force came out of the closet specifically to challenge the military's ban on gay servicemen. In 1974, after reading an *Air Force Times* interview with Frank Kameny (who had acted as a mentor to gay servicemen), Matlovich decided to reveal his homosexuality in a letter to his commanding officer, which he sent March 6, 1975. The Air Force began discharge procedures, leading to a Matlovich lawsuit. The case became a major news story with Matlovich becoming the first identified gay man featured on the cover of a news magazine, *Time*, on September 8, 1975. Matlovich fought an expensive five-year battle to be reinstated. He prevailed in a U.S. District Court, but knowing that the case could drag on for years, he reached a financial settlement. NBC broadcasted a sympathetic television movie based on the case, *Sgt. Matlovich vs. the U.S. Air Force* in 1978, but Matlovich's life would have no happy ending. He devoted himself to advocating for gay civil rights, but contracted AIDS and died shortly before his 45th birthday in 1988.

THE INEVITABLE BACKLASH

Even with the small advances in gay civil rights in the 1960s and early 1970s, few segments of American society remained as anti-gay as the bare-knuckled world of electoral politics, where even a tangential connection to homosexuality meant political death. Just 10 days after his election as governor of California in 1966, former Hollywood actor Ronald Reagan gathered his advisors at his Pacific Palisades home to discuss a run for the presidency. A so-called homosexual scandal, however, scuttled these plans. The newspaper columnist Drew Pearson revealed that gay men worked on Reagan's staff. The fact that the governor had gays working for him was enough to alter his immediate political future. Even though Reagan purged gays from the state government, journalist and author Theodore White observed, "From this blow, the Reagan campaign never recovered." The former movie star would have to wait until 1980 to run successfully for the nation's highest office.

Religious conservatives reacted with alarm as employment barriers to gays fell and more voices called for tolerance of homosexuals. The religious right, describing themselves as defenders of "traditional values," launched a counteroffensive against the still infant gay civil rights movement. A gay-rights ordinance in Dade County, Florida, sparked a repeal campaign led by singer and former Miss Oklahoma Anita Bryant, who had a Top 40 hit song, "Paper Roses," in 1960. In that decade, Bryant had become a fixture in TV commercials for Tupperware, Coca-Cola, Holiday Inn, and the Florida Citrus Commission, for whom she promoted orange juice. After Dade County passed a law banning discrimination based on sexual orientation in employment, housing, and public accommodations, Bryant led a repeal effort, arguing that social acceptance of gays would lead to widespread child molestation and a decline in American society. Calling gays "human garbage," at one point she declared, "As a mother, I know that homosexuals cannot biologically reproduce children, therefore, they must recruit our children," she said. "If gays are granted rights, next we'll have to give rights to prostitutes and to people who sleep with Saint Bernards and to nail biters." Bryant formed a group called "Save Our Children" that persuaded nearly 70 percent of Dade County voters to overturn the anti-discrimination ordinance in a referendum June 7, 1977.

Within the next year, voters reversed anti-discrimination ordinances in Eugene, Oregon, St. Paul, Minnesota, and Wichita, Kansas. The most important battle came in California where conservative state Senator John Briggs placed a referendum on the state ballot that would have allowed school districts to fire gay employees or anyone discovered to be publicly or privately "advocating, imposing, encouraging or promoting homosexual activity." Another loss by gay civil rights advocates in the nation's most populous state might set back the movement for decades. The gay community, however, effectively organized against the "Briggs Initiative." Labor organizations rallied to the defense of gay members belonging to teacher unions, the largest-circulation newspapers in the state editorialized against the proposed law, and even Governor Reagan opposed the initiative, calling it an attack on free speech. In an editorial, Reagan (who as a Hollywood actor had befriended many gays such as Rock Hudson) asked what would happen if a student upset about a bad grade made a false accusation of homosexuality against a teacher. More than 58 percent of voters cast "no" ballots on November 7, 1978. The anti-gay tide stalled, and in 1980 the Democratic Party for the first time included a gay rights plank in its national platform. However, anti-gay sentiment remained at daunting levels. According to a 1977 Gallup poll, only 27 percent of the American public believed that gays should be allowed to teach in elementary schools, while a mere 26 percent said in 1978 that they would vote for a "well-qualified" gay candidate for president. For three years following her anti-gay crusade, readers of *Good Housekeeping* named Anita Bryant the nation's "Most Admired Woman."

HARVEY MILK AND HIS LEGACY

Harvey Milk's political career captured the triumph and tragedy of gay politics in the 1970s. A Navy veteran and former Wall Street investment banker, Milk moved to San Francisco and established a camera shop on Castro Street in the heart of the city's thriving gay community in 1972, organizing the Castro Village Association, a merchants' network. He lost three times as an openly gay candidate in races for the Board of Supervisors, which governed both the city and county of San Francisco, when elections were held on a city-wide basis. However, he led a successful effort to amend local election rules. Milk finally won an election on January 8, 1977, after the county races were separated into individual districts and his gay constituency, with help from labor unions, could make the decisive difference. He received many letters of praise, particularly from gay people who saw him as an inspiring example. "I thank God," read one letter from a 68-year-old lesbian, "I have lived long enough to see my kind emerge from the shadows and join the human race." However, he also dealt with chilling threats mailed from across the country, such as one note that said, "Maybe, just maybe, some of the more hostile in the district may take some potshots at you—we hope!!!" Milk took such threats in stride. One of his biggest accomplishments was passage by the board of an anti-discrimination ordinance that prohibited businesses from firing individuals based on sexual orientation. Never a one-issue candidate, he also supported free public transportation and called for a citizens' commission to oversee the San Francisco Police Department.

Yet, "The Mayor of Castro Street" seemed to sense that his days might be numbered. He made a tape recording on November 18, 1977, leaving a note asking that the message be played only following his death. "If a bullet should enter my brain, let that bullet destroy every closet door," he said. Milk was assassinated just nine days later by Dan White, a conservative Catholic former police officer who served on the Board of Supervisors and who increasingly clashed with Milk and other board members. White had recently resigned his office, citing inadequate supervisor pay and general disgust with the allegedly corrupt state of city politics, but then changed his mind and became enraged when San Francisco Mayor George Moscone, at the urging of Milk and others, would not reinstate him. On November 27, White snuck into city hall armed with a handgun and fatally shot the mayor in his office before finding and killing Milk. Insult was added to injury at Dan White's trial when defense attorneys successfully kept gays and people of color off the jury. Further, they argued that at the time of the murders, White suffered from diminished mental capacity caused by eating too much junk food, which soon became infamous as the "Twinkie defense." The jury convicted White of voluntary manslaughter rather than first-degree murder, and he was sentenced to only seven years and eight months in prison. A mob of 3,000 gay men and women rioted the night of the verdict, May 21, 1979, leaving more than 160 hospitalized, including 61 police officers, and more than $1 million in damages across the city.

Milk made a lasting impact on state and national politics. Across San Francisco, buildings bear his name, and the municipal landscape now includes a Harvey Milk Plaza at the intersection of Castro and Market streets. An LGBT magnet school in New York serving at-risk students is called Harvey Milk High School. In the wake of his assassination, the Harvey Milk Gay Democratic Club became the party's largest organization in California and one of the most effective get-out-the-vote operations. The San Francisco Board of Supervisors controls the city's airport, and the county gay civil rights ordinance that Milk guided to passage required major airlines to no longer discriminate against gay and lesbian employees. His political rise as an openly gay man inspired countless others to be honest about their sexual identities and to battle for legal reforms granting equal legal rights to the LGBT community. "There were always gay teachers, gay nurses, gay health-care people who lived quiet little lives and feared for losing the security of the jobs that they had," as Walter Caplan, who served as Milk's attorney, noted. However, as a result of Milk's life and political crusades, he said, "You could just see that people stood a little taller." Milk proved that gay politicians could pull together a diverse coalition and win elections without concealing their identities, opening the door for the approximately 600 gay elected officials currently serving in public office in the United States, including Tammy Baldwin of Wisconsin, the first openly gay U.S. senator, who was elected in 2012.

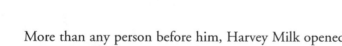

More than any person before him, Harvey Milk opened a national dialogue about the worth and dignity of LGBT people, but his violent death and the light sentence given his murderer revealed the depth of anti-gay hatred still reigning in the United States. On July 12, 1979, a Chicago disc jockey named Steve Dahl held a "disco demolition night" during a Chicago White Sox game at Comiskey Park, which began with the destruction of disco records and ended in a small riot. Many observers believe that the rage expressed that summer night had much to do with the economic frustrations of a working-class crowd that resented the perceived political advances of two groups deeply associated with disco music— African Americans and gays. As the 1970s ended, a conservative movement led by Christian televangelists Jerry Falwell and Pat Robertson rose in part to oppose gay rights. Anti-gay political groups like the Moral Majority catapulted Ronald Reagan into the White House in a landslide in 1980, threatening the baby steps taken by LGBT toward political equality in the previous three decades. The worse was yet to come as gay men in cities like San Francisco began to show mysterious symptoms like fever, rapid weight loss, pneumonia, and the rare cancer Kaposi's sarcoma. The epidemic that would eventually be called Acquired Immunodeficiency Syndrome (AIDS), which would kill about 700,000 Americans by 2014, had already reached the country's shores. Like the 1970s, the 1980s would be a time of heartbreak and resilience for LGBT Americans.

Chapter 5

HIV 101

What is HIV? What is AIDS? How does someone contract HIV? Who is at highest risk? These may be questions that you have pondered as you begin to learn about the important relationship between HIV and the gay community. In previous chapters, we have focused on LGBT civil rights through the nineteenth and late twentieth centuries. During the late 1970s, however, the LGBT civil rights movement shifted radically as a new disease first known as, "Gay Related Immune Disorder" (GRID), began killing gay men by the thousands.

This chapter will help readers understand more about the bio-psychosocial HIV/LGBT relationship. To better ensure that readers will have a basic understanding of HIV as a disease, the present chapter will outline what HIV is, the difference between HIV and AIDS, and explain how HIV can be contracted, as well as explain the differences in treatment for HIV/AIDS in the 1980s versus the available treatments of today. After reading this chapter, readers will have a better understanding of these basic concepts as a backdrop to Chapter 6, which will explore in more detail HIV's complex relationship with the LGBT community over the past three decades.

SCOPE OF THE PROBLEM

While HIV/AIDS is a major American public health issue, the disease's impact on global populations has varied greatly, from a minimal effect on some countries to potentially devastating catastrophes in others, especially African nations. According to UNAIDS (a program of the United Nations), by the year 2007, there were 33 million people who had been infected worldwide (with 2.7 million new infections taking place that same year alone). Of those infections, 45 percent involved youth and young adults from 15 to 24 years of age. Overall, more than 25 million people have died from complications of HIV/AIDS, with developing countries suffering the most. Africa bears 68 percent of the global AIDS burden. Sub-Saharan Africa alone accounts for 22.5 million adults and children over the age of 15 that are living with HIV, including 1.7 million newly infected individuals.

Historically, infection has most frequently occurred through male-to-male sex, intravenous drug use, and lastly, heterosexual contact. Most recent estimates indicate that about 30,000 HIV infections occurred during male-to-male sexual contact in 2009, representing more than half (53 percent) of all infections for that year. Gay and bisexual men account for nearly half of all persons living with HIV in the U.S. and also account for more than half of new HIV infections. The Centers for Disease Control (CDC) estimates that the rate of infection for sexual contact is 44 times higher than that of any other risk group. Gay men represent the only risk group with rates of new HIV infections increasing. (Since the early 1990s, complicated statistical models have been used to predict current and future rates of HIV infection based on historical data, and scientists have developed laboratory testing capable of approximating how long someone has been infected.)

Given recent medical advances, the unique and intimate relationship that gay men have to the HIV epidemic is often difficult to fully understand. One illustration of this comes from the concept of "survivor's guilt" found in the early 1990s among gay men. This clinical phenomenon occurred in gay men who watched their friends die of AIDS while they remained healthy. Consequently, these high levels of bereavement were significantly related to posttraumatic stress disorder (PTSD) symptoms, sleep disturbance, and other stress related factors. Other studies indicated similar findings of depression, anxiety, and stress symptoms among survivors and those who watched and cared for sick or dying friends, partners, and family members. The PTSD-like symptoms occurred due to the fact that, by 1990, three times more San Franciscans had died of AIDS than died in the four major American wars of the twentieth century combined.

What is HIV?

"HIV" stands for Human Immunodeficiency Virus. Broken down more specifically, the term consists of three parts. First, "human," meaning the virus can only infect humans. Second, "Immunodeficiency," explaining that it weakens an infected person's immune system by destroying the important cells that fight disease and infection—the resulting deficiency renders the immune system incapable of protecting the person. Finally, the infectious agent is a "Virus," which can only reproduce itself by taking over a cell in the body of the host.

The fact that HIV is a virus rather than a bacteria is important for a number of reasons. First, bacterial infections are single-celled creatures that can reproduce on their own and do not require the cell of a host for replication. Viruses, on the other hand, are much smaller and consist of a protein coat and a core of genetic material. Unlike bacteria, they cannot survive without a host and can only reproduce by attaching themselves to cells. Viruses also tend to be specific to the cells they attack. Additionally, while bacteria can often be treated through medications (including antibiotics), viral infections are often untreatable and usually left to "run their course." Since the beginning of the twentieth century, vaccines have been developed to reduce the rate of viral infections. For instance, diseases such as polio, measles, and the chickenpox all now have vaccines to prevent transmission. More recently, vaccines to prevent hepatitis A, hepatitis B, and human papillomavirus (HPV) have been released and commonly used. Although no vaccination for HIV exists, treatment methods have advanced significantly in the past decade.

Most viruses, including the common flu (influenza), can be cleared by the immune system over time. In the case of HIV, however, the immune system cannot overcome it, and the infected individual is affected by the virus for life. In addition, HIV replicates itself within an important part of the immune system (within T-Cells or CD4 cells). These cells are necessary for the body to fight other infections and disease, but as HIV replicates itself, it destroys these cells and leaves the body open for what are known as "opportunistic infections."

Scientists believe that HIV initially came from a chimpanzee in Western Africa. Most likely, humans contracted the virus after hunting and eating an infected animal. More recent research indicates that HIV may have been found in humans as far back as the late 1800s, but became much more prevalent only in the late 1970s in the United States. A brief overview of the history of HIV in the U.S. is provided later in this chapter, while Chapter 6 specifically covers the experience of HIV in the LGBT (primarily gay) community.

How is HIV Contracted?

HIV can be contracted through a number of methods involving the transfer of certain bodily fluids, including blood, semen, pre-seminal fluid, rectal fluids, vaginal fluids, and breast milk. Contrary to common belief, HIV does not survive well outside of a host. Therefore, for transmission to possibly occur, these fluids must be injected directly into the bloodstream, or come into contact with damaged tissue or a mucous membrane (found inside the rectum, the vagina, the opening of the penis, and inside the mouth).

In the United States, HIV is primarily spread through sexual intercourse and the sharing of needles by intravenous drug users. Anal sex is the highest risk behavior, with receptive sex being riskier than the insertive role. Vaginal sex is less risky than anal sex. Oral sex (contact between a person's mouth and another person's sex organ) is the least likely sexual transmission method. Much less commonly, HIV can be passed from an infected mother to a child during birth or breastfeeding. With advances in medical treatments for HIV-positive individuals and good prenatal care, perinatal transmission has become nearly non-existent. In very rare instances, transmission can result from deep kissing an HIV-positive person with open sores or bleeding gums, being bitten by a person with HIV when the skin is severely damaged, or eating food that has been pre-chewed by an HIV-infected person with oral bleeding. As mentioned, HIV does not survive long outside of the body, and it cannot reproduce outside a human host. Therefore, the virus does not spread through the air (such as through sneezing or coughing) or water. One cannot contract HIV through insects, such as mosquitos or ticks, or through saliva, tears, or sweat. Additionally, closed-mouth or "social" kissing cannot transmit HIV, nor can using a toilet after a person who has HIV.

Many people do not realize that there are multiple strains of HIV, and that an individual who is already infected with one type can become a carrier of another strain. Such a case is called an HIV superinfection. The new strain can replace the original strain or remain alongside it. The effects of superinfection differ for each individual, however, approximately 4 percent of superinfections become hard to treat with traditional antiretroviral medications.

What Are the Symptoms of Infection?

Generally, immediately after becoming infected with HIV, a person will have no symptoms at all. Within two to four weeks, many people develop a brief flu-like illness that they often do not recognize as the early stages of HIV infection. Like a common flu, individuals may experience symptoms such as fever, swollen glands, sore throat, fatigue, headache, and muscle/joint aches and pains. These symptoms can last for just a few days to several weeks. Although the symptoms of primary HIV infection may be mild and escape notice, the level of virus in the bloodstream (i.e., viral load) is particularly high during this time. Because of this, HIV infection spreads more efficiently during primary infection than during the next stage of infection. It should be noted that some individuals who become infected with HIV will not have any symptoms at all for ten or more years.

After the primary infection stage, individuals enter what is known as the clinical latency phase of infection. During this time, many people experience no symptoms at all. Clinical latency infection can last for eight to ten years, with exceptions of progression both longer and more quickly occurring. However, if left untreated, HIV continues to infect white blood cells, reducing the body's ability to prevent other infection and disease. By approximately ten years into infection, most individuals will progress to AIDS.

How Does One Discover if They Have HIV?

If a person is sexually active, they have generally heard that they should use protection and get tested regularly. This is important, particularly in the case of HIV, because a person can be HIV-positive and not know it for many years. The most common test for HIV is actually a measure of the antibodies produced to fight off the virus. Generally, the immune system takes between three to eight weeks to begin creating these antibodies. So while receiving this type of HIV test is less expensive, it may also provide a "false negative" if conducted too close to the time when the virus was initially transmitted. Approximately 97 percent of people develop antibodies within the first 3 months after infection. This common HIV test is called an antibody screening test (immunoassay), which looks for antibodies in the system. The Patient Protection and Affordable Care Act provides for HIV screening through health insurance without a co-payment. For those without medical insurance, there are places where individuals can be tested for free or a reduced cost. Whether conducted in a lab or as a rapid test (which takes approximately 20 minutes) at a testing location, the choices are either a blood or cheek swab test. Most blood-based tests can detect HIV sooner because the antibody level is higher in the blood than in oral fluids.

More recently, tests that detect both the antibodies and the antigen (part of the virus) have been released. These tests can find recent infection earlier than those that only detect antibodies but are available only for blood tests, which is a more invasive procedure and may deter individuals from being checked. The recently released rapid test is also an immunoassay (a quick test to detect the presence of specific molecules) used for screening and provides results in less than 30 minutes. If the immunoassay shows a positive result, a follow-up test would be needed for confirmation. This second round of diagnostic exams includes antibody differentiation tests (which can distinguish between HIV-1 and HIV-2) and either the HIV-1 nucleic acid test or the Western blot antibody test.

There are a number of emerging home-testing kits as well, including the Home Access HIV-1 Test system and the OraQuick In-Home HIV Test, which were recently approved for widespread use. The Home Access kit involves pricking one's finger to collect a blood sample, sending the sample to a licensed laboratory, and then calling for the results the next business day. This test is anonymous, and the manufacturer can provide confidential counseling and referral for treatment. The OraQuick home test provides results within the home and involves swabbing the mouth for an oral fluid sample and using the kit to examine it. If the results are positive, the individual will need to complete follow-up testing, but he or she can call the manufacturer for confidential counseling and referrals to testing sites.

What is AIDS?

Over time, and if left untreated, HIV can destroy so many of the CD4 cells that a person becomes unable effectively to fight infections and diseases. After ten years with HIV, an untreated person will progress to AIDS, which stands for Acquired Immunodeficiency Syndrome. The condition is "acquired," meaning that the illness was not inherited or genetically related; "immunodeficiency" refers to a deficient immune system (that is, the system that fights off infection and disease); and the term "syndrome" describes a complex collection of symptoms and illnesses. A person is considered to have progressed to AIDS if they have one or more specific opportunistic infections, certain cancers, or a very low number of CD4 cells. Individuals with AIDS need medical intervention and treatment to prevent death.

AIDS is considered a syndrome, rather than a single disease, because people tend to experience a number of opportunistic infections as a result of the disease, which create significant health issues. Generally, people with a well-functioning immune system can be exposed to viruses and have no reaction to them, but when a person who has HIV is exposed, the results can be serious and sometimes fatal given their compromised immune system. These infections are called "opportunistic" infections because they take advantage of the person's weakened system. There are more than twenty opportunistic infections that the CDC recognizes as associated with HIV infection including various types of lymphoma, cervical cancers, and recurrent pneumonia.

Treatment of HIV

The earliest treatments for HIV infection came out in 1987, when azidothymidine (AZT), a drug that inhibits the enzyme that HIV uses to synthesize DNA, was approved by the Food and Drug Administration. Since then, a number of new treatment options have become available. There are currently five different classes of HIV drugs. Each attacks the virus at a different point in its life cycle. HAART (Highly Active Antiretroviral Therapy), the practice of mixing together multiple antiretroviral medications (ARV's), is more commonly known as "the cocktail." Generally, a person prescribed medications takes 3 antiretroviral drugs from at least two classes.

In 2014, new guidelines were released that suggested all people infected with HIV should begin a treatment regimen. However, just because a person is HIV-positive does not mean that he/she must take HIV medications. Whether a person begins medications is dependent on a number of factors, including that person's CD4 count and viral load. However, it is critical that once a person begins medication, the protocol needs to be followed with a high degree of

Class	Description
Nucleoside/ Nucleotide Reverse Transcriptase Inhibitors (NRTIs)	Sometimes called "nukes." These drugs work to block a very important step in HIV's reproduction process by acting as faulty building blocks in the production of viral DNA. This blocks HIV's ability to use a special type of enzyme (reverse transcriptase) to correctly build new genetic material (DNA) that the virus needs to make copies of itself.
Non-Nucleoside Reverse Transcriptase Inhibitors (NNRTIs)	These are called "non-nukes." They work in a very similar way to "nukes." Non-nukes also block the enzyme, reverse transcriptase, and prevent HIV from making copies of its own DNA. Unlike the nukes (which work on the genetic material), non-nukes act directly on the enzyme itself to prevent it from functioning correctly.
Protease Inhibitors (Pis)	When HIV replicates inside cells, it creates long strands of its own genetic material. These long strands have to be cut into shorter strands in order for HIV to create more copies of itself. The enzyme that acts to cut up these long strands is called *protease*. Protease inhibitors (stoppers) block this enzyme and prevent those long strands of genetic material from being cut up into functional pieces.
Entry/Fusion Inhibitors	These medications work to block the virus from ever entering your cells. HIV needs a way to attach and bond to CD4 cells, and it does that through special structures on cells called receptor sites. Receptor sites are found on both HIV and *CD4* cells (they are found on other types of cells too). Fusion inhibitors can target those sites on either HIV or CD4 cells and prevent HIV from "docking" into your healthy cells.
Integrase Inhibitors	HIV uses your cells' genetic material to make its own DNA (a process called reverse transcription). Once that happens, the virus has to integrate its genetic material into the genetic material of your cells. This is accomplished by an enzyme called *integrase*. Integrase inhibitors block this enzyme and prevent the virus from adding its DNA into the DNA of CD4 cells. Preventing this process prevents the virus from replicating and making new viruses.
Fixed-dose combinations	These are not a separate class of medications but combinations of the above classes and a great advancement in HIV medicine. They include antiretrovirals which are combinations of 2 or more medications from one or more different classes. These antiretrovirals are combined into **one single pill** with specific fixed doses.

Source: U.S. Department of Health and Human Services

fidelity. When a person does not take the HIV medication regularly, the virus can become highly resistant, leading the mutations to become non-responsive to the drugs being used to control the disease. Research has indicated that taking 3 drugs concurrently does the best job of controlling reproduction in the body, assuring that many individuals achieve "undetectable" status.

THE HISTORICAL EXPERIENCE OF HIV

As described in detail in Chapter 4, the 1970s were a time of liberation (including, of course, sexual liberation) for the gay community in the United States. Mass numbers of gay men were moving to San Francisco, where an openly gay man, Harvey Milk, had been elected to city supervisor. Additionally, fueled by stigma and discrimination, public sex venues (i.e., bathhouses) began opening throughout major cities. The movement, however, quickly slowed in the early 1980s when the first outbreak of HIV was discovered. In 1981, the "gay cancer" or "Gay Related Immune Disorder (GRID), as it was known at this time, was found primarily in gay men, and medically known as a form of skin cancer called Kaposi Sarcoma.

Although cases had been increasing since the late 1970s, the CDC did not issue an official recognition of the new disease until June 5, 1981. Initially, this report was named "Pneumocystis Pneumonia in Homosexual Men—Los Angeles," but the CDC was reluctant to include the reference to gay men for fear of connecting an outbreak to a specific community, leading to further prejudice. Thus, all references to homosexuality were subsequently omitted. The first report to directly correlate the disease with gay men was not published until July 1982.

During the early 1980s, few attempts were made to address the disease, especially from the federal government. President Ronald Reagan did not publicly mention the epidemic until 1985. The earliest known mention of the disease in a political setting, in 1982, occurred at a press conference with White House Press Secretary Larry Speakes. Even here, AIDS was mentioned only in jest, with a reporter calling the disease a "gay plague" and Speakes asking a questioning reporter, "Do you have it?" Although more than 200 individuals died of AIDS in 1981 alone, no significant policy strategy existed until 1985. In 1983, the U.S. Public Health Service stated that AIDS was "no threat to the public." This same year, the CDC also officially announced that it had identified four groups that appeared to be at higher risk of HIV infection: homosexual men, intravenous drug users, Haitian immigrants, and hemophiliacs. The Haitian community, fearful of negative attention, protested the classification and was removed from the list in 1985.

THE DEVELOPMENT OF PUBLIC POLICY ON HIV

Why did public policy develop so slowly for HIV/AIDS? Further, why was the gay community so strongly correlated with HIV risk, and how did this contribute to the lack of policy initiatives? Examining other epidemics of the time, as well as the government response to them, can be valuable in seeing the alternative approach taken with HIV. For example, the discovery of cyanide in Tylenol capsules in the fall of 1982 led the *New York Times* to publish one article per day for the entire month of October on the scare. At this same time, the major press had published only a handful of articles on HIV. Additionally, the FDA coordinated the testing of more than 1.5 million Tylenol capsules in a national effort. Johnson & Johnson, the company that produces Tylenol, was committing $100 million to the process. Meanwhile, less than $1 million had been spent on the entire effort against HIV transmission. Notably, the Tylenol scare led to the deaths of only seven people. By this time, AIDS had killed 260 Americans.

As HIV was so closely associated with gay men, the political process was laden with moral and value-driven sentiments. As an illustration of the political perspective at the time, when asked in 1987 how HIV policy might affect the larger population, Senator Lawton Chiles of Florida replied: "I guess you can say that as long as this disease is confined to homosexuals, no real danger." Additionally, liberals and conservatives strongly disagreed on how to respond to the disease, with the political right arguing that gay men had brought the disease upon themselves with promiscuous, perverted behavior. "Just Say No," was a slogan First Lady Nancy Reagan had promoted to urge children to reject drug use, and social conservatives wanted gay men to similarly renounce homosexuality, which they viewed as unnatural and sinful, entirely if they wanted to avoid AIDS. The LGBT community was certainly in conflict with the conservative political atmosphere of the Reagan administration. Unfortunately, it was the AIDS-related death of movie star Rock Hudson that helped bring the disease to the forefront of American minds (and to Ronald Reagan, an old Hollywood friend). At this time, the FDA began HIV antibody testing, and finally, in 1987, President Reagan's administration, at the strong advice of Surgeon General C. Everett Koop, sent an 8-page booklet, "Understanding AIDS," to every household (over 100 million) in the U.S.

FEDERAL FUNDING FOR HIV PREVENTION AND TREATMENT

Federal funding for research in the prevention and treatment of HIV was minimal through much of the early 1980s. Congressional appropriations greatly increased after AIDS was redefined as a public health concern in 1985, although comprehensive legislation did not pass until 1990 when the Ryan White CARE Act (RWCA) was signed into law by President George H.W. Bush.

The law was named after Ryan White, an Indiana teenager with hemophilia who contracted AIDS after receiving a blood transfusion that carried the virus. White was diagnosed in December 1984, and his diagnosis became publically known when, after a long medical absence, he tried to return to class, only to face hysteria and harassment from parents and teachers at his school in Russellville close to his hometown of Kokomo. The local community feared that AIDS could be transmitted by casual contact and that White would cause a local epidemic. He was temporarily barred from attending school. His fight to be allowed to be readmitted made him an international celebrity. He won the support of music superstars like Michael Jackson and Elton John, and political figures like Nancy Reagan and Surgeon General Koop. Because of his youth and his disease, a homophobic public did not blame him for catching AIDS the way they did gay men and intravenous drug users. White inspired calls for better treatment of AIDS patients, more research into the syndrome and funding for treatment, and helped reduce misperceptions of the AIDS and its victims. White died April 8, 1990, at the age of eighteen.

No prior policy strategy had ever been passed by Congress specifically to assist those affected by a disease rather than other socioeconomic factors (i.e., age, income, race). The RWCA allocated funding to states, cities, and community-based organizations to impact those living with AIDS, or because of their risk status for contracting the disease. Though not the only source of funding for research on HIV prevention and treatment, the RWCA is the largest. In 2008, the law authorized the spending of $2.8 billion across all programs, while total CDC funding, the next largest amount, is slightly less than $1.6 billion for HIV and STD services combined.

The bill was sold as an effort to combat an "urban disaster," initially named the Ryan White Comprehensive AIDS *Resource Emergency* Act. In order to avoid the political implications of being seen as welfare spending, it was re-labeled as disaster relief. Thus, even in the earliest years, HIV was seen as a socially based illness with welfare implications. The legislation included four parts (Title I-IV), each with distinct initiatives. Title I provided relief directly to cities that had been the most affected by HIV/AIDS cases at the time, setting the stage for where "people should worry." Only sixteen cities qualified for initial funding, called eligible metropolitan areas (EMA's). Eligibility requirements dictated a cumulative caseload of 2,000 HIV affected individuals, or at least 0.0025 percent of its total population. Once qualified, funding from Title I was distributed based on the number of cumulative cases (or "need"). This portion of the bill also required EMA's to create HIV Planning Councils, which examine the specific needs of the community and distribute funding based on their findings.

Title II of the grant ensured money was made available to all fifty states, at no less than $100,000 per state. Again, the law based funding on the number of cumulative cases of HIV; however, this money was distributed through states rather than the EMAs. Title III and IV funding went directly to community-based projects by public and private nonprofit organizations that worked with at-risk populations. Title III funding was intended to provide prevention and early intervention services (such as HIV testing, social services, education) to individuals in the community. Often underfunded (or not funded at all), Title IV funding was specifically designated to the provision of family-centered services to children, youth, and women who were living with HIV. The Ryan White CARE Act was reauthorized in 1996 and 2000. In the 2006 reauthorization, the law was renamed the Ryan White HIV/AIDS Treatment Modernization Act while also reiterating the intent that Ryan White funds were intended to be (at least politically) a health care bill rather than a social service (welfare) program. In this new bill, at least 75 percent of funding through Titles I-III must be used for core medical services, drastically changing the landscape of services, and shifting the focus even further from prevention into the treatment and maintenance of health for HIV positive clients. In 2014, Congress removed the mostly unfunded Title IV since the majority of these services were already accounted for under other components of the bill.

HIV/AIDS continues to be a public health problem in the United States, with more than half of all infections continuing to occur in men who have sex with men. Recent advances in medicine have made what was a terminal illness into a chronic, but treatable disease. Part of the reason why HIV was so readily transmitted in the early part of the epidemic was the fact that the early signs of infection mirror that of many other viruses, including the common flu. However, unlike most other viruses that can be cleared by the immune system over time, HIV affects the infected individual for a lifetime.

With federal funding increasing through the 1990s, and medical and social science research being more commonly funded throughout this time, treatment and prevention efforts have been expanded with great success. In fact, when the White House released the National HIV/AIDS Strategy (NHAS) in 2010, government officials estimated that prevention efforts had already averted more than 350,000 infections across the country. The NHAS envisioned that the "United States will become a place where new HIV infections are rare and when they do occur, every person, regardless of age, gender, race/ethnicity, sexual orientation, gender identity or socio-economic circumstance, will have unfettered access to high quality, life-extending care, free from stigma and discrimination."

Although this goal paints a wonderful image for the future, the idea has only recently become a possibility.

Chapter 6

SOCIOCULTURAL AND HISTORICAL IMPACT OF HIV/AIDS IN THE GAY COMMUNITY

It is difficult to conceptualize a volume on the history of the LGBT community without addressing the overwhelming influence of HIV/AIDS. The disease remains a critical public health issue in the United States. The most recent estimates indicate that the overall rate of HIV diagnosis in the 33 reporting states to be 18.5 per 100,000 people. Gay men remain the largest community affected by the HIV virus, with more than 50 percent of the cases involving men who have sex with men.

In the early 1980s, when HIV first became a public health concern, the disease was almost exclusively associated with homosexuality, specifically the sexual behaviors of gay men. This association was conveniently attached to existing discrimination, homophobia, and heterosexism. Despite increased public awareness and improved prevention and treatment techniques developed over the last twenty years, HIV continues to be a concern for LGBT people, especially among gay men. The (quite literally) intimate association between HIV and the gay community, in many ways, has embedded itself within the fabric of the gay community and its culture.

This chapter concerns the constellation of historical, political, social, and cultural factors that influence the ways in which gay men in the early twenty-first century perceive HIV, their risk for contracting the virus, and potentially harmful behaviors in which they engage. The ways in which medical advances in HIV treatment have changed both the understanding of the disease and the best practices for its prevention will also be examined. Given that a subset of

73

the population reports being less careful when having sex or using drugs due to advancements in HIV treatment, public health officials have needed to develop innovative HIV education and prevention strategies to address these new attitudes and practices.

This discussion opens with an overview of the epidemiological impact of HIV on gay men before offering a brief history of the HIV epidemic. After defining pertinent terminology and examining several theories that can contribute to an understanding of how gay culture may influence HIV risk-taking behaviors, the chapter culminates with evidence that describes how a number of characteristics (i.e., age, race/ethnicity, substance use, social settings and socio-sexual norms) may impact gay men's risk behavior, specifically as they are influenced by the culture of (and in some instances promoted by) the gay community. The chapter concludes with a consideration of the educational, policy, research, and practice implications of these factors.

STIGMA, HIV, AND
GAY CULTURE

The initial lack of Centers for Disease Control (CDC) recognition did not prevent further stigmatizing of the gay community. The negative attention of this disease served as fuel for extremist "evidence" against homosexual practices. In 1985, Gallup polled households across the U.S., finding that 37 percent of Americans had their opinion of LGBT people changed for the worse, and only 4 percent stated to feeling sympathetic to the cause or undecided.

Wrapped in the history of HIV are unique cultural implications. Because sexuality (and subsequent sexual behaviors resulting from sexual orientation) is central to the experience of being an older youth and adult, there became a heightened sensitivity to governmental involvement in approaches to the disease's identification, treatment, and prevention. Before AIDS was irrefutably identified as a deadly illness that disproportionately affected gay men, most did not adhere to safe-sex guidelines concerning their sexual behaviors. For instance, given the sexual "revolution" described in chapter 4, many gay men were already getting a number of other sexually transmitted infections (STIs) such as hepatitis B & C, as well as experiencing an increased prevalence of gonorrhea, chlamydia, and syphilis. Gay men were disproportionately diagnosed with STIs due to frequently unprotected sexual acts such as rimming, or "Oral-Anal contact." However, as most of these STIs are treatable, many gay men were repeatedly diagnosed with multiple STIs, placing them at risk for antibiotic resistance and complicating treatment. At this time, condoms were generally used to prevent pregnancy, a protective message not applicable for gay men. Reacting to continued bias and stigma in the mainstream media, and following the first CDC report on the relationship between HIV and homosexuality, gay newspapers often described the disease as a medical oddity that was blown out of proportion by homophobes in the scientific community and the media.

Bathhouses were also a thriving business of the early 1980s, bringing in more than $100-million a year in America and Canada. An outspoken doctor, Dan William, MD, commented to the New York City magazine *Christopher Street* in 1980 "one effect of gay liberation is that sex has been institutionalized and franchised. Twenty years ago, there may have been a thousand men in any one night having sex in NY baths or parks. Now there are ten or twenty thousand—at the baths, the back room bars, bookstores, theaters. . . . The plethora of opportunities poses a public health problem that's growing with every new bath in town." In short, many gay men believed that the new "crisis" was simply a heterosexual plot to undermine the sexual liberation of the gay community, especially as the disease was initially called the "Gay Cancer" and was so strongly being associated with the group.

The first educational messages directed at gay men also came long before public policy, from AIDS Service Organizations (ASOs) such as the Gay Men's Health Crisis (GMHC). Many of these agencies existed within the gay community and met with a surprisingly unreceptive audience. In fact, messages were often greeted with anger and denial rather than interest. As noted in the widely known book and movie "And The Band Played On," the gay community "didn't need some moral majority doctors telling them what to do with their sex lives."

Fueling this distrust were medical researchers who suggested "promiscuity itself, together with multiple bouts with sexually transmitted diseases produced such catastrophic clinical results." Although many physicians were promoting safer sex, their message suggested a curtailment of promiscuity itself, which did not resonate well with gay men, having recently experienced a distinct sexual liberation in the 1970s. Similarly, HIV risk reduction could not be handled with the same policy approaches as other diseases. Generally, the goal of public health and policy is to find individuals who are infected and then simply limit their ability to spread the disease further. As sex holds an additional symbolic meaning for the gay community, it was much more difficult to find effective ways to reduce the spread of HIV in the community. Gay men felt that they had been singled out by the larger (heterosexual) community and were largely unwilling to make changes in their sexual behaviors because of this mistrust.

Additionally, because the disease was so closely associated with the "gay lifestyle," there was difficulty in finding a prevention policy message that would both scare people enough into making safer decisions while not ostracizing those who had fallen ill to HIV from receiving medical attention or otherwise alienating the gay community as a whole. Finding an effective policy strategy to encourage individuals to see their personal risk while not creating widespread panic was an arduous task. Ultimately, two strategies were debated and remain to the present day. Both hold implications on the way individuals perceive their risk and ultimately engage in, or do not engage in, risky behaviors.

Abstinence and Harm Reduction:
Competing Models

Prior to the AIDS epidemic, behavioral interventions for physical diseases were considered unnecessary, as medical responses often sufficed. Longstanding research has established that behavioral interventions can effectively reduce unwanted practices, even those that had been previously thought unchangeable. Once scientists identified the HIV virus, and understood its transmission routes, prevention became the primary goal while waiting for "a cure."

Proponents of the abstinence model believe that behaviors themselves are a problem and must be eliminated in order for an intervention to be successful. HIV transmission, for example, was proliferated by homophobic ideologists as a symptom of a deeper inability for the person to control his or her behavior. Often the inability to abstain is seen as a character flaw that must be corrected. As sex practices are inextricably connected to sexuality, this model may conflict with norms within the gay community. For gay men, already experiencing prejudice based on their sexual behaviors, the abstinence approach seemed deeply rooted in moral and value-based discriminatory practices.

Alternatively, proponents of the harm reduction model stress that behaviors are not necessarily bad but that harm can occur by virtue of the behaviors. Within the harm reduction model, negative outcomes of sex (i.e., HIV, other STDs, and unwanted pregnancy) occur because of "unsafe" sex, as opposed to "bad" sex. People who engage in behavioral interventions using a harm reduction approach believe that behavior falls on a continuum, with the ultimate goal of protection from STIs and other risky situations. Within such an approach, policies are designed to reduce the harmful consequences associated with drug use or other high-risk behaviors, such as unsafe sexual practices. This model views behaviors along a continuum of risk, allowing for incremental change for the individual. Encouraging one to use condoms rather than going unprotected, or decreasing the number of sexual partners, minimizes risk for contracting HIV or other STIs.

Around 1986, the public debate over how to best prevent the spread of HIV began in the U.S. Senate. Jesse Helms of North Carolina, along with his colleague Lawton Chiles of Florida, organized *against* the production of materials that promoted safer sex (i.e., condom wearing) between men. Their belief was that only educational materials promoting abstinence were appropriate, couching the argument against the use of public dollars that "promoted" homosexual sex or intravenous drug use. Helms proposed Amendment 956, which would prohibit the CDC from "providing AIDS education, information, or prevention materials and activities that promote, encourage or condone sexual activity outside a sexually monogamous marriage (otherwise known as No-Promo-Homo) or the use of intravenous drugs."

During the mid-1980s, the CDC was also scrutinized for the agency's handling of information dissemination about the disease. In 1986, the CDC made it a policy that local panels would be convened to review and approve educational materials created by publicly funded AIDS Service Organizations. These panels were intended to "[ensure] all educational materials were to be understandable by those to whom it was directed but not offensive when judged by a 'reasonable person'. . . [and] avoid [the] overt depiction of the performance of 'safer sex' practices." In 1988, the CDC began supporting HIV/STD education in schools but promoted an abstinence-only education model for prevention.

Organized groups with their own political agendas supported each of the competing strategies. HIV activists and community organizations, who sought to warn people while avoiding any negative stigma about the sexuality of those affected, backed the harm reduction approach. Meanwhile, conservative politicians and fundamentalist Christian groups largely supported an abstinence-based policy.

Policymakers, of course, were expected to take a stance. When Surgeon General C. Everett Koop sent an 8-page brochure to 107 million homes, his mention of "condom use" left him branded as a "harm reductionist," resulting in an immediate backlash. Although Koop stressed the value of abstinence, the press only noted his willingness to consider alternative models.

The importance of ASOs also became much clearer during this time. While the government debated the merits of different HIV prevention approaches during the 1980s, people (gay men in particular) continued to die from the disease. Mostly unfunded by the federal government, ASOs began offering educational information to at-risk groups. As it became clear that HIV was spread through blood and semen, the messages became more specific, with recommendations to practice "safe sex," graphically depicting "safer" sexual scenarios (often with explicit accompanying pictures) in a positive light.

In this model, community norms drove the prevention approach and were better received by the gay community than were so-called "Moral Majority" tactics aimed at eliminating homosexual activities. (The Moral Majority was a highly conservative political group established in 1979 by television evangelist Jerry Falwell and others that promoted right wing political candidates and fiercely opposed the "gay lifestyle" and LGBT civil rights legislation.) Because many politicians felt that the epidemic was largely a "gay disease," the tactics employed within the community were largely left without comment. Although these messages may have been particularly effective in the 1980s for preventing the spread of HIV among this cohort of gay men, the lack of other community-centered information may (at least in part) have led to the hyper-association of HIV with the gay community. ASOs would later move towards the prevention of HIV with other populations, in part because of epidemiological trends and partly to encourage fresh funding towards the effort due to increased prevalence in other groups.

Some Thoughts on "Culture" and HIV Among Gay Men

The word *culture* implies the established patterns of human behavior that include thoughts, communications, actions, customs, beliefs, values, and institutions of racial, ethnic, religious, or social groups. More than 100 definitions of "culture" have been proposed, with little agreement among scholars. In general, culture includes worldviews and common features of a group of people. Likewise, multiple levels of culture impact the view that an individual will take on their world experience, including common universal characteristics, group-specific characteristics, and individual variable characteristics.

In the United States, culture has often been associated with race and ethnicity, but diversity is taking on a more expansive meaning to include the socio-cultural experiences of people including language, sexual orientation, gender identity and neighborhood. This can include differences in gender, social class, religion and spiritual beliefs, sexual orientation, age, and physical and mental ability. Further, this definition allows for a broad interpretation that can include behaviors (including substance-use patterns) and interpersonal social settings, such as alternative schools, low-income housing, and centers for LGBT health promotion.

Attempting to define the "culture" of HIV as it relates to gay men is difficult and can be stigmatizing. At some time in the early 1990s, the term "men who have sex with men" (MSM) became popular among HIV educators and practitioners as a more accurate way to describe populations of men who engage in sexual behaviors with other men and thus are at increased risk for HIV infection. This term was more commonly used when referring to groups of men from ethnic and racial minorities, as well as those who may not identify themselves as gay while having sex with other men. Further, those in support of the term believed that there were three distinct advantages: the label indicates only behavior without challenging sexual identity; it eliminates culturally charged connotations that "gay" may have for some individuals; and it squarely places the risk for contracting HIV on the behavior, rather than the sexual orientation of the individual.

Although the benefits are enticing, there are significant concerns with the blanket use of the MSM term. Within the context of HIV prevention, there are a plethora of differences between gay-identified and non-gay identified MSM, which can complicate messages. The term MSM is often "loosely used for grouping categories of at-risk populations whose only shared characteristic is that they are men who have sex with other men." Culturally different groups of "men who have sex with men" do not share similar knowledge and behaviors or may experience stigma differently.

Further, in terms of prevention implications, the emotional, romantic, and personal needs of an individual (and whether they are met or not) will, in large part, determine if an individual negotiates safer sex practices. Additionally, power dynamics within relationships may be different for those experiencing discrete elements of stigma. Therefore, how individuals identify (heterosexual, homosexual, both, neither, etc.) and the relationship that they have with their sex partner (intimacy, connectedness, necessity, etc.) will greatly influence their perception of the sexual act.

Cultural Concerns for
HIV Risk

Embedded within HIV risk for gay men are certain cultural norms and practices that increase the risk for contracting the virus. While all (or even a majority) of gay men do not engage in these activities, literature identifies several common social contexts including bathhouses, sex parties, and the use of the internet (and recently geolocating phone applications) to facilitate sexual activities. Public sex environments are defined as public or semi- private meeting spaces for men to have sex with men, often advertised discretely or known by word of mouth

Since the advent of the internet, information about sex parties and finding anonymous sexual partners have become more accessible. For many gay and bisexual men, these environments present chances to meet people. For others, these venues increase access to places and situations with opportunities for drug use and other risks that lead to unprotected sex. Three environments often described are bathhouses, sex parties, and smartphone applications because they offer both the opportunity for meeting potential sex and drug use partners, and serve as a venue for health promotion interventions.

Bathhouses

Bathhouses date as far back as the sixth century, BC, with records indicating their existence in ancient Greece. In western cultures, bathhouses have been the location of sexual activity since the late nineteenth century when homosexual acts were declared illegal and often resulted in arrest. Existing in the United States since at least 1888, The Everard, a New York City bathhouse, began to be regularly frequented by gay and bisexual men (it finally closed in 1986). In general, bathhouses charge a "membership fee" for entry and operate under the pretense of a private club; therefore, law enforcement officials are often unable to disrupt the activities occurring within them. As a result, law enforcement tends to focus on public sex environments, such as parks or beaches, while leaving commercial environments, like bathhouses, alone. Critics of bathhouses suggest that they have not faced much legal intervention because of the high cost of undercover police, homophobic law enforcement personnel, and public disinterest in prosecuting victimless crimes.

Aside from the debates about the merits espoused by advocates and faults laid by critics against bathhouses, these sites have been traditionally one of the most common venues for gay and bisexual men's risky sexual behavior because they provide an anonymous setting for sex and the sexual fantasies of those men who frequent them. Thus, locations such as bathhouses have played an important role in the sex lives of gay and bisexual men by permitting gay and bisexual men to escape from the homophobia and heterosexism experienced in their everyday lives. For HIV-positive gay and bisexual men, bathhouses are venues to escape from the pressures and difficulties of living with HIV because of their "don't ask, don't tell" nature. Thus, these establishments serve as an emotional reprieve from the stigma felt from global sentiment and within the gay community itself. At the same time, many are aware of the risks that these venues bring to themselves and others. For example, individuals may recognize in a testing session that their risky behaviors are "unhealthy" but may disregard these perceptions when they are in unique environments, such as the bathhouse.

Sex Parties

Sex parties are alternative venues to bathhouses, taking place not in public spaces but, rather, in discretely private locales in which gay and bisexual men (as well as non-gay identified men) attend for the explicit purpose of engaging in sex with multiple partners. Unfortunately, sex parties are a poorly understood area of HIV prevention and intervention because of their hidden nature. Of what is known, some sex parties encourage condom use by making them readily available to party attendees. Beyond providing condoms to participants, some parties are actively targeting those people interested in having sex without condoms, also known as "barebacking." Some barebacking parties provide attendees with a range of substances, including methamphetamine, to increase sensory stimulation and decrease inhibitions. Thus, in some sex parties, drug use becomes an additional socially accepted risk factor for men. From the little research available, we can infer that sex parties are similar to bathhouses in that some gay and bisexual men engage in risky sexual behaviors, however, further research is needed to untangle cultural features that foster gay and bisexual and other MSM's involvement in these venues.

The Internet

Some research reports that the internet and social networking sites specifically are becoming an increasingly useful setting to engage in sex with others. Internet access, although not directly causal of unsafe sex practices, is an important facilitator to consider in the practical application of interventions to MSM. Over the last several years, the use of the internet and smart phone technology has increased the ability for potential partners to find each other. Geolocation is another new feature specific to smartphone online social networking applications, allowing people to find sex partners within specific and proximal geographic locations. Especially within the gay and bisexual men's community, the freedom to find sexual partners through chat-service websites and social networking applications such as Gay.com, Craigslist, Grindr, and Manhunt increase the potential for anonymous and, in turn, riskier sex practices. Studies are mixed regarding the proportion of protected vs. unprotected sex with partners met online. However, as the use of internet chat rooms, social media, and other venues increase, a new language is emerging that permits easy identification of the risky sexual activities in which users are interested.

Considerations for HIV
Risk Practice

Recent research indicates that social factors, such as personal networks, social capital, cultural contexts, and social networks have an impact on HIV-risk behaviors. Additionally, although often referred to as a broader "LGBT community," the subgroups within this population find that their experiences and issues differ substantially from each other. Stigma typically associated with women's consumption of alcohol would compound perception of use by lesbians, but may not similarly apply to gay men's drinking behaviors. Such factors that contribute to differences in substance use and intervention needs among the LGBT community underpin the need for more research attention to this area. Likewise, HIV prevention research and strategies are nuanced and a one-size-fits-all approach fails to address unique experiences of different subgroups.

Age

Some empirical evidence suggests that younger gay men are at higher risk for HIV transmission today. Most evidence for age as a risk factor suggests it is related to the experience of the HIV epidemic and overexposure to intensive safer sex prevention efforts that fail to address their complex needs.

One explanation for increased sexual risk-taking in young men is related to their experience, or lack thereof, with HIV as an epidemic. For gay men, the impact of watching those around you die cannot be easily overlooked. As proponents of "survivor's guilt" suggest, the posttraumatic stress disorder (PTSD) symptoms, and the effects of personal experience, can have a profound impact on behavior. Young gay men born in the 1980s (or after) may not have experienced this and were additionally not exposed to the same level of fear-based HIV prevention messaging as their older cohorts. For example, research suggests that many young MSM who express less concern for the seriousness of HIV are significantly more likely to report high numbers of partners (10 or more) than their more concerned peers. Additionally, high rates of unprotected sex have been documented in recent years across young gay men. For example, several studies have found that young gay men (18-25) had engaged in unsafe sex within the prior six months at rates as high as 43 percent. One study found that as many as 45 percent of young men 18-24 were engaging in at least occasional unprotected sexual intercourse. Another found 37 percent engaging in this behavior. Other research suggests that young men feel inundated with prevention materials, become burned out, and seem disinterested in more antiquated prevention messages.

Research on age has shown that younger cohorts of gay men are, in fact, engaging in higher-risk sex. No studies have examined how community norms impact this, however, lack of social and familial support and level of knowledge about the disease have been associated with higher risk practices. More research is needed to understand how the experience of membership within the gay community influences each age cohort's decision-making.

Race

HIV disease was initially found mostly in white, affluent gay men but has increasingly become a concern of socioeconomically disadvantaged individuals. Communities of color now carry the heaviest burden of disproportionately high HIV infection rates. The HIV prevalence rates for blacks and Hispanics are 7.6 and 2.6 times the rate for whites, respectively. Furthermore, the majority of those living with HIV are nonwhite (65.4 percent), and nearly half (48.1 percent) are men who have sex with men. African-American males now bear the highest incidence of HIV and the highest rate of STIs when compared to all other racial and ethnic groups. Hispanics also represent one of the fastest growing populations affected by HIV. As such, race appears to be a potential risk factor that must be assessed when addressing HIV in gay men, especially those who consider themselves a part of other minority populations.

HIV and Hispanic Men

Hispanic men, in general, have additional socio-cultural pressures that impact their HIV risk. First, Hispanics will reach 25 percent of the U.S. population (about 97 million) by the year 2050, with one-third identified as youth under the age of 19. In 1970, only 9.1 million persons of Hispanic origin resided in the U.S. Ten years later, the Hispanic population totaled 14.6 million. By 1990, the population grew to 22.4 million, representing 9 percent of the total U.S. population. Central Americans represented the largest proportion of newly arrived Hispanic immigrants during the 1980s, with 70 percent entering the country between 1980 and 1990. Furthermore, whereas many Hispanics emigrate to the U.S. from rural areas, recent immigrants (second and subsequent generations) are residing in more geographically concentrated and urban areas in which jobs and services are more readily available. Also, higher density households and living arrangements in Hispanic urban neighborhoods have had the effect of increased family and individual levels of stress, leading to a need for more specialized prevention interventions targeting this community.

HIV disproportionately affects Hispanics in both prevalence and mortality as well. Recently, HIV was the 6th leading cause of death for Hispanic men ages 25-44. Although Hispanics currently account for 17 percent of the total U.S. population, in 2012, they accounted for 19 percent of all HIV infections and were three times as likely to be infected when compared to non-Hispanic whites. The CDC's analysis indicates that men made up three-quarters (76 percent) of new infections among Hispanics/Latinos, and their incidence was more than double the rate of white men (43.1 vs. 19.6 per 100,000). Hispanic women represented a quarter (24 percent) of new infections among Hispanics/Latinos in 2006, nearly four times the rate of white women (14.4 vs. 3.8 per 100,000). HIV is the 5th leading cause of death for Hispanic women ages 25-44. As such, the HIV epidemic poses a serious health concern to the Hispanic population. In general, Hispanics report lower use of condoms. In a July 2009 report, the National Survey on Drug Use and Health found that 9.4 percent of Hispanics, aged 12 and older, were in need of treatment for alcohol or drug use. The report also found that Hispanics born in the U.S. were 6.4 percent more likely to need substance abuse treatment when compared to Hispanics not born in the U.S.

Hispanics also have higher rates of untreated mental health concerns, which are connected to increased HIV risk-taking behaviors. Recent epidemiological studies utilizing the data from the National Latino and Asian American Study also show different trends for mental health disorders across Hispanic subgroups. Specifically, among Cuban, Puerto Rican, Mexican, or other Hispanic decent, Puerto Ricans were found to have a higher prevalence of lifetime and past year psychiatric disorders. In addition, Puerto Ricans had the highest prevalence of co-morbid psychiatric disorders (presence of one or more additional disorders). The length of time that Hispanic immigrants spend in the U.S., acculturation, and generational status has been shown to be important factors related to increased risk for mental disorders and HIV.

In addition to increased risks associated with being Hispanic, men who are also gay encounter unique stressors related to culture that are empirically linked to their risk for HIV. For example, the traditional gender role of *machismo* has positive aspects that include protecting the family, however, studies have indicated that this same concept of masculinity through dominance can lead to increased risky behavior and internalized homophobia, especially among gay Hispanic men. One pivotal study found several variables associated with the contraction of HIV among Hispanic gay men. In addition to some variables common to other groups (demographic, developmental, social cognitive, and behavioral), the study postured that cultural variables should be included in the assessment of risk among Hispanic men. For example, Rafael Diaz and his colleagues found that high levels of *machismo* among Hispanic gay men reflected strict gender-role behaviors, including positioning during anal sex, a perception of low sexual control (and use of condoms), as well as a disassociation with being considered "gay" as long as he played the insertive role during sex.

Cultural expectations (including *machismo*) are often played out by gay Hispanic men against the backdrop of discrimination from the outside (towards both homosexuality and Hispanics) and from within (with strong negative stigma towards homosexuality by other Hispanics) the community. One study found that high feelings of discrimination might lead to a distancing from the gay community, potentially decreasing exposure to HIV prevention messages.

As noted above regarding concerns about the use of the term MSM, Latino individuals face identity crises, increased anxiety, and high rates of drug and alcohol consumption if they also experience high rates of internalized homophobia. Another study found that men who reported higher rates of discrimination and internalized homophobia were at increased risk.

HIV and African-American Gay Men

African-American men have the highest incidence of HIV/AIDS when compared to all other racial and ethnic groups. Though representing only 13 percent of the U.S. population, blacks nevertheless account for more than 50 percent of all HIV diagnoses. African Americans are ten times more likely to be diagnosed with HIV than whites. There are significant disparities that exist for African-American men, in addition to the added stressors related to being gay.

Although HIV/AIDS results in similar medical outcomes for whites, distinct environmental and culturally related factors among African-American men may enhance experiences both directly and indirectly related to HIV-related risks. Factors such as homelessness, incarceration, and poverty are related to disproportionate rates of HIV among African-American men. Racism, stigma, and homophobia are additive factors contributing to disproportionate burden of HIV among both gay, bisexual, and heterosexual black men. In fact, socioeconomic status is the most documented factor contributing to health disparities in minority groups. As African Americans represent a poverty rate 2.5 times higher than whites and a median household earning rate 70 percent lower than that of whites, it is clear that socioeconomic status (SES) plays an important role in the HIV transmission. As with gay men in general, the closed nature of many African-American men's sexual networks creates an increased risk of HIV transmission. Additionally, gay African-American men must contend with homophobia within African-American communities and racism within gay communities, which can isolate them from systems of support.

Although there has been a recent increase in research attention to the impact of HIV in African Americans, little empirical research has been directed at African-American MSM. As previously argued, MSM should not be used to group those who identify as "gay" and those who identify as heterosexual but who engage in male-to-male sexual contact. However, for many black men who have sex with other men, stigma has prevented them from being out within their own community. Although a commonly heard term is "being on the down-low" (i.e., black men who consider themselves straight but have sex with other men anonymously), recent researchers have found that there is no empirical evidence to support that the "down-low" exists and has an impact on HIV on black gay men. Some experts within the field believe that this concept is a "sexy yet stigmatizing" way to explain away HIV/AIDS in black men but all cultural groups have something similar to the "down low." However, other socioeconomic factors such as poverty, racism, and homophobia are more predictive in HIV risk.

Nevertheless, a number of authors do cite that a subculture exists within the African-American male community, that the "down low" does exist, and that it uniquely impacts black men in the United States beyond other risk factors. Black MSM account for a larger proportion of HIV cases than other racial groups and are five times more likely to contract HIV than Caucasian men. Some research has also examined the difficulty of negotiating sexual orientation and religion. This dissonance may cause significant stress for black men while creating an increased risk, as many sources of support are perceived to be unavailable.

Substance Use

Higher rates of substance abuse exist among samples of gay individuals when compared to the general population. Youth who identify as gay or lesbian have nearly three times the risk of using illegal drugs than their heterosexual peers. Unfortunately, few interventions have been developed to address controlled substance use problems among gay men, likely due to methodological challenges associated with research among hidden populations.

Research has shown a clear connection between sexual orientation, substance abuse, and sexual risk behaviors. One of the largest flaws in these studies is the extensive reliance on convenience samples from social outlets such as bars and clubs. Because these samples are far from representative of the larger gay community, it is hard to determine how such use relates to the larger gay community. However, there is some promising evidence on how gay men make decisions to engage in the use of controlled substances.

A growing body of research suggests that there are cultural elements related to gay or bisexual men's initiation into drug use. Gay or bisexual men's initiation typically begins in social settings. Several studies suggest qualitatively that the use of controlled substances enhances social skills, minimizes anxiety and reduces inhibition within new social and sexual situations. Initial drug use often occurs in social settings where social pressures to use drugs are enhanced despite intentions among novice users to abstain. For many gay men, drug use was seen as part of an event or party, enhancing the probability of use. Moreover, these social settings provide an opportunity for non-users casually to initiate use, without traditional peer pressures. In this way, drugs can be seen as a feature of the social setting, not an essential requirement for participating in the activity.

If drugs are available but their use is not required for participation in the social setting, why do some gay and bisexual men initially choose to use controlled substances in these settings? Research suggests that the physical environment not only affects the setting and nature of drug use, but also the social contexts and the network of persons surrounding an individual. Additional research suggests that the social settings where drug use is most prominent encourage "escapist" practices such as anonymous sexual activities, and, therefore, are appropriate settings in which gay and bisexual men are able to lose themselves. Hence, for gay and bisexual, initiation of substance use may be culturally driven and associated with a need to escape from the stress and oppression that gay men experience in everyday life. Many researchers suggest that gay and bisexual men's drug use juxtapose sexuality, drug use, and sexual risk against feelings of social and sexual risk against feelings of social and sexual isolation. Experts argue that the connection between social settings and the drug use of gay and bisexual men mitigates the experience of oppression and stress that they experience in daily life and their attempts to escape the oppression.

IMPLICATIONS FOR FUTURE POLICY, RESEARCH AND CLINICAL PRACTICE

This chapter reviewed many components that impact HIV risk among gay men. The purpose was to investigate the historical factors that may impact gay men from other communities in a unique way. This is not to say that the HIV disease does not impact other minority groups. Rather, prevention activities that focus on gay men as a risk group must be aware of the way that HIV disease has affected gay men. No other risk group is more associated with the disease. At the historical, public policy, and cultural levels, no other group is more directly affected in the United States. In general, we know that interventions that are culturally based are the best for minority communities; however, research for this group continues to lag far behind other subgroups. What follows are some concluding thoughts on the practical, research, and policy-based recommendations for the future of this emergent field.

Policy

As stated by two HIV researchers in 1991, "In general, HIV prevention programs have been hampered by the inclusion of moralistic, social policy, or other goals that bear no necessary relationship to HIV infection prevention: for example, the elimination of intravenous drug use, the elimination of same-sex behavior or adolescent sexual behavior, the encouragement of monogamy or sexual abstinence, or the attempt to alter the living habits of the urban poor." The policy strategies that the U.S. has taken with HIV prevention were mismatched with communities that are most affected by the disease.

Another concern in today's HIV prevention policy and practice arena is the changing face of those who are at highest risk for HIV infection. For gay men living during the 1980s, prevention efforts were often geared toward the unique needs of their age cohorts (i.e., younger gay men received different messages than older men). However, as Eric Rofes has discussed, prevention efforts often assume that now, because these younger men have grown up and become the same age as men were when the epidemic first hit, their relationship to the epidemic is similar to that of men from a dozen years earlier. In other words, the way that men perceive their risk for contracting HIV has changed over the last twenty years, and new methods for preventing transmission must be developed in order to meet the growing needs of new populations. Fortunately, fresh policies that allow for prevention programs to be adapted to meet the needs of culturally diverse populations are now being developed to reach at-risk groups.

Additionally, policy advocates should recognize the extensive research suggesting that harm reduction approaches are effective in reducing high-risk behaviors. Policies should be assessed based upon their actual impact on reducing a target risk behavior, rather than their consistency with cultural norms such as the abstinence only approach. The long history of associating HIV risk with particular, marginalized populations must be overcome in order to design and implement a comprehensive HIV policy strategy that will work for all affected groups.

Research

There are some significant limitations that must be addressed for further research to continue. First, most of the studies mentioned above have relied on snowball and convenience sampling rather than utilizing a representative national sample. (Snowball sampling occurs when researchers ask test subjects to recruit future test subjects. Convenience sampling is when researchers use subjects simply because they are easily accessible, because of geographical proximity or quick willingness to participate.) Researchers have suggested that it is possible for health issues to be misunderstood due to relying on convenience or purposive samples to make inferences on hard to reach groups. Also, as a part of a marginalized population, being willing to participate in a study may mean that participating individuals are inherently different from those not represented in research, making it difficult to generalize results for others within their community.

Future research is needed to develop more representative samples of gay men and to understand the mechanisms for behavior change in this group. Currently there exists a fair amount of literature that discusses the prevalence of risk factors (substance use, HIV risk, depression, etc.) in gay men. However, few researchers attempt to understand how these risk factors are developed, and how protective factors (such as family, community bonding, school environments) can protect gay youth from engaging in risky behaviors.

Additionally, research is needed to understand the relationship between age, behavioral risk factors, and environmental risk factors. Although the experience of living through the AIDS crisis in the 1980s was a highly charged experience, very little research actually exists to describe the influence that being younger (or older) had on decision-making and perceptions of risk. Research on risk behaviors are prevalent, however, we are continually seeking to advance understanding of how sex negotiation and communication, intimate partner violence, lack of comprehensive sexual health education in schools, religion, and homophobia impact treatment and promote healthy behaviors among young gay and bisexual men.

Clinical Practice

Research widely asserts that interventions are more effective when they are matched to the culture of the community that they are intended to assist. Unfortunately, little research exists which examines the specific needs of unique communities of gay men. The failure of available interventions can also be linked to the lack of culturally nuanced strategies that speak to the unique experience of diverse groups of gay men. What follows are insights gained from the preceding literature review that can be used to propose guidelines for practitioners working with gay men.

One area of clinical importance is the relationship between drugs and sex, as well as how clinicians use this relationship within the context of culture. That is, do clinical staff understand what a "bathhouse" or a "sex party" is? Can they really relate with the experience that gay men go through when they experience discrimination based on policy and service availability? Lastly, what type of judgmental undertones are displayed by practitioners or perceived by gay men. For example, although sexual impulse and interest is often increased in conjunction with drug use, the ability to climax during intercourse is often reduced. Where this may sometimes seem like a negative, this is often seen as a benefit to the men who are using drugs, as the experience can last longer. It has also been reported, however, that after a time the sexual enhancement can be inhibited, particularly after being awake for several days. Related to the perception of enhancement is an allied concept that sex may be perceived as "not as good" or "boring" when it is done in a sober setting. It is necessary that clinicians have a clear understanding of the relationship between sex and the client's substance use, in order to understand the perceived "losses" associated with discontinued use.

As studies are increasingly looking at the relationship between drug use and social venues, it is clear that use of methamphetamine specifically is embedded within a social context, and that the drug has an important role within this milieu. Starting with assessment, through intervention, and into termination, clinicians can engage clients in an organic- or ethnographic-based process in which they collaborate with social workers to identify the cultural features that underpin drug and sexual risk-taking behavior so that they can develop strategies to either manage or eliminate use, or to prevent the initiation of use. Finding ways to replace the benefits of substance use with other strategies may enhance health outcomes beyond termination of the client-practitioner relationship.

As social service providers engaged in cross-cultural service provision, it is imperative that we understand the historical, cultural, and sociological factors associated with HIV risk among gay men in an effort to better serve their unique service needs. Lastly, we must also acknowledge that interventions and research also needs to address community factors associated with HIV in order to develop community-level and individual-level strategies that enhance opportunities of support, combat white heteronormative prevention strategies, and focus on building self-efficacy and enhancing the resilience of individuals.

Chapter 7

TRANSGENDER AND BEYOND
An Essay by Matt Kailey

On August 7, 1995, in Washington, D.C., a 24-year-old woman, Tyra Hunter, was in a serious car accident. As paramedics began to treat her for her life-threatening injuries, they discovered that Ms. Hunter had a penis and testicles. At that moment, the paramedics stopped medical intervention, instead standing back and laughing at her and making jokes and racial slurs (Ms. Hunter was African American), even as bystanders pleaded with them to continue treatment. When she was finally taken to the hospital, a doctor on staff refused to adequately treat her, and she later died from her injuries. Her family won a lawsuit of almost $3 million in connection with her death.

RATE YOURSELF

If I asked you to rate your knowledge of transgender people and issues on a scale of one to three, with three signifying that you know pretty much everything there is to know about the topic, two connoting that you know something about the topic, but could stand to know more, and one indicating that you're thinking "Trans-what?"—which would you choose? I ask this question at the beginning of every talk or class that I present on transgender issues, and I always get a wide range of responses. I get a "three" every once in a while, but not as often as you might think. In fact, even many people who identify as transgender will raise their hand at "two." If I was in a similar situation, I might raise my hand at "two" as well—and I transitioned from female to male in 1997, and have been teaching, training, and writing about the topic ever since. While that might not instill a lot of confidence in the reader, there is a very good reason why transgender people might choose "two"—and why I might choose "two," even though I have written

91

several books on the subject and have even created a three-credit, full-semester university course, Transgender Studies, on the topic.

The reality of this field of study is that it is changing all the time—even the term "transgender" is relatively new. Fresh identities and labels are constantly popping up in and around the transgender community. Scientific discoveries are being made about possible "causes" of transgenderism and transsexualism. Meanwhile, new laws and policies are being created in order to address the concerns of transgender and transsexual individuals. So what we know today could easily change tomorrow. That's why, no matter how much you know or think you know, choosing "two" is almost always your safest bet. It is also why you will want to keep learning, even after you have finished this book.

It is not that the *concept* of transgender is new. In fact, people who we in the Western world might consider transgender have appeared in every culture, in every geographic region, in every time frame throughout history. It is just that different cultures look at gender differently. Each culture has specific language, labels, and social concepts that it applies to gender-diverse populations, or those people who do not "fit" that culture's gender norms and expectations.

Even in the United States, which is where I live, language, labels, norms, and expectations around gender vary based on geographic region, age, race, ethnicity, social and economic class, and a host of other variables. It is important to note that I am white. I was born in 1955 and raised in the Midwest in a middle-class household. I transitioned from female to male at the age of 42. The information that I relate is informed by that background and my personal experiences. No two experiences are alike, which is why, regardless of how long I have been writing, teaching, and training about these issues, if I am honest about the constantly changing landscape of gender diversity, I will almost always rate myself as a "two."

So if you are a "three," good for you! While this introductory information might be a big yawn for you, hopefully you can help others in your classroom and in your community understand the ideas that are presented here. If you are a "two," join the crowd. Some of this information will be familiar, and some might be new or different from what you have heard before. If you are a "one," never fear! It is time to open your mind to some novel ideas to which you may be unaccustomed, but that will eventually fall into place. If you have questions, talk to the "threes."

Regardless of where you fall on this basic rating system, learning the language of the transgender community can be slightly overwhelming. It has been for me, and I have been a member of that community for almost two decades. But because it is ever-changing and evolving, and because there are so many terms and concepts to understand, I suggest that you read and memorize this little statement below, and keep it handy in your mind, because you will probably eventually need it:

I know what that means to me. Tell me what that means to you.

This simple phrase can make a world of difference when communicating with a person who comes out to you as transgender, transsexual, or one of the many other gender-diverse identities that I will discuss in this chapter. As a teacher, therapist, doctor, employer, coworker, neighbor, or friend—whatever role you find yourself in with relationship to a gender-diverse person—being able to say this and mean it tells the person not only that you have working knowledge of gender diversity, but that you also recognize that the person has a specific identity and meaning behind the terms that the person is using. It also shows that you are willing to honor and respect that meaning and that identity.

You might be wondering how you can get to that place where you can say, "I know what that means to me"? You can start by reading this chapter. Let's do it!

In January 2010, Amanda Simpson became the first openly transgender woman to be a U.S. presidential appointee. President Barack Obama appointed Simpson to senior technical adviser in the Commerce Department's Bureau of Industry and Security.

I KNOW WHAT THAT MEANS TO ME

Definitions might be the easiest place to start, although they can also be the most complicated. Why? Because as transgender people, we have pretty much had to create our own language, since little has been available to us through academic, scientific, medical, or psychiatric channels—the usual suspects who create a lot of the language we use every day. The positive thing about developing our own language is that we can craft a vocabulary that reflects our identities, without having to rely on others—people outside of our communities—to decide our language for us. The downside is that it can make things difficult for those outside of our community to understand who we are. When the language is unfamiliar, some people have a harder time figuring it out, and some give up altogether—especially when they find out that many transgender people use varying definitions as well. But that is the fun of learning a new language, right?

Sex and Gender

It helps to start by understanding the difference between sex and gender. *Sex* is generally considered a biological trait having to do with aspects of a person's physiology—chromosomes, reproductive organs, and sometimes secondary sex characteristics, such as breasts, facial hair, and muscle and fat distribution. Sex is what a doctor assigns to you at birth, usually based on what that doctor sees—or does not see—between your legs when you come out of the womb. The most typical sex designations are "male" and "female." Your sex designation generally follows you throughout your life, and there are many expectations put upon you based on which sex your birth certificate says you are.

Gender, on the other hand, is something different. Gender starts with a *gender identity*, or who you think you are with regard to being a boy/man, girl/woman, both, or neither (yes, I said both or neither—we will come back to that). Gender also consists of *gender expression*, or how you present your gender identity to the world—through clothing, hairstyle, mannerisms, hobbies, interests, and even the car you drive. Some people call gender expression "doing" gender or "performing" gender, because it is the way in which you are putting your gender identity out there in the world—for an audience, as well as for yourself. A third component of gender is *gender roles and expectations*—your culture's assumptions and presumptions that are put upon you based on your physical appearance and the way you are expressing your gender.

Western culture is considered a binary culture with regard to sex and gender. We identify two sexes, male and female, and we identify two genders, boy/man and girl/woman, which are also the two possible choices for gender identity that we are given. We also identify two gender expressions, masculine and feminine, and two sets of roles and expectations that go with those genders and gender expressions. For many people in our culture, two is enough (possibly because most have not been given the opportunity to consider anything else). Also, for a majority of people in our culture, their gender identity, or their man-ness or woman-ness, tends to match up with their physical sex, or their maleness or femaleness. Not only is their gender identity in alignment with their physical body, but the way that they express their gender identity and the way that they carry out their gender roles is at least somewhat consistent with the culture's expectations. But for some people, this is not the case.

*On December 31, 1993, in Humboldt, Nebraska, a 21-year-old individual whose legal name was Teena Brandon, but who went by Brandon and was known to identify as male, was murdered by the same pair of men who had raped him on Christmas Eve. When Brandon reported his rape to the police, questioning centered more around his sexual orientation and gender identity than the actual rape itself, and Brandon refused to answer some of the questions or did not answer them sufficiently for the police. The men who raped him were not arrested, and they proceeded to track him down and kill him. The award-winning movie **Boys Don't Cry** is based on Brandon's story. Brandon was discredited by police and killed by former friends when it was discovered that he had breasts and female genitalia. Brandon is now known as Brandon Teena, and based on what we know about him, we assume that he would have identified as transgender, although he was killed before he could fully express or explain his personal identity.*

Transgender

There are people whose gender identity does not align with their physical sex. Their body says one thing, and their mind says another. These people are often referred to as *transgender people*—at least in modern-day, Western terminology. "Trans" means "across" or "on the opposite side"—a transatlantic flight takes you across the Atlantic Ocean, while a transcontinental railroad runs across the continent. In its most basic and narrow definition, *transgender* refers to a person whose gender identity and physical sex are "across" from each other—they are not in alignment, based on what our culture tells us they should be.

For example, a person might have a body that led doctors to say, "It's a boy," at birth, but that same person might have a gender identity that says, "No. I'm a girl,"—or vice versa. Why does this happen? We do not know for sure. There are several theories, and the most logical one at this point has to do with the interaction of sex hormones, or androgens and estrogens, with chromosomes on a developing fetus. We do know for sure that this phenomenon is not a choice, that it is most likely a medical issue rather than a psychiatric one, and that, for some people, it is extremely difficult or impossible to live with.

Thus, in its narrowest sense, transgender can be defined as having a gender identity and a physical sex that do not match up. But there is a broader definition, one that is actually more popular today—that transgender refers to anyone who challenges gender roles, expressions, or expectations, usually on a regular basis, and particularly when that person experiences repercussions for doing so. This broader definition is often referred to as the "transgender umbrella." Crossdressers, drag queens and kings, bigender people, genderqueer people, and many other identities—even "masculine" women and "feminine" men—can fall under this larger "umbrella."

People who fall under this narrow definition of transgender are included under this umbrella. There are also people whose gender identity and physical sex do not necessarily match, but they are not "opposite" or "across" from each other. That is, there are people with a body that led doctors to say, "It's a boy," at birth, but that same person might have a gender identity that says, "No. I'm not a boy. But I'm not a girl, either. I'm both (or I'm neither or I'm something else entirely)."

No matter how anyone identifies, however, I should point out that this umbrella only covers you if you choose to lie underneath it. Many people whose identities are routinely placed under this umbrella do not see themselves as transgender, so only those who actually identify as transgender should be considered as such.

The term "transgender" tends to be more flexible, as do people's choices as to whether to adopt it for themselves, because it is a socially created term that evolved over several decades. Variations on the term were found beginning in the late 1960s and early 1970s, but those variations did not necessarily reflect the way the term is used today. It is important to remember that language that is constructed within and by particular communities is far more flexible than language constructed by "authorities."

Now we have a narrow and a broader definition of transgender. We also know that we have not pinpointed a cause for this as yet—but does that really matter? The sun "comes up," even for people who do not know how or why it does. A flower blooms (unless you are like me and accidentally kill every plant you try to grow), even for someone who does not know the process behind it. Because we have not yet determined a "cause" for something that the culture has determined is outside of its norms, many people in the culture delegitimize transgender people and their experiences. We do not need to identify a cause to know the phenomenon occurs. All we need to do is to accept the fact that it does—that transgender people exist, that they have always existed, and that they will continue to do so. We do not have to understand something in order to acknowledge that it is real.

In January 2009, Diego Sanchez became the first openly transgender person to work on Capitol Hill when he was hired as a legislative assistant for Representative Barney Frank. Sanchez was also the first transgender person on the Democratic National Committee's Platform Committee in 2008.

Transsexual

We know that a mismatch between a person's gender identity and that person's physical sex is not a choice. That fact can be very painful for some people, and there are those who would prefer not to live at all rather than to live in a body that they feel is not correct for them. We also know that many prominent professional organizations, including the American Medical Association, the American Psychological Association, and the American Psychiatric Association say that, for some people, changing the body to match the gender identity is a recommended and successful treatment. The U.S. Tax Court has determined that such treatment can be a medical necessity. In the case of *O'Donnabhain v. Commissioner of Internal Revenue* decided in 2010, the Court ruled in favor of Rhiannon O'Donnabhain, who appealed an Internal Revenue Service's decision that she could not claim medical care for a transition from male to female on her income taxes as a medical deduction.

This is where we get to another term that is probably familiar to some of you— *transsexual.* Once again, there are a couple of definitions for the label, although "transsexual" was created by the medical community during the 1940s with a specific meaning in mind. The term's medical origin and specific focus allows for less flexibility and adaptability. It is important to note that the "sex" in transsexual refers to biology—the physical body—and not to any sex acts or to sexual orientation (more on that later).

Historically, when Western culture has identified people who are suffering because their gender identity and physical sex do not align, we have tried to change the gender identity to match the body. We know now that it simply does not work. Many have tried electroshock treatments, talk therapy, psychotropic medications, hormones—none of these things have made a difference. What has made a difference is changing the body to match the gender identity.

For many people, this has been a life-saving process. Research has shown us that for those who were clinically depressed, and even suicidal, because of a misalignment or "mismatch" between their body and their gender identity, changing the physical sex through the use of hormones and/or surgery has reduced or eliminated depression and suicidal ideation. It is called *transition*, and people who go through the process are often called *transsexual people*.

Now we have the most narrow, basic definition of transsexual—a term that describes those who experience a misalignment between their body and their gender identity and who change their body with hormones and/or surgery to match their gender identity. Another part of this definition includes those people who cannot or do not want to transition—those who cannot take hormones or have surgery due to health or financial reasons, or who simply do not want to alter their body, but who still live full time in the gender that matches their identity. Many of these people fall under a broader definition of transsexual.

Some transsexual people might identify as transgender prior to transition and as transsexual during and after transition. Others identify as both transgender and transsexual after transition. Some people might identify as transsexual prior to transition and as a man or a woman after transition, leaving anything to do with "trans" off completely. For these people, being transsexual is a temporary medical situation that has been corrected by transition, and they are no longer trans in any way. They have corrected the "problem." Now, it is time to move on with life as a man or a woman.

On July 17, 2008, in Greeley, Colorado, 18-year-old Angie Zapata was beaten with fists and a fire extinguisher, then covered with a blanket. When her killer, Allen Andrade, heard gurgling from under the blanket, he continued to beat her head with the fire extinguisher until she was dead. Andrade apparently attacked and killed her when he discovered that she had a penis, later telling a friend, "All gay things must die." Andrade was charged with first-degree murder and a hate crime, and was found guilty of both, making him the first person in the United States ever convicted of a hate crime for killing a transgender person. The district attorney who filed and fought for a hate crime conviction against Andrade was a conservative Republican.

Trans Man and Trans Woman, FTM and MTF

While some people who might be considered transgender or transsexual by others no longer identify in any way with the transgender or transsexual community, there are others who use *trans* as a specific identifier. Those people might consider themselves transgender, transsexual, or both.

When I was going through transition, even after hormones and chest surgery, I was having difficulty seeing myself as a "man" and using that specific label for myself. My therapist at the time suggested that I try "trans man" instead. It does not work for everyone, but it did for me, and I maintain that label to this day. It allows me to be a "man" in a way that might not be completely in sync with my culture's definitions and expectations, but in a way that is completely in sync with my own.

For me, "trans man" is short for "transsexual man." I see myself as a transsexual man because I have had medical intervention that has altered my body, or my physical sex. Prior to my transition, I identified as transgender. I do not anymore, but if someone calls me that, it is fine with me. With all the language confusion and the many identities and labels in our community, I do not expect everyone to pay attention to and specifically know my own personal identity.

But people can get confused about the concepts of trans man and trans woman, particularly because the media gets it wrong so much of the time (and they have had guidelines for many years). Unless you are told differently by the person you are talking to or referring to, a transgender man, transsexual man, or trans man refers to a person who was designated female at birth and identifies as male, lives as male, and/or has transitioned from female to male. A transgender woman, transsexual woman, or trans woman refers to a person who was designated male at birth and identifies as female, lives as female, and/or has transitioned from male to female.

FTM is an acronym that means Female-to-Male, and MTF is an acronym that means Male-to-Female. While some people will refer to themselves as FTM or MTF, usually these acronyms are used to designate a direction in which the person is moving, such as a female-to-male transition or a male-to-female transition. However, if someone says to you, "I'm MTF," that person is referring to the fact that she was designated male at birth and is now female—and vice-versa with FTM.

It is important to note that, although this term is still seen and heard with some frequency in the media and elsewhere, "tranny" is considered a derogatory term by the vast majority of transgender and transsexual people. It should not be used for any reason unless a specific person identifies as such, and then it should only be used to refer to that specific person.

On January 17, 1999, in Toccoa, Georgia, 53-year-old Robert Eads died after more than twenty doctors refused to treat him for his illness. Some even refused to have him in their waiting room. Mr. Eads died of ovarian cancer. An award-winning documentary, **Southern Comfort***, documents the last year of Mr. Eads' life.*

Trans and Trans*

"Transgender and/or transsexual people" can be a mouthful, which is why many people talk about the *trans community*. *Trans* is shorthand, and it allows us to easily refer to a very diverse community of people, making sure that we are being as inclusive as possible. When most people talk about the trans community, they are generally referring to transgender people, transsexual people, and others who might fall under the transgender umbrella.

Even more inclusive is the newest term adopted by the community—trans*. Easy to write, but not as easy to say, *trans-asterisk* evolved in order to include those who do not necessarily identify as transgender or transsexual, but who do identify with the concept of "trans"—being "across" from, or maybe not in complete alignment with, the gender identity, expression, roles, and/or expectations that are expected of them based on their physical sex. Transgender and transsexual people can also identify as trans*. Note that sometimes the asterisk is not verbalized, but saying it can differentiate between the trans community and the larger and seemingly more diverse trans* community.

On June 16, 2001, in Cortez, Colorado, 16-year-old Fred Martinez was repeatedly bashed in the head and body by a large, heavy rock until he died. Five days later, in a canyon on a dirt road near town, his body was found. The killer bragged to a friend that he had killed a "fag." Martinez, who was Navajo, could be considered two-spirit, a distinctly Native American term describing those who engender both a male spirit and a female spirit, and one which does not translate into Western cultural thought. In Navajo, Martinez could be considered nádleehí, a term that does not translate specifically into English or into Western cultural parameters. Westerners sometimes refer to Martinez as "transgender," the closest term in Western culture that might describe him. The award-winning documentary **Two Spirits** *is about Martinez's life.*

Other Identities

Transgender, transsexual, trans, and trans* are not the only identities that you might run into in gender-diverse communities. There are many others, and it would probably take several books to cover them all. As we discussed earlier, new terms and new descriptions for identities are coming into existence all the time.

They are being created because established language used to refer to sex and gender has been so restrictive that many people have not been able to fully discover their own identity, simply because they have had no language available with which to describe it.

Now that language in the trans and gender-diverse communities is becoming more fluid and malleable, and now that people are being "given permission" (at least in gender-diverse communities) to identify in ways that are comfortable for them and that seem right to them, people are finding community in groups whose names and identities make sense to them—or they are making up their own labels if they cannot find an existing one that fits. Some other terms that you might hear in trans, trans*, and gender-diverse communities:

Genderqueer: This means different things to different people who identify in this way (which is why you are lucky to have that phrase I taught you earlier), but it is generally used to describe a person who identifies with both genders, with neither gender, or with a variety of genders. Genderqueer people often see the world as consisting of more than two genders—as do quite a few non-Western and indigenous cultures, as well. Some genderqueer people consider themselves part of the transgender or trans* community, and some do not.

Bigender: This generally refers to a person who identifies as a man and a woman, but at different times. Bigender indicates some adherence to the binary gender system, but a person who is bigender often goes back and forth between what we would consider the gender expression of a woman and the gender expression of a man.

Androgynous: Again, this can mean different things to different people, but it generally refers to a person who is expressing both masculine and feminine gender characteristics at the same time and appears to be "in-between" genders, or whose gender expression cannot be read as masculine or feminine. Some androgynous people might identify as transgender or trans*, and some might not.

Neutrois: This term is less common than some, but refers to people who are gender neutral—who do not have a specific gender. Agender can also be used to refer to gender-neutral people. However, as with genderqueer, this identity means different things to different people. Some people who identify as neutrois might see themselves as transgender or trans*, and some might not.

Gender Fluid: This generally refers to a person who expresses gender in a fluid way. A gender-fluid person does not move back and forth between two genders, as a bigender person does, but might mix masculine and feminine gender expressions, and might lean more towards masculine gender expression one day or for one period of time, and feminine gender expression at another time. Gender fluidity allows a person to express masculinity and femininity in whatever ways are comfortable for that person. Some gender fluid people might identify as transgender or trans*, and some might not.

Crossdresser: This term has historically referred to a heterosexual man who dresses in clothing typically reserved for women, and who wears makeup, wigs, nail polish, and other accoutrements designed specifically for women on an occasional basis in order to express a feminine side of himself. Most crossdressers identify as men and do not want to transition to female or live as female at all—except on the occasions when they "dress." This could be once a day, once a month, or once a year. It depends on the individual. Crossdressers are often put under the transgender umbrella, but there are many crossdressers who do not see themselves as trans. "Transvestite" is a word that has been used in the past to refer to crossdressers (and sometimes to transgender and transsexual women). This is considered a derogatory term and should not be used under any circumstances unless a person specifically identifies as such, and then it should be used only in reference to that particular person.

Drag Queen/King: Drag queens are generally gay men who dress in traditional women's clothing, often outlandishly, for the purposes of entertainment. Most drag queens are not transgender, and most have no interest in transitioning or living as women in any way. Drag kings are women—frequently lesbians—who dress in traditional men's clothing, often outlandishly, for the purposes of entertainment. Most drag kings are not transgender, and most have no interest in transitioning or living as men in any way. Drag has a long history in the gay and lesbian community, and it is done specifically for entertaining others by lip-synching to popular songs and sometimes imitating popular recording artists.

Two-Spirit: A term used by some Native American or First Nation people to describe those who embody both masculine and feminine, man and woman, male and female. Two-spirit people were often considered gifted or special because they carried two spirits—those of male and female. They were sometimes given special status because they were two spirits. Some tribes had particular gender names for two-spirit people in their tribe, connoting a separate gender entirely. Some had different names for two-spirit female-bodied people and two-spirit male-bodied people. "Transgender" could be seen as a Western term for two-spirit people, but in reality, the concept does not translate across cultural lines, because, as you can see, many tribes identified more than two genders.

There are many more identities that exist that are not listed here. And, as with all identities that do not conform to the traditional Western binary gender system, whether an individual person identifies as transgender, transsexual, trans, or trans* is strictly up to that person. It is always best to keep an open mind, refrain from making assumptions, and listen to each individual that you meet and accept that individual's personal explanation of who that person is and how that person identifies.

In 1886, We'wha, a member of the Zuni tribe, was invited to Washington, D.C., and met with President Grover Cleveland. We'wha became a famous and celebrated individual in the nation's capital, and was seen as a woman by the president and others. No one apparently realized We'wha was what Native people might refer to today as two-spirit.

Never Give Up!

You might feel confused or overwhelmed by all of these terms, and now you realize that there are even more terms out there that you might encounter. It is easy to feel like you want to give up, particularly if all of this information is completely new to you. But you should not give up—and you really cannot. The reason that you should not give up is because you will change and grow as a person as you become increasingly familiar with trans and gender-diverse communities. And that is what learning is all about.

More and more people are coming out as trans or gender-diverse in some way, laws are changing to protect transgender and transsexual people and other specific gender identities, and as you go out into the work world, you will eventually come across trans and gender-diverse people—as clients, customers, coworkers, bosses, employees, neighbors, and friends. The person who does your taxes might be trans. The person who delivers your mail (or your baby) might be trans. The person who operates on you, drills your teeth, fixes your car, or fixes your computer might be trans. The more knowledgeable and comfortable you are with these concepts, the better you will be able to function in an increasingly diverse society. Because new laws are being passed every year that protect transgender, transsexual, and gender-diverse people, including restroom laws, other public accommodations laws, and employment laws, you need to be aware of your legal standing as a coworker, employer, or business owner.

The primary reason that you should be aware of gender diversity, however, simply has to do with acceptance. Becoming an open-minded and accepting person will allow you to feel comfortable and at ease around anyone, and will allow everyone to exercise the rights to which they are entitled as citizens, without facing prejudice and discrimination from you. Once you know about and begin to understand the concepts of gender identity and gender diversity, you can help educate others who might not know as much as you do. And you can make the world a better place for everyone. We can eliminate, or at least reduce, the number of Tyra Hunters, Robert Eadses, Brandon Teenas, Angie Zapatas, Fred Martinezes, and countless others who have been victimized and have died due to being trans or gender diverse. Although some of these deaths occurred quite a while ago, the tragedies have not stopped. Every November, the transgender community comes together for Transgender Day of Remembrance, a day to observe the tragic deaths that have occurred in the prior twelve months, due simply to people being trans or gender diverse.

On June 12, 2012, attorney Kylar Broadus, founder of the Trans People of Color Coalition and a law professor at Lincoln University of Missouri, made history by becoming the first openly transgender person to testify before the U.S. Senate. Broadus was testifying on behalf of the federal Employment Non-Discrimination Act (ENDA), which would prohibit employment discrimination on the basis of sexual orientation and gender identity.

One More Label!

But wait! We forgot one more term—one more definition, one more label. And that one is for you—*if* you are not trans or gender diverse. That label is *cisgender*. This is also a relatively new term that has risen to common use in trans communities. The term is used to refer to non-trans people—those whose gender identity and physical sex "match" based on cultural expectations. If you have what our culture considers to be a female body (or a male body) and you "feel like a woman" (or a man), you are considered to be cisgender.

Like trans, *cis* is a Latin root and it means "on the same side as." If transgender people have a gender identity that is across from their physical body, then cisgender people have a gender identity that is on the same side as their body. In other words, their gender identity and physical sex are congruent—they "match." So if you are not trans or gender diverse, and you were getting a little jealous about all these cool words and identities out there, now you know that you have your own!

WHO PUT THE T IN LGBT?

So with all these different definitions and concepts, where does sexual orientation fit in? You have probably heard the acronym LGBT, and if you have not, it stands for lesbian, gay, bisexual, and transgender. Does that mean that transgender is a sexual orientation? Does that mean that gay men identify as women and lesbians identify as men? Does that mean that bisexual people are more likely to fall in love with or want to have sex with transgender people? No, no, and no.

Although "T" was added to "LGB" quite a while ago with regard to the names and services of various organizations, as well as with regard to legal, social, and educational issues, none of the above questions are true with regard to the inclusion of the "T" in "LGBT."

Transgender is not a *sexual orientation*. As discussed earlier, it is a term or label used to refer to a person whose gender identity and physical sex do not "match up," or to a person who transgresses traditional gender identities, expression, roles, and/or expectations in some way. Transgender and transsexual people can be any sexual orientation. If a person who was designated female at birth transitions to male and is attracted to men, he might consider himself gay. If he is attracted to women, he might consider himself straight or heterosexual. Or he might not use these traditional labels to identify his sexual orientation. He might choose another label, such as *queer*, or he might not use a label at all. The same thing is true of a person designated male at birth who transitions to female.

It is important to remember that gay, lesbian, bisexual, straight, and even queer are not sexual orientations—they are simply labels for sexual orientations or attractions. For example, I transitioned from female to male. Because I was attracted to men and was considered a straight woman prior to transition, I had friends in two camps when I transitioned—those who expected me to be attracted to women, and those who expected me to be attracted to men.

One of my female friends, when she found out that I was transitioning, said, "Well, I guess you'll have to start liking women now."

"Why?" I asked.

She said, "Because you're straight, and everyone knows that people can't change their sexual orientation."

She had confused the concept of sexual orientation with the label for a particular sexual orientation. She had assumed that because I was a "straight" person as a woman, I would have to be a "straight" person as a man.

Then there were others who assumed I would be a gay man. I was one of those people. When I transitioned, I entered the gay male community, because I assumed that, since I was attracted to men, I would be "gay." While this is technically true if we are going by labels, it is important to remember what I eventually found out myself—that "gay" signifies much more than who a person falls in love with or sleeps with. Gay cisgender (or non-trans) men had a whole history of experiences that I never had and never will have.

Community is built around shared experiences, particularly those that can be traumatic or troubling. I did not grow up getting beaten up or even getting dirty looks in the school locker room. I did not grow up hearing gay slurs directed at me and fearing for my life or safety because of this type of hate. I did not grow up afraid to look at a person I was attracted to, or hold hands with a date in public. These are the types of experiences that join people together and cause them to form a community identity that exists under a particular label. And these are the types of experiences that I did not have as a "gay" man, because I did not grow up as a gay man.

That does not mean that I cannot use the label "gay" to describe my sexual orientation. I use it frequently. But it does not always fit, and sometimes I just describe myself as a trans man who is attracted to men. It is long and clumsy to say, but it reflects my life and situation much better than "gay" does—at least for me. Other trans guys might feel differently, and many describe themselves as gay if they are attracted to men. There is nothing wrong with that. Everyone should have the right to identify themselves with the terms that are most comfortable and make the most sense to them. That is what freedom of gender expression and freedom of sexual orientation is all about.

Not only is transgender not a sexual orientation, but it does not necessarily represent the experience of gay men, lesbians, or bisexual people at all. Gay men are happy being men. Gay men do not want to transition or to live as women. They are simply men who are attracted to other men and sometimes those men are gay trans men. Lesbians are happy being women. Lesbians do not want to transition or to live as men. They are simply women who are attracted to other women and sometimes those women are trans women who are lesbians.

Bisexual people generally recognize a binary sex and gender system. Basically, bisexual people are attracted to men and women, but, contrary to the myths surrounding bisexual people, they are not attracted to everyone all of the time. Just like anyone else, bisexual people see a person they are attracted to and decide to ask that person out or get to know that person. The only difference is that the person might be a man or a woman, whereas with a gay man or a straight woman, the person will likely be a man, and with a lesbian or a straight man, the person will likely be a woman.

When I transitioned, friends advised me to seek out bisexual people as potential partners, because as a man with "standard female genitalia," I could offer the "best of both worlds." That is a nice thought, but it demonstrates a misunderstanding of bisexuality. While bisexual people might be more flexible in their attractions, and therefore more willing to explore different sexual avenues, bisexual people tend to expect that their men have "standard male equipment" and that their women have "standard female equipment." This is not true for all bisexual people, just as it is not true for all gay, lesbian, or straight people. All people have their own preferences and their own "list" of what works and what is a "deal-breaker." Trans people have those lists, too. The one thing that we can be certain of is that nothing is certain in anyone's gender identity or sexual orientation.

Like gender identity, we do not know the mechanisms behind sexual orientation. We do know that it is not a choice, and there are many indications that it is biological, and likely genetic, in origin. But once again—does it matter? Cause is really of little consequence when a behavior or way of being is accepted as natural, normal, and just another part of human experience and this is the place we have to get to as a culture with regard to sexual orientation and gender identity.

Straight, or heterosexual, is considered the majority sexual orientation, although a great deal of research has indicated that many people, even those who identify as straight, are not exclusively attracted to the "opposite" sex. Many trans people also identify as straight, and quite a few of those do see themselves as part of the mainstream—straight men and women, like anyone else in mainstream straight culture. In fact, it might surprise you to know that there is both transphobia in the gay and lesbian community and homophobia in the trans community.

Transphobia among gay men and lesbians is generally a result of misunderstanding, just as it is in the straight mainstream culture. But one particular concern among gay men and lesbians that can result in transphobia has to do with mainstream perception of trans people, as well as having the "T" tacked onto "LGB." This incorrect perception is that gay men and lesbians are really trans people who are afraid to or do not want to transition, or that trans people are really gay men and lesbians who transition in order to make their sexual orientation acceptable to the mainstream culture.

We have already seen that this is not true, but a lot of people who are not as knowledgeable as you are now tend to get these things confused. We already know that gay men are happy being men and that lesbians are happy being women. We already know that trans people can be any sexual orientation, and transitioning from male to female or from female to male would be quite a big step to take just to have an "acceptable" sexual orientation. But not everyone understands these things. The bottom line is that gay men and lesbians who experience transphobia are generally concerned about being confused with or conflated with trans people, and their argument is: "We're not like you. You're weird and strange. You will bring us down and prevent our acceptance by mainstream society. You will keep us from getting our rights."

In some cases, this is not a completely illogical argument (except the part about "weird and strange"). A prominent example of this argument lies in the federal Employment Non-Discrimination Act (ENDA), which, at the writing of this book, has been languishing in Congress and has not passed. Many people say that this is because transgender protections have been added to this bill, and Congress is reluctant to pass it with these protections. Some members of Congress have even said that they would vote to pass the bill if it were just for gay men and lesbians, but that they will not pass it and give employment protections to trans people. This way of thinking has certainly contributed to transphobia in gay and lesbian communities.

While the trans community has seen more than its share of transphobia, another phenomenon persists—*homophobia* in the trans community. Yes, there are trans people who are not particularly fond of being teamed up with the gay and lesbian communities, and their argument is much the same: "We're not like you. You're weird and strange. You will bring us down and prevent our acceptance by mainstream society. You will keep us from getting our rights."

This attitude has also been borne out in some circumstances. In the past, and still today, trans people have transitioned from male to female or from female to male, assimilated into mainstream society, and lived their lives as men or women. These people often identify as straight, find straight partners, and set up a home and family in the 'burbs without any problem. Many medical personnel have long seen transgenderism and/or transsexualism as a medical situation and have treated it as such. Once that "problem" has been corrected, that person is free to go off and live his or her life in the gender that matches his or her identity. But once the "T" became attached to "LGB," even these assimilated trans people started to come to the attention of the mainstream public. People started to wonder—"Is that short man who lives next door trans?" or "Is that tall woman on the PTA committee trans?" Probably not, but it certainly is possible, and assimilated trans people began to feel as if they were suddenly in the public eye. They felt that they had rights before as straight men and women, and now they were being seen as something else. Homophobia in the trans community might have at least a portion of its roots here—in the sudden visibility of the LGBT community.

I have had both transphobia and homophobia directed at me—transphobia from gay men and lesbians who did not understand trans people and did not want to be associated with us, and homophobia from trans people who assumed I was "straight" or attracted to women and became angry and hateful when they found out that I was attracted to men. So while the LGBT community is a "community" for political reasons, such as getting inclusive bills passed and supporting each other in activist undertakings, it is really too large to be a real "community, " with every member supporting the all-inclusive acronym.

But if transgender is not a sexual orientation, and if some gay men and lesbians do not want the "T" on the end of their acronym, and some trans people do not want to be there, then why did this unlikely joint venture take place? What do gay, lesbian, bisexual, and transgender people have in common that would even cause these initials to be united in the first place?

The simple answer is gender. Trans people are discriminated against because of gender. In a binary gender system, they are not "doing" their gender correctly, because they are adopting the appearance and behaviors of the "opposite" gender. Those who do not understand that trans people are adopting the appearance and behaviors of the gender with which they identify tend to see this as intentionally misleading or as a deliberate affront to traditional gender concepts and roles. For some trans and gender-diverse people, particularly those who do not recognize a binary gender system, their presentation could indeed be a deliberate affront to tradition. But even in cases of rebellion intended to produce change, these people are still, at the very heart of the matter, expressing their true gender identity.

In many cases, trans women have it far worse than trans men with regard to discrimination based on gender. Not only are they discriminated against as women, because women are still considered second-class citizens in Western culture (and in many others), but they are also discriminated against for being trans. And trans women seem to make mainstream culture even angrier than trans men do, a phenomenon that is due, in large part, to continuing *misogyny* (hatred or dislike of women or girls) in our culture.

It is difficult for anyone who does not understand the concept of transgender to understand why a "man" would want to take a step down in society—to relinquish "his" power and privilege by becoming a woman. If a "man" would do this (and the fact is that trans women are not men, or else they would not transition), then maybe that power and privilege is shaky at best. Maybe it is not everything that it is cut out to be. And that can be frightening to those who have embraced it for so long.

Where trans men are concerned, it might make sense to misogynists in our culture that a "woman" would want to be a man, but the idea can still infuriate those who think that trans people are trying to trick or deceive others. Trans men can anger those people who believe that we transition in order to gain male privilege and that we do not deserve it by virtue of having been designated female at birth. Of course, we know that trans people transition not to take a step down or to gain male privilege, but because we simply cannot live in a body that does not match our gender identity. But these are just some of the beliefs that lead to transphobia and discrimination in society, and they are based in gender.

For gay men and lesbians, gender is also a dominant factor in their experience of discrimination. They are also not "doing" their gender correctly, because many gay men and lesbians express characteristics and behaviors that are associated with the "opposite" gender. A gay man walking down the street who is alone and not wearing rainbow-flag decals on his backpack or rainbow beads around his neck still can be, and often is, attacked for being gay. How did the attackers know? They didn't. They guessed by the way he was expressing gender. He might have been walking a certain way that his tormentors associated with "femininity." His clothes or his hairstyle might have reflected something "feminine," or at least something that was not "masculine" enough. Straight men who do not subscribe to particular "masculine" ways of expressing themselves are also often targeted. Boys who are bullied at school for being gay are not always gay. They are simply expressing one or more gendered behaviors that are not considered masculine or masculine enough.

Lesbians and straight women who express a more traditionally "masculine" gender are often subject to the same treatment. And again, it is based in misogyny. Any man who expresses a "feminine" side of himself, based on our culture's norms and values, is automatically suspect and can suffer enormous negative consequences. Any woman who does not "know her place" and expresses a more "masculine" persona can also be targeted. Discrimination based on gender has its roots in misogyny and negatively impacts trans people, gay men, and lesbians.

This is the common denominator that joins these diverse communities under one acronym for the purposes of political action and change. This is the basis for discrimination faced by every letter in LGBT and the main reason why it is important for these communities to work together. We are all facing the same types of discrimination. We are all facing the same types of violence. While some of our needs are vastly different, in the political arena, they can overlap substantially, creating a strong need for large numbers, distinct voices, and unity in diversity.

The Other Letters

Oh, yes, there are definitely other letters that have been added to the alphabet soup. Some of you may have seen this: LGBTQQIA. In a Queer Sexualities class that I taught, we eventually managed to come up with about fifteen letters or so that we could add to this acronym. Because we know that language, labels, and identities are always changing, there will no doubt be more in the future. Some of the more common ones that we see today include:

Q, which can stand for queer or questioning (or both), is commonly added to the LGBT acronym today. *Queer* is generally seen as a sexual orientation that goes beyond bisexuality and embraces the notion that there are more than two sexes and/or more than two genders. Queer goes beyond binary bodies and gender expressions to the root of attraction—"I am attracted to that particular person, whoever that person might be, whatever that person might look like clothed or naked, whatever expression that person might have."

But queer does not always refer to sexual orientation. Like all the other terms we have discussed, queer has a particular meaning to each person who adopts it as an identifier. For some, it can simply mean living outside of mainstream society's parameters for sex, gender, and sexuality or sexual practices.

Queer is a word that once had a very derogatory meaning and was used against a group of people—specifically gay men. It has been reclaimed by a younger generation, but it is important to remember that it still has negative connotations in some communities, particularly in those who have suffered discrimination, and even physical violence, while being taunted with this word.

Questioning refers to people who are questioning their sexual orientation, gender identity, or both. A questioning person might find answers in the LGBT or queer community or continue to question throughout life. We all question certain aspects of ourselves. In a way, questioning people are just seekers of inner knowledge.

I, which stands for *intersex*, is a letter that has been recently added to the lexicon. In some instances, you might see intersex listed under the transgender umbrella, and although I personally do not know any intersex people who identify as transgender, I am sure that there are some out there. Intersex, which is also referred to as disorders of sex development (DSD), generally refers to a situation in which a person is born with a body that is not "standard" in some way, based on our standard medical models of "male" and "female" bodies. An intersex condition might involve sex chromosome combinations that are different from the standard XX and XY, such as XXY or XYY or XO, or reproductive organs or genitalia that vary from the medical "standard." Some intersex people like having the "I" added to the LGBT acronym and some do not. You might be familiar with the word "hermaphrodite," which in the past has been used to refer to people with intersex conditions or DSD. This is considered a derogatory term now that should not be used unless a person specifically tells you that this is how that person identifies.

A, which generally stands for allies, is also sometimes seen in the LGBT acronym. Allies are cisgender people who align themselves with the trans community in order to help secure equal rights and equal treatment for trans and gender-diverse people. "A" can also represent agender people, or those who do not identify with any gender, and asexual people, or those who do not have sexual attractions.

You might see other letters associated with this acronym, and there is no harm is asking what those letters stand for. There is also no harm in asking what specific terms and identities mean if you are not familiar with them. There are times, places, and ways to ask people about their identities. There are certain situations when it is not appropriate.

For now, the important thing to remember is that we are all individuals, with many different identities and many different labels for those identities. You might not know or understand them all. I certainly do not. But you now have a base from which to branch out as you continue to study and learn about gender and sexual diversity.

Chapter 8

TRANSGENDER ISSUES

In recent times, some of the most cosmopolitan and presumably sophisticated societal institutions have been cruel to those who do not neatly fit into the artificial male/female binary. Consider, for instance, the case of Maria José Martínez-Patiño, considered Spain's top female hurdler going into the 1988 Olympics. World sports governing bodies, such as the International Olympic Committee (IOC), began requiring a certification from a doctor that athletes competing as women in the games were biologically "female" and that men were biologically "male."

The IOC and other sports organizations based their judgment regarding an athlete's gender solely on whether DNA tests found the person had an "XX" chromosome pair (indicating a female birth sex) or an "XY" genetic profile (indicating a biological male). Expecting nothing surprising, Patiño submitted to the required test and prepared to compete the next day with her teammates in the 1985 World University Games in Kobe, Japan. She was stopped by officials who informed her that there were problems with her results and that further testing would be needed. In the meantime, she could not compete and was encouraged by her team doctor to fake an injury. Patiño had lived her whole life as a woman, but she soon discovered that her cells contained Y chromosomes. Doctors later determined that Patiño had a condition called androgen insensitivity syndrome, which meant that her cells were unable to detect the hormone testosterone that directs the body to develop male sexual characteristics. Instead, because of the estrogen that all men and women produce, Patiño developed what externally appeared to be a female body. She was what scientists refer to as an "intersexual," someone with both male and female biological characteristics.

Planning to compete in the Spanish national championships in January 1986, she was told once again to feign injury but this time she refused. After entering the competition and winning the 60-meter hurdles, her test results were leaked to the press. A media frenzy erupted and her life began to fall apart. Embarrassed and ashamed, she lost friends, and her fiancé broke off their engagement. The

Spanish Athletic Federation stripped her national titles and barred her from the 1988 Olympics and other future competitions, and her university scholarship was revoked.

The Spanish sports authorities based their harsh decision on two flawed assumptions widely shared by the larger society. First, they assumed that all humans were either male or female. Because Patiño had some biological traits associated with men, she was therefore a man. Secondly, the officials confused sex with gender. Even though Patiño had lived all her life as a woman and identified as a woman, and even though she had developed breasts and the narrower waist, wider hips, and higher voice associated with women, they insisted that she was a man on the basis of her Y chromosomes.

Patiño went through her ordeal at the same time that the first transgender civil rights groups were forming in the 1980s to break society out of the male/female binary prison. Leaders such as Leslie Feinberg, who wanted to unite all gender nonconforming people in one cause, helped to popularize the term "transgender" in the 1990s.

As a result of the efforts of political activist groups like Transsexual Menace, Transgender Nation, and the American Educational Gender Information Service battling against transphobia, awareness has grown in the general public for the broad range of people who do not fit into the male/female binary—not just intersexuals, but also transsexuals, as well as those who identify neither as male nor female and now often refer to themselves as genderqueer. This activism has resulted in some dramatic changes. The IOC now considers claims of androgen insensitivity syndrome when it considers who is eligible to compete as a man or a woman in the Olympics. (After spending three years away from the sport successfully petitioning to have her eligibility reinstated, María Patiño failed to qualify for the 1992 Spanish Olympic team.) The IOC has also begun to allow transgender athletes to compete in accordance with their gender identity if they have undergone sex reassignment surgery, have had hormone treatment for at least two years, and have received legal recognition of their gender identities.

Such advances are primarily the work of trans activists. The battle for greater acceptance of trans men and women in the larger society has even received measured support from a group that has sometimes acted more as an enemy—the American psychiatric profession.

MEDICAL AND MENTAL HEALTH ISSUES

The DSM and "Gender Dysphoria"

In the past, transgender identity was considered a symptom of mental illness. Trans people were confined involuntarily in mental hospitals where they often suffered abuse and neglect and, like gays and lesbians, found themselves subjected to such supposed "cures" as hormone treatments, electroshock therapy, lobotomies, and nausea-inducing drugs. However, just as the psychiatric profession ceased categorizing homosexuality as a mental illness in 1973, psychiatrists as a group no longer regarded transgender men and women as suffering from a mental disease.

Under the fourth edition (published in 1994) of the *Diagnostic and Statistical Manual of Mental Disorders* (DSM), transgender men and women were still diagnosed as suffering from Gender Identity Disorder (GID). Psychiatrists used the DSM to diagnose patients and to submit claims to health insurance companies. Defining transgender men and women and transsexuals (those who have received surgery to transition from female to male or vice versa) as mentally ill had terrible economic and legal consequences. Trans fathers and mothers saw their parental rights terminated, with the supposed science of the DSM used as a rationale. The Federal Aviation Administration required prospective transgender pilots to undergo costly psychiatric evaluations at their own expense to get licenses. Anti-LGBT groups like the Family Research Council used the DSM legally to battle efforts to protect trans men and women from housing and employment discrimination.

In spite of the stigma attached to mental illness, however, eliminating GID from the psychiatric manual posed a dilemma. Medical treatments that make gender transition possible, such as hormone injections and gender reassignment surgery, are catastrophically expansive. Male to female (MTF) surgeries can cost as much as $24,000 in the United States, while female to male (FTM) surgery can create bills of between $50,000 to $100,000. Without a concrete psychiatric diagnosis, insurance companies will not cover the costs of these procedures.

The authors of the latest edition (2013) of the manual, the DSM-5, tried to split the difference between labeling transgender men and women as suffering from a disorder and satisfying the demands of insurance companies for a defined medical condition. Instead of describing trans identity itself as an illness, the new manual focuses on the emotional turmoil that can possibly result from "a marked incongruence between one's experienced/expressed gender and assigned gender," —a condition that the DSM-5 now designates as "gender dysphoria" or "the distress that may accompany the incongruence between one's experienced or expressed gender and one's assigned gender."

Thus, the person is not ill, according to the new manual, simply because the individual's gender identity does not match that person's birth sex but because of the barriers—financial and otherwise—that the individual faces in making a transition from male to female or female to male. The new diagnosis suggests that the condition is impermanent—that once gender transition has taken place, the dysphoria will go away.

The gender dysphoria diagnosis met broad approval within the psychiatric and psychological professions. The new DSM criteria for a gender dysphoria diagnosis vary slightly for children and adults. Therapists are instructed to diagnose children as being gender dysphoric if they have a strong desire to be a gender other than what they were assigned at birth or already believe themselves to be; if they express a strong preference for dressing in clothes not associated with their assigned sex or assuming cross-gender roles while engaging in make-believe; if they strongly prefer games and toys typically associated with a gender different from the one that they have been assigned; and/or if they express a desire for the secondary sexual characteristics that differ from those associated with their birth sex. Such diagnostic criteria, however, still rely on stereotyped notions of male and female behavior and preferences.

Before its publication of the DSM-5, the American Psychiatric Association (APA) issued a statement favoring civil rights for transgender men and women and supporting those who seek transition surgery. According to the 2012 declaration, the APA now "[r]ecognizes that appropriately evaluated transgender and gender variant individuals can benefit greatly from medical and surgical gender transition treatments" and "[a]dvocates for removal of barriers to care and supports both public and private health insurance coverage for gender transition treatment" while opposing "categorical exclusions of coverage for such medically necessary treatment when prescribed by a physician." Finally, the APA statement condemned public and private discrimination against trans people in employment, housing, health care, education, and licensing.

Standards of Care

Trans men and women seeking gender transition can anticipate a long wait. Those who have found doctors wishing to help them will often begin hormone treatments while some, but not all, seek a variety of sex reassignment surgeries. Jennifer Diane Reitz, who operates the website Transsexual.org., suggests that, in a best-case scenario, it might take a patient two years to begin the medical process and often more than five years for the various surgeries—breast removals for FTMs, breast augmentations for MTFs, phalloplasties (construction of a penis) for FTMs, penis removal and the construction of a vagina for MTFs, and so on. Gender transition is never really finished. Patients must continue, if they can and so desire, to take testosterone or estrogen for the rest of their lives.

Many doctors who agree to provide transition care for transgender patients conform to the standards established by the World Professional Association for Transgender Health (WPATH)–an international multidisciplinary professional association dedicated to promoting evidence-based care, education, and respect in transgender health—in their manual *Standards of Care for the Health of Transsexual, Transgender, and Gender Nonconforming People*. The standards are not legally binding but have become commonplace for medical professionals treating trans patients. WPATH's guidelines have been criticized for reinforcing the traditional male/female binary. "[An] individual was expected to assert that they had always identified as the 'other' gender, to be willing to live as the 'other' gender before commencing medical interventions, to present in ways that were conventional for the 'other' gender, and to be heterosexual as the 'other' gender to receive medical care," noted Laura A. Jacobs, an activist and psychotherapist specializing in LGBT issues. These standards, she suggests, constitute a narrow definition of male and female identity and ignore that gender represents a broad spectrum of identity with many points between the extremes.

The WPATH eligibility criteria for a patient seeking hormone treatments (testosterone for FTMs and estrogen or progestogens for MTFs), breast removal ("top surgery") for FTMs, or breast augmentation for MTFs, include: persistent and thoroughly documented indications of gender dysphoria, the mental capacity to make a fully informed decision to agree to and start the procedures, and legal status as an adult.

Adults seeking hormone treatments need documentation of gender dysphoria or a supporting letter from a health care professional. These letters might need to include the results of extensive psychosocial testing, information on how long the medical professional writing the letter had worked with the patient, the profession-al's reasons for supporting hormone treatments, statements from the professional that the patient has been fully informed of the consequences of the treatment(s) and has freely agreed to them, and a promise of availability to coordinate all care from the health care professional.

According to WPATH standards, to become eligible for a hysterectomy, and/or the removal of ovaries, and the removal of testicles, the transitioning patient must not only meet the requirements already listed but also to have undergone "twelve continuous months of [appropriate] hormone therapy," unless a medical condition makes this impossible or the patient is unable or unwilling to partake in such treatments. Finally, before patients can undergo genital alteration, many doctors require that they experience twelve straight months living in the gender role that conforms with their gender identity, a so-called "Real Life Test." Breast augmentation surgery or breast removal will further require referrals from a mental health professional while genital surgery will require two letters from psychiatrists, psychologists, or some other credentialed person in the field.

The concept of "informed consent" developed in reaction to WPATH's rigid definition of those deemed to be prepared for transition care. The Tom Wadell Health Center in San Francisco pioneered this approach, later offered at Fenway Health in Boston, Callen-Lorde in New York City, and the Mazzoni Center in Philadelphia. Such clinics offer hormone replacement therapy without the elaborate other steps required by WPATH after the patient learns the details of the medical procedure and the physical consequences of the treatments.

Medical Abuse of Trans People

Transsexuals intersect with the medical community not just when they seek a gender transition. They need the same standard care that all people do—for the illnesses, aches, pains, and injuries of everyday life. "Transsexual people need routine medical care," as Matt Kailey, a FTM, wrote in *Just Add Hormones: An Insider's Guide to the Transsexual Experience.* "We get pneumonia, we break bones, we cut ourselves, we get cancer, we have heart attacks—just like everybody else."

Regardless of the advances in the psychiatric profession regarding tolerance toward transgender people, the medical profession still often treats trans men and women with hostility, confusion, and worse. A doctor visit can be a nightmare. Females-to-males, including those who do not want or cannot receive genital surgery for financial or other reasons, endure stares as they sit in the waiting room for a gynecological exam and often feel violated during the exam itself. "Yes, it's embarrassing to make an appointment with an ob/gyn in a baritone voice," Kailey said. "Yes, it's embarrassing to sit in a waiting room in a full beard. I pretend that I am waiting for my wife until I am called in."

Unfortunately, doctors, nurses, and other care providers live in a society rife with homophobia and transphobia, and they are not immune from these prejudices. As Lambda Legal (an LGBT civil rights organization) observed, gay and transgender patients commonly encounter "disrespectful attitudes, discriminatory treatment, inflexible or prejudicial policies and even refusals of essential care" when seeking medical care. About 27 percent of transgender people have experienced a direct refusal of health care services by medical professionals while another 21 percent say that doctors, nurses, and/or paramedics at some point used demeaning and abusive language toward them.

Intersexual Children and Sex Assignment Surgery

One group that does not fit within the male/female binary has been more victimized by medical abuse than any other. According to biologist and science historian Anne Fausto-Sterling, author of *Sexing the Body: Gender Politics and the Construction of Sexuality*, perhaps as many as 1.7 percent of all children are born intersexual, in other words, with sexual or reproductive anatomy that clearly does not align with the conventional definitions of either male nor female.

Intersexual children are usually subjected to surgeries very early in life to force them into the male or female category. Doctors who refuse to accept intersexuality often pressure parents soon after the birth of their intersexual children to choose a gender identity for their babies, and parents have imposed male or female personae upon children based on physically ambiguous external evidence. After an initial gender assignment surgery, the child is often subjected to repeated follow-up operations, which often leave them incapable of orgasm and with increased scarring.

There are numerous ways that an individual can be born outside the male/female binary. Genetically, males have an X and Y chromosome in each cell and females have two X chromosomes. However, some have an XO chromosomal pattern (called Turner Syndrome), which results in the individual not developing secondary female characteristics such as breasts, menstrual cycles, or the ability to have children. Others have an XXY profile (Kleinfelter's Syndrome) characterized by small penises, little body hair, and developed breasts. Yet another group displays what some scientists call mosaic genetics where they have an XY chromosome pair in some cells and XX in others. Individuals with XX chromosome pairs but with the gene for congenital adrenal hyperplasia (CAH) have typically masculine external genitalia but their internal reproductive organs are female and potentially fertile.

The parents of intersexual children are often traumatized and are urged by their physicians to take hasty and drastic actions, leading them to simply guess whether their child should really be a boy or a girl, never considering the possibility that the child could be both or neither. Such children go through numerous grueling operations to become externally male or female, and the initial round of surgeries must be followed up by other procedures as the child's body grows. When the child becomes old enough to express an identity, it is often at variance with what the parents decided. The adult intersexual then often has to accept an identity that does not match internal perception, pay out-of-pocket for catastrophically expensive surgeries to reverse earlier incorrect parental choices, or make uncomfortable compromises.

By then, extensive physical damage already has been done to the patient. When they reach adolescence and adulthood and have had male or female bodies imposed on them, intersexual teenagers and adults bear scar tissue not only physically but also mentally. "Multiple genital surgeries can have negative psychological as well as physical effects," Fausto-Sterling warned. "Many intersexual adults report that repeated genital examinations, often with photographs and a parade of medical students and interns, constitute one of their most painful childhood memories."

Transitioning

Transgender men and women depend on the medical community to align their bodies with their identities. With supportive doctors, the experience can be challenging and exciting. At the same time, it can be disorienting and disappointing. Some trans people report frustration at the length of time it takes before the hormones they take result in a noticeable physical transformation. "There's a myth that the shot produces some kind of 'high,' or that you instantly transform from mild-mannered reporter into superhero, giving the impression that all trans men are walking around in a drug-induced state of hypermasculinity," Kailey wrote. "In fact, the hormone sits in the muscle and slowly disseminates into the bloodstream over the course of several days. There are definite highs and lows as testosterone levels wax and wane in the system, but the hormone affects everyone differently."

For those taking testosterone to transition from female to male, some changes can be reversed if the person decides to stop the transition, but other changes are not reversible. "Clitoral growth, facial hair growth, voice changes, and male pattern baldness [for those with the genetic predisposition] are not reversible," write the authors of *Trans Bodies, Trans Selves*, a noted resource for the transgender community.

FTMs taking testosterone shots will also notice that their skin will transform, becoming thicker and secreting oil, and that, like cisgender males experiencing adolescence, they will often develop acne. Body odors will change and perspiration may increase. FTMs sometimes undergo slight breast pain. Hips will not change in width because hormone injections do not change the structure of the skeletal system, but muscle mass will increase in size and definition though some FTMs also sometimes develop a paunch as well. FTMs' faces become more angular and, as the vocal cords thicken, their voices deepen. Vocal changes sometimes occur shortly after injections begin, though the register at first may go up and down as with an adolescent boy. Body hair patterns will resemble that of the FTM's male relatives, with some having a sparse hair covering, others developing thick hair on their chest and back, but it may take up to five years for hair growth to completely develop.

Some FTMs see surgery as the next logical step while others view it as a financial impossibility. It would usually be a mistake to think there is one step involved. FTMs potentially face "top surgery" involving the removal of breasts, a hysterectomy, and removal of the ovaries. The surgical reconstruction of the genitals involves several stages including removal of all or part of the vagina (vaginectomy), a reconstruction of the urethra (vessel through which urine passes after leaving the bladder), alteration of the scrotum (scrotoplasty), and construction of a penis (phalloplasty) or the separation of a hormone-enlarged clitoris from the labia minora so it can be placed near the typical position of a penis (a metoidioplasty). Doctors often insert a penile prosthesis and a testicular prosthesis to aid with erection a year after the construction of a penis, when feeling has returned to the tip.

Transgender women also rely on hormone treatments—estrogen, testosterone blocker, and progesterone—taken in pill form, by injection, or through skin patches, gels, creams, or sprays. Trans women who take estrogen injections often experience mood swings including anxiety, intense headaches, hot flashes, and weight gain. The first physical change experienced by trans women undergoing hormone treatments is dryness of skin and an increased tendency toward bruising and skin splitting or cracking. Some of the sensory perceptions change as well.

"Other than my breasts, the most significant changes for me were psychological," said one transitioning woman. "My sense of smell and taste have grown somewhat more acute, and my sense of touch has changed immensely . . . I feel far, far more in touch with my body, connected, with a much clearer, sharper sense of touch. It's kind of analogous to wearing gauze over my ears for twenty years and suddenly having it removed." For trans men, typically, menstruation ceases by the end of the third cycle after testosterone treatments begin.

Within a few weeks of estrogen or progesterone treatment, breasts begin to develop in male to females. This metamorphosis can be slightly painful. Some trans women have breast augmentation surgery as part of their transition. As with transgender men, as a result of the hormone treatments, weight redistributes, with trans women experiencing an increase in fat around the hips and thighs. Some will have laser treatments or electrolysis to deaden hair follicles to eliminate facial hair. Erections will become less firm and not last as long. Orgasms also change, sometimes lasting longer but with less peak intensity. In a few month's time, trans women become sterile as the hormone therapy reduces sperm count.

As with transgender men, not all trans women want or have financial access to gender-affirming surgery. Many transgender people do not feel surgery is necessary to "complete" them. Also, as with men who choose to be surgically altered, the process for women is long, complex, and expensive. They face the removal of their testicles, the inversion of the penis and foreskin to form a vagina (a vaginoplasty), and the alteration of the glans of the penis to form a clitoris. Trans women may also opt for plastic surgery to give their faces a more feminine appearance or to reduce the size of their Adam's apple through a thyroid cartilage reduction, also known as a "tracheal shave." Patients must work with their doctors to prevent the new vagina from closing due to the body's healing process, using vibrators and dildos to keep the cavity open.

Surgeries for FTMs generally cost between $5,000 and $10,000. Breast augmentation for MTFs can run between $6,000 and $8,000. The bill for an orchiectomy (testicle removal) ranges from $3,000 and $5,000. Vaginoplasties are complicated and can cost between $15,000 and $30,000. Scrotoplasties—the creation of a scrotum—may cost as much as $5,000. Phalloplasties are the most expensive procedure and can add up to between $30,000 and $100,000. In addition to the high costs of the surgeries themselves, transgender men and women often must pay for travel, hotel, and aftercare costs, as well as footing the bill for numerous follow-up visits to their general practitioners, gynecologists, urologists, and surgeons. For a variety of reasons, including discrimination and loss of parental support at an early age, transgender men and women are often poorer than the general population and are frequently without insurance, leaving them unable to scrape together the huge funds needed for affirming surgery.

Health Risks

Transition can be emotionally liberating but does not come without health risks. Hormone treatments for FTMs can cause pelvic pain and also cramping after orgasm. Testosterone treatments can cause high hemoglobin, which can result in impaired thinking and an elevated risk of a thrombo-emoblism. Testosterone can also result in high cholesterol (increasing the odds of strokes and heart attacks) and, because of the tendency of the hormone to increase belly fat and overall weight, it can be a contributor to Type II diabetes. Trans men who have not had their uteruses, ovaries, or breasts removed might face an elevated risk of cancer in these organs.

A small number of trans women taking testosterone blockers face the danger of sudden heart stoppage resulting from a jump in blood potassium levels and such patients should have their potassium levels checked regularly. Estrogen treatments increase the risk of blood clots for MTFs as well as high blood pressure that, in turn, can contribute to kidney disease, coronary disease, and blindness. Silicone injections for breast enhancement carry many dangers, including the possibility of the substance migrating from the injection site to other parts of the body and causing painful lumps; injection site infections; damage to organs when lumps of silicone become lodged in blood vessels leading to the heart, the kidney, the brain and so on, and pulmonary embolism when silicone enters the bloodstream and blocks blood vessels in the lungs. Chest surgery will leave significant scars, some of which may not significantly fade.

Up to about eighteen months after beginning testosterone treatments, transgender men who still have their female reproductive organs are capable of conceiving children and carrying them to term although the child is more likely to suffer from birth defects because of exposure to the hormones. Trans men who do not want a child should continue to practice birth control and should immediately stop hormone therapy if they discover they are pregnant.

The likelihood of pregnancy complications is also significantly higher for trans men who are on hormones. The longer the testosterone treatments continue, the harder it is for the ovaries to release eggs, and infertility will often result. Trans men often suffer from polycystic ovary syndrome, a condition that frequently causes infertility.

The Challenges of Aging

Trans men and women face unique challenges as they enter their senior years. A lack of financial savings presents a major challenge. According to a 2013 study, transgender workers experience twice the unemployment rate of the general population and are far more likely to have unpredictable living arrangements. Because they often cannot find stable employment at decent wages after transition, retirement is not an option for many transgender people. As their health and mobility decline due to age, they live in poverty, especially if they incurred the catastrophic costs of gender-affirming operations.

For a variety of reasons, transgender people more frequently experience poor health as they age, they are more likely to be disabled, and, as they become elderly, they suffer more from social isolation, depression, and suicidal thoughts. If they transitioned at an older age, they are also more likely to be isolated from friends and family when they most need a support system.

Medical problems increase as someone ages, but doctors are often ill-informed on health issues related specifically to transgender people. According to a 2011 study in the *Journal of the American Medical Association*, medical students in this country spend an average of just five hours during their entire stint in medical school covering any LGBT-related health issues and even less time on matters specifically concerning trans patients. Doctors often, for instance, do not know much about the effects of hormone therapy on elderly trans men and women. "In general, most of the information or data on hormone replacement therapy is based on experiences twenty-five years ago for postmenopausal women," June LaTrobe, a 72-year-old trans woman living in Chicago told the Al Jazeera cable television network in 2014.

Access to health care for transgender patients did improve as a result of provisions of the recently-passed Affordable Care Act, which prohibit insurance companies from denying coverage based on pre-existing conditions. Previously, insurance companies would categorize what used to be termed Gender Identity Disorder as a pre-existing mental illness as a rationale to deny coverage to trans men and women.

The trans elderly face not only more health and financial problems, but also (if they transitioned late in life) the hostile reactions of family members. "It's the loss of the grandchildren," said Loree Cook-Daniels, a trans activist who founded FORGE, a support group for the trans community that focuses on the needs of aging trans men and women. "Oftentimes the adult children freak out and cut off access to the grandchildren. And that is incredibly painful to these people . . . It's really hard to describe the feeling of not belonging anywhere. The best I can describe it is standing out in the rain, looking through a window at the rest of society and knowing they won't accept you."

LEGAL ISSUES

Transgender Employment Protections

There are federal laws that provide some protection for trans men and women. For instance, Title VII of the Civil Rights Act of 1964 explicitly prohibits sex discrimination in employment by any employer of fifteen or more people. The U.S. Equal

Employment Opportunity Commission (EEOC), tasked with enforcing this law, and the federal courts have ruled that Title VII applies to discrimination against gender non-conforming individuals. This allows trans men and women and other gender non-conforming persons working for sufficiently large companies anywhere in the country to file discrimination complaints with the EEOC. Also, Executive Order 13762 (issued by President Barack Obama in July 2014) bars anti-LGBT discrimination by all federal contractors.

As of July 2014, 19 of the 50 states—California, Colorado, Connecticut, Delaware, Hawaii, Illinois, Iowa, Maine, Maryland, Massachusetts, Minnesota, New Jersey, New Mexico, Nevada, Oregon, Rhode Island, Utah, Vermont, and Washington—plus Washington, D.C., and Puerto Rico specifically ban discrimination against transgender men and women. In addition, about 200 cities and counties have banned discrimination against trans people, including Atlanta, Austin, Buffalo, Cincinnati, Dallas, Kansas City, New Orleans, New York, Philadelphia, Pittsburgh, and San Francisco. Furthermore, executive orders in Delaware, Indiana, Kansas, Kentucky, Maryland, Michigan, New York, Pennsylvania, Utah, and Virginia ban gender identity discrimination in state employment. In December 2014, the Department of Education ruled that discrimination based on gender identity is prohibited under Title IX of the Civil Rights Act of 1964.

Even the Pentagon, which only recently allowed gays and lesbians openly to serve, seems to be moving toward transgender inclusion. In 2014, three retired generals called for an end to the ban on trans men and women serving in the U.S. military, saying that such a change would not harm the country's military effectiveness. They issued a joint statement that said in part, "allowing transgender personnel to serve openly is administratively feasible and will not be burdensome or complicated." According to a 2014 report by the Williams Institute, "Transgender Military Service in the United States," 15,500 trans men and women were currently serving in the U.S. military, reserve forces, or the National Guard, and there were 134,000 transgender veterans.

However, in most of the country, no state laws or executive orders are in place to protect transgender people. Meanwhile, the proposed Employment Non-Discrimination Act (ENDA), which would ban discrimination based on sexual orientation or gender identity, has languished in Congress. Without legal protections, trans men, women, and even children have suffered extensive hardships at the workplace, in the housing market, and at school. The 2011 National Transgender Discrimination Survey (a joint project of the National Gay and Lesbian Task Force and the National Center for Transgender Equality) indicated that 26 percent of trans people had been fired at some point because of their gender identity, 50 percent endured harassment at their jobs, about 20 percent either could not obtain housing or were evicted, and that almost 80 percent of trans students had experienced harassment or physical assaults while at school. At the same time, as many as 17 percent experienced being passed over for promotions because of their gender expression.

Insurance Coverage

Even though the diagnosis of gender dysphoria did not completely remove the stigma of mental illness from transgender men and women, the debate on whether trans people were "abnormal" by definition and the APA's gradual public shift on this attitude undoubtedly has opened some doors for the transgender community. The American Medical Association endorsed hormone treatments and transition surgery for those categorized as suffering gender dysphoria. According to the Human Rights Campaign (HRC), a pro-LGBT organization, when it started lobbying companies in 2001 to provide transgender-inclusive health insurance plans (including coverage for gender transition surgeries and hormone treatment), the group could not find a single firm that provided such benefits. In 2011, the HRC reported that 207 of the 636 surveyed businesses either provided trans-friendly insurance coverage for employees or planned to do so by the next year.

Among the corporations that expanded their health plans to defray the costs of transition treatments were Apple, Dow Chemical, General Mills, Kellogg, Levi Strauss, Nordstrom, Sprint, Volkswagen's U.S. division, and Whirlpool. Many company health plans, however, still categorized transition surgery, including breast removal for FTMs, as cosmetic and a matter of choice. In December 2014, New York Governor Andrew Cuomo declared that insurance companies in the state would not be allowed to deny customers coverage for gender transition hormones and surgeries, thus becoming the ninth state to issue such guidelines. Earlier that same year, the U.S. Department of Health and Human Services also ended a 33-year ban on Medicare coverage of gender reassignment treatments that had been in place since 1981 because such surgeries were considered "experimental."

The policy shift came in response to a lawsuit filed by Denee Mallon, a 74-year-old trans woman and Army veteran. The endorsement of the AMA and APA for such treatments for gender dysphoria also prompted the change by the HHS board. Judith Bradford, the co-chair of the Fenway Institute, a Boston LGBT research institute, was overjoyed. "This is long overdue," she said. "It brings government policy in line with the science around trans people's health care needs." The move was significant and not just for trans men and women on Medicare, because the HHS board's decisions often influence the policy of private health insurance companies. The change brought an angry response from Christian conservatives, such as Leanna Baumer, the Family Research Council's senior legislative assistant. "Real compassion for those struggling with a gender identity disorder is to offer mental health treatments that help men and women become comfortable with their actual biological sex—not to advocate for costly and controversial surgeries subsidized by taxpayers." Baumer's comments, however, are in direct contradiction of most clinical experience and research.

Access to Public Accommodations and Housing

If the early twenty-first century has marked an era of rapid advance in the fight against anti-gay and anti-lesbian discrimination, the results for transgender people in the same era were far more mixed. In January 2014, California passed land-mark legislation codifying the right of trans men and women to use the restroom that aligns with their gender identity. This kind of law, however, sparked a fierce backlash from the Christian right that claimed such statutes would result in sexual assaults. During an already fierce debate over a controversial Equal Rights Ordinance, conservatives successfully pressured Houston Mayor Annise Parker (herself a lesbian) to delete language providing transgender people's access to appropriate restrooms in public buildings.

In the spring of 2015, the Texas State Legislature debated three bills concerning trans men and women and their access to public restrooms. One proposed law, introduced by Republican State Representative Debbie Riddle of Tomball, would have made it a crime to enter a public restroom, locker room, or shower not designated for a person's birth sex. Another Republican, State Representative Gilbert Peña of Pasadena, filed a bill that would allow bystanders to sue trans men and women who used bathrooms not designated for their birth sex for up to $2,000. The bill also allowed financial compensation for "mental anguish" that the cisgendered person might suffer as a result of the encounter. "I've got four granddaughters, and I'm not interested in anybody that has a question about their sexuality to be stepping in on them," said State Representative Dan Flynn, R-Canton, a co-author of Riddle's bill. Meanwhile, the same year, the state legislatures of Florida and Kentucky debated measures similar to Riddle's. The Kentucky legislature considered but rejected a provision that would have provided a cash award of $2,500 to anyone who discovered a transgendered person in the "wrong bathroom."

These types of laws were rationalized on the premise that sexual predators might stalk women's restrooms disguised as transgender women and that encountering trans men and women in restrooms might traumatize youngsters. The proposals ignored the lack of any known cases of predators masked as trans women. Meanwhile, 59 percent of transgender students reported being denied access to the bathrooms, showers, and locker rooms corresponding with their gender identity in a survey issued by the National Center for Transgender Equality. Many also experienced harassment and even assaults while using restrooms aligned with their birth sex.

In spite of the 1964 Civil Rights Act and the protections provided by specific states, cities, and counties, transgender people still suffer substantial discrimination in employment and housing. For instance, the United States Department of Housing and Urban Development noted in January 2011, "there is evidence . . . that lesbian, gay, bisexual, and transgender individuals and families are being arbitrarily excluded from some housing opportunities in the private sector." Nineteen percent of transgender men and women have reported being denied a home or apartment because of their gender expression. About 11 percent said their landlords or property owners kicked them out of their homes because they were transgender. Nineteen percent at some point became homeless due to their transgender identity, a much higher rate than for the cisgender population. Trans men and women of color face even greater barriers.

Trans people reported suffering regular humiliation at the hands of landlords during a March 2011 hearing of the U.S. House Judiciary Committee on the Fair Housing Act. "In October of 2007, I lived in an apartment that I'd occupied since May, having just pulled myself up from homelessness," one witness said. "I was looking for a job daily, and getting help to pay my rent. I paid my rent a tad bit late in October, and then went full time as a woman shortly after that. I let the apartment management know what was going on with me, including showing them my letter from my therapist, which was copied and included in my file. I started going to school after that. In November, I went in to pay my rent and it was refused. I was evicted a few days before Thanksgiving."

Such housing discrimination results in a much higher rate of homelessness for trans men and women, which leads to other tragic outcomes. According to the National Gay and Lesbian Task Force and the National Center for Transgender Equality, transgender men and women who end up homeless experience a far higher incidence of imprisonment, are more likely to turn to prostitution out of financial desperation, are more likely to become HIV positive, and to attempt suicide.

Marriage Equality

Transgender marriage rights have been tied directly to the battle for marriage equality for gays and lesbians. On June 26, 2015, the United States Supreme Court, with its *Obergefell v. Hodges* decision overturned all state bans on same sex marriage, ruling that such marriages were a fundamental right under the Fourteenth Amendment's guarantee of "equal protection under the law" for all citizens. Writing for the 5-4 majority, Justice Anthony Kennedy declared, "No union is more profound than marriage, for it embodies the highest ideals of love, fidelity, devotion, sacrifice, and family . . . It would misunderstand [gay] men and women to say they disrespect the idea of marriage. Their plea is that they do respect it, respect it so deeply that they seek to find its fulfillment for themselves. Their hope is not to be condemned to live in loneliness, excluded from one of civilization's oldest institutions. They ask for equal dignity in the eyes of the law. The Constitution grants them that right." It was not clear immediately after the ruling whether this decision applied to trans men and women seeking marriage. Previously, some courts have denied transgender people the right to marry, basing the decisions on prohibitions against marriage by same-sex couples and because some states do not legally recognize gender transition.

However, an early marriage ruling favorable to trans people came in the 1976 New Jersey decision *M. T. v J. T.*, which involved a transgender woman (M.T.), who had married a cisgender man (J.T.) shortly following sex-affirming surgery, and shared a dwelling with him for two years until he moved out. M.T. filed a suit seeking financial support and maintenance, but J.T. countered that M.T. was a biological male and that their marriage had no legal standing. M.T., however, prevailed when the court ruled under "no legal barrier, cognizable social taboo, or reason grounded in public policy" could M.T. not be considered a female.

In 2012, in the *Radke v. Miscellaneous Drivers & Helpers* decision, a Minnesota court upheld the validity of a marriage between a transgender woman (Christie), whose birth sex was male, and her husband because Christie had legally changed her birth certificate, which now stated she was female. This made Christie eligible to marry a cisgender man under Minnesota law. Her husband's health insurance company had denied Christie health coverage based on Minnesota's ban on same-sex marriage. The court ordered the insurance carrier to provide coverage, ruling that it was "not the [company's] role to impose its own definition of gender and marriage upon its participants." Instead, the court said, the company must acknowledge Christie's birth certificate amendment and her marriage.

In the cases noted above, the courts relied on surgery as the determinant of the trans litigants' legal sex. This does not reflect the view of the medical and psychiatric community, nor even of the federal government. For instance, as of 2010, the U.S. State Department no longer requires a person to undergo gender-affirming surgery in order to change the gender designation on their passport. The State Department now considers "appropriate clinical treatment" when it designates an individual's gender on passports. Meanwhile, three states, California, Washington, and Vermont, allow individuals to change the listed gender on birth certificates without mandating surgery.

On the other hand, in *Littleton v. Prange* (1999) and *In re Estate of Gardiner* (2002) (in Texas and Kansas respectively), courts have ruled that only the gender that originally appears on the birth certificate matters in determining the legal sex of litigants and their rights to marriage and spousal benefits. *Obergefell v. Hodges*, however, might have set a precedent that could eventually make earlier transphobic decisions moot.

Parental Rights

A dearth of case law pertains to the parental rights of transgender people. In some cases, judges have rejected the assumption that trans identity automatically makes someone an unfit parent. A Colorado appeals court in the *Christian v. Randall* case (1973) reversed a trial judge's decision to remove a child from the custody of the biological mother because that individual had transitioned to male. According to the appellate court, "the record contain[ed] no evidence that the environment of the [transgender parent's] home . . . endangered the children's physical health or impaired their emotional development." Other cases have gone horribly wrong for trans mothers and fathers. In a 1982 Ohio case, *Cisek v. Cisek*, a trans parent lost visitation rights because their "transexualism . . . would have a sociopathic affect [sic.] on the child." The court did not rely upon expert testimony to reach that conclusion but simply asserted "[c]ommon sense dictates that there can be social harms." In other cases, courts have ended all of the parents' parental rights based on the mother or father's transgenderism or have made a parent's continued visitation or shared custody contingent on the trans mother or father hiding their gender identity from their children.

The American Civil Liberties Union recommends, based on past cases, that parents who are considering transitioning follow these recommendations, as they "where feasible could be helpful in the event the parent ends up in a dispute over child custody issues because courts are likely to look favorably on these actions":

- Plan the transition under the guidance of doctors and/or therapists.
- Prior to coming out to a child as transgender, consult child psychologists, social workers, or other experts for guidance on how to make the adjustment as smooth and positive as possible for them.
- If the other parent is cooperative, make sure they are part of the plans for coming out.

Transgender parents in a fight over custody should be ready to provide testimony from psychiatrists and other mental health professionals as to their stability and the emotional impact that loss of contact with a trans parent might have on the child. They should also have family friends and other witnesses available who can testify regarding the state of the relationship with the child. Finally, if the offspring is mature enough, be ready to have the child testify in court regarding custody arrangements.

"A court may not limit custody rights based on a parent's gender transition or transgender status in the absence of evidence demonstrating harm to the child," according to the ACLU. In cases such as *Stanley v. Illinois* (1972), *Quillan v. Walcott* (1978), and *Troxel v. Granville* (2000), the U. S. Supreme Court has held that parents have a constitutional right to maintain their family relationships. Based on precedents, a court cannot terminate parental rights in order to supposedly shield a child from being exposed to transphobic prejudice.

Hate Crimes

The Southern Poverty Law Center (SPLC), which tracks hate crimes, says no reliable numbers exist for how many violent attacks take place against transgender men and women each year. However, it is clear that trans people are assaulted and murdered far out of proportion to their numbers in the population. "Although official statistics on attacks on transgendered people do not exist, it seems clear that they are almost certainly the most victimized members of that LGBT community, and therefore the most victimized group in American society," the SPLC reported in 2011. In 2003, a wave of anti-trans violence swept Washington, D.C. On August 12 of that year, Stephanie Thomas, 19, Ukea Davis, 18, Bella Evangelista, 25, and Emonie Kiera Spaulding, 25, all trans women, were murdered in the U.S. capital. Such cases are not uncommon across the country.

Hate crimes against transgender men and women became a federal crime under the Matthew Shepard and James Byrd Jr. Hate Crimes Prevention Act of 2009, but many hate crimes go unreported because trans people believe that police are hostile toward them. In one national study, 37 percent of the cases of verbal abuse reported by transgender men and women involved police officers as the offender. According to one study, the most common reason for not reporting a hate crime was the belief that the individual would not be taken seriously. This breakdown of trust between trans people and law enforcement personnel complicates the job of protecting the transgender community from pervasive bullying and violence.

SOCIAL ISSUES

Interactions with the Cisgender World

Transitioning at Work

Transgender men and women get fired more often than their cisgender peers and have a harder time finding new jobs, so the process of transitioning at work is fraught with risk. Some employers have existing policies regarding workers undergoing gender transition. The authors of *Trans Bodies, Trans Selves* recommend that a trans employee about to transition raise the issue with the employer first.

Transitioning is not something that a transgender employee can do with privacy, so the authors of *Trans Bodies* recommend that several decisions be made in advance such as whether to adopt a different name; which pronouns the trans employee wants to go by; whether and when to wear different clothing; which bathrooms, locker rooms or other gender-segregated on-site facilities to use; and finally, how many peers to inform about the transition and whether to come out with each co-worker individually or to make an announcement to the entire staff.

Even if the employee is ready to transition immediately, the company might ask for time to take administrative actions necessary to accommodate the worker's new identity, such as making a new ID card or address other workplace issues. The company may also want to formulate a strategy with the employee on how to inform clients about the transition. Of course, some work places might be unhelpful or even hostile, and the trans employee might consider speaking with an attorney, if one is affordable, to discover what state or local legal protections are provided trans people.

Living and Working with Transgender People

The transgender man or woman in the transition process can expect a lot of questions that are sometimes condescending, ill-informed, or annoying, so patience is advised. At worst, peers might ask about genital surgery, a trans person's sex life, and other highly personal information. Because gender transition is such a public process, some people wrongly assume trans men and women have lost the right to any privacy. This might be a by-product of ignorance rather than malice.

Work peers, friends, relatives, and strangers might refuse to acknowledge an individual's gender expression, calling a MTF "he" or a FTM "she." A trans man or woman might be addressed by a longtime acquaintance by a name used before transition. It might be best to address these issues with the person in question in private and to realize that this person is experiencing a learning curve.

The most painful encounters can be with longtime friends and family members who undergo a mourning process for the person they thought they knew and feel betrayed because they feel like a secret was kept from them. Matt Kailey noted the kinds of anger and bargaining the members of a trans person's most intimate circle might express. "Why didn't you tell me this before?" they might ask. "You haven't been honest with me. Why are you doing this to me?" Spouses and romantic partners might try to blame themselves for the transition and promise to be better, more passionate, more attentive partners. Sometimes, they will accuse the trans person of selfishly inflicting pain on them, other family members, and especially children, who—in spite of their elders' fears—are often the ones most accepting of change.

In some sad cases, acceptance never occurs. "The whole ordeal can be especially difficult for spouses and partners," Kailey warned. "Many transpeople are involved in a romantic and sexual relationship before transition. Some relationships do not survive. Some grow stronger." Almost all who have had a close relationship with a transitioning person, however, will experience some confusion, anxiety, and will have a lengthy list of questions. People in transition automatically become educators to others in their lives, and the attitude trans men or women themselves have toward the changes in their lives will often shape the reaction of others in their orbit. Kailey suggested:

The important thing for transpeople to remember when dealing with friends, family, partners, or complete strangers on the street is that most people will take their cues from us. If we see our transexuality as shameful or disgusting, they will too. If we're uncomfortable, we'll make those around us uncomfortable. But if we see ourselves as the normal, intelligent, diverse people that we are and, if we act our lives accordingly with many interests and outlets other than our transexuality . . . well, I can't guarantee that everyone will follow suit, but at least we'll set the stage for others and, most importantly, for our own self-acceptance.

Etiquette with Transgender Individuals

If transgender men and women enter a new world when they physically transition, the cisgender majority has also entered a new reality in which trans men and women are more visible and expect to be treated with a long-denied respect. For members of the transgender community, the rules of etiquette when dealing with a trans person are self-evident: respect the gender expression of the trans person. When addressing a MTF, call the person "she" and if she has a new name, use that name. When addressing a FTM, call the person "he." Realize that the language to describe relationships within families has changed and acknowledge that a longtime "brother" has become a "sister," and vice versa. On the other hand, trans people should realize that mistakes will be made and little will be gained by publically calling the person out if no ill will was intended.

When individuals present as both "masculine" and "feminine," it is generally considered acceptable to ask such people which pronouns they prefer to be addressed by when the choice is not obvious. Many will consider such questions a sign that the stranger is trying to be respectful of the trans person's feelings. But often the clues are there, and the confused stranger should be sensitive to them. "[T]he standard rule is to use the pronoun of the gender the person is presenting," Kailey said. "If someone who looks obviously male is in a dress, wig, and high heels, 'she' is the appropriate pronoun every time. For a person born female, a masculine appearance and dress can sometimes go either way, but if the name is masculine, if there's any facial hair, or if there are any other clues to masculinity, 'he' is the way to go."

Two questions are almost always considered rude by trans men and women: "Why did you do it?" and "Have you had the operation?" the latter question implying that somehow the person is not a "finished" human being and that a person's identity depends on a surgeon's knife and hormones. The question about motive implies that the decision might have been frivolous or impulsive.

Trans men and women are increasingly accepted as part of American life but the language trans and cisgendered people use to communicate with each other is still evolving. As Kailey concludes:

In an ideal world, there would be no need for trans etiquette—simple etiquette, extended to all people, would do . . . Transgendered and transsexual people would be assumed to be just like everybody else, and issues of gender diversity would be addressed along with other diversity issues, like sexual orientations, race, ethnic heritage, and physical abilities. Children would grow up understanding that there are some people who just don't naturally fit into male and female molds, and people would be used to seeing a selection of genders or a fill-in-the-blank gender question on every form. But that world has yet to come, and it will arrive only through the visibility of transpeople who are willing and able to show others our humanity.

A Troubled Alliance: Transphobia in the Gay Community

The battle against transphobia in the general society is further complicated by the intolerance shown toward trans men and women in the gay, lesbian, and bisexual communities. Clearly, there should be unity among all components of the LGBT community, as Matt Kailey observed. "For all of us—gay, lesbian, bisexual, it's about gender," Kailey said. "It's not about the gender we're attracted to—it's about the gender we are."

That self-evident common ground is not always obvious, however. "Many in the gay and lesbian community have rejected transfolk in the larger scheme of things, arguing that the communities have nothing in common and that 'weird' and 'crazy' transpeople will destroy the credibility of the mainstream GLB community." For instance, some lesbians have rejected common cause with MTFs because they are not "real" women and FTMs because such people have supposedly entered the socially privileged male caste. Kailey stated the intolerance within the LGBT community cuts both ways. Some trans men who form relationships with women and trans women who form relationships with men identify as straight and do not believe that they have anything in common with gays or lesbians. Kailey has said that he heard trans men make comments like "I'm not going to a gay bar. I'm not a fag." Such trans men believe they have assimilated into mainstream life and that allying with LGB people will only disrupt their transition. "They are transmen who feel that any alliance with the gay and lesbian community is wrong and can only lead to trouble," he said. "They've transitioned into straight, middle-class lives with wives and children. They want no identification with a population that they see as 'different' or 'deviant.'"

This fragmentation of the LGBT community has clearly made more difficult the job of battling shared hardships such as workplace discrimination, anti-LGBT violence, and the dangerous insistence by many that humans can fit in one of only two rigidly defined categories—males and females—whose behaviors and proper romantic and erotic choices are narrowly proscribed as well.

In spite of the violence and the still high level of intolerance faced by trans men and women, the ground has shifted, and there are abundant signs that the American culture increasingly accepts non-gender conforming people. American pop culture has always played a contradictory role in shaping attitudes toward marginalized people, sometimes reinforcing the most demeaning stereotypes and sometimes directly challenging long-held prejudices. The years 2011-2015 in many ways marked a watershed for trans men and women.

Millions applauded as Chaz Bono, the transgender man born as the daughter of 1960s and 1970s pop stars Sonny and Cher, competed in the game show *Dancing with the Stars* in 2011. In 2013, Laverne Cox became the first trans actor to ever be nominated for an acting award at the Emmys for her performance in the prison drama *Orange is the New Black*. Pop star Thomas James Gabel of the band Against Me! came out as transgender in 2012. Now performing as Laura Jane Grace, the guitarist helped pen a well-received punk rock album *Transgender Dysphoria Blues,* featuring tracks like "True Trans Soul Rebel," which brought the desires and pain of the trans community to a new audience. On the other hand, Jared Leto's Oscar for best supporting actor was seen, at best, as a mixed blessing. Leto played a trans woman in the film *Dallas Buyers' Club*, but many in the trans community believed the character he played reinforced ugly old stereotypes of trans people as frivolous emotional wrecks prone to criminality.

Nevertheless, transgender men and women have never before experienced such visibility. On April 24, 2015, an estimated 17 million viewers watched the ABC news program *20/20* as the 1976 decathlon Olympic gold medal winner Bruce Jenner (soon to be known, as Caitlyn), explained in a two-hour interview why she decided to transition from male to female. It was the show's highest ratings in 15 years, and it was the highest-rated program on broadcast television for the entire week.

Decades of work by activists have made a dramatic impact. According to a 2011 study by the Public Religion Research Institute (PRRI), 89 percent of Americans "agree that transgender people deserve the same rights and protections as other Americans." Support for transgender rights was high across the political spectrum, with 94 percent of independents, 92 percent of Democrats, and 86 percent of Republicans supporting equal rights for trans people. Meanwhile, approximately three-quarters of Americans want Congress to enact employment nondiscrimination laws that protect transgender men and women. Part of this groundswell of support is grounded in personal relations. About 11 percent of those responding to the poll told interviewers that they had a close transgender friend or relative. As with the gay and lesbian community, the early twenty-first century has been a time of dizzying change for trans men and women.

Chapter 9

CREATING AN AMERICAN LGBT
LITERARY TRADITION

Gay, lesbian, and bisexual literature flourished in the United States even before the term "homosexual" was coined in an 1869 German pamphlet advocating the repeal of an anti-sodomy law in Prussia. From the earliest days of the American republic, the genre of gay, lesbian, and bisexual arts and letters has been dominated by two overriding themes—coping with the mainstream culture's characterization of homosexuality as diseased, destructive, and sinful; and countering definitions of "masculinity" and "femininity" that required heterosexual orientation. For the most part, until after World War II these authors insisted that gay men were as manly and lesbians as womanly as their heterosexual peers. After World War II, homosexual writers more loudly and persistently insisted that gay identity was normal and a thing of beauty. In the post-war era, gay and lesbian writers also increasingly challenged the dominant definitions of masculinity and femininity, arguing that gender was a product of the imagination, a set of behavioral expectations imposed on men and women in order to preserve an existing power structure dominated by straight people. Meanwhile, a new and emerging literature produced by members of the transgender community began to arise asserting their gender and sexuality.

Many of the nineteenth- and early twentieth-century writers who would be described as gay or lesbian today left only indirect clues about their bedroom behaviors or private desires. Nevertheless, the evidence is convincing that many of the most innovative and influential writers such as Walt Whitman, Herman Melville, Henry David Thoreau, and Henry James were likely gay or at least bisexual, according to today's terminology. In classics ranging from *Leaves of Grass* to *Moby*

Dick to *Go Tell It on the Mountain,* gay and lesbian writers concerned themselves not only with sexual identity, homophobia, the beauty of the human body, the meaning of family, and gender roles but also racism, war, poverty, inequality, and what it meant to be an American.

PROMINENT WHITE GAY AND BISEXUAL WRITERS

Walt Whitman

Gay writers in the first half of the nineteenth century toiled in an era in which white people bought and sold human beings, Native Americans faced genocide, and women lacked any political power and almost entirely were denied an independent economic existence. Convulsive economic upheaval also marked the antebellum period. The country shifted from subsistence agriculture to a more capitalist way of life. One of the most influential poets in American history, Walt Whitman, flew in the face of the emerging discipline of the marketplace with poetry that celebrated the languid beauty of the body, spontaneity, and—most controversially—sexuality. Born into a poor family in West Hills, New York, in 1819, Whitman received little formal education. On his own, he pored over books, teaching himself about history, music, literature, and theater. As young as twelve years of age, he began writing stories for newspapers in Brooklyn and New York City before teaching in one-room schoolhouses in ten different isolated communities on Long Island. Whitman rejected many of the cruel ideas common to teaching in those days, such as paddling students or using canes to physically punish children who misbehaved or answered questions incorrectly. He allowed his students to discuss possible answers to questions rather than merely provide memorized answers. In 1841, Whitman commenced a career as a journalist, editor, and publisher for a number of publications, including the *Long Islander,* the *Brooklyn Daily Eagle,* and the *New Orleans Crescent.* His time in New Orleans marked his first extensive exposure to slavery. He joined the abolitionist ranks, shocking readers of one poem by juxtaposing the images of a gruesome amputation with the auction of a slave girl. "The malform'd limbs are tied to the surgeon's table; What is removed drops horribly in a pail; The quadroon girl is sold at the auction-stand, the drunkard nods by the bar-room stove."

Whitman began his ascent as a major American literary force upon the publication of *Leaves of Grass* in 1855. Whitman celebrated individualism and the brotherhood of all races, declaring, "In all people, I see myself." In a society marked by ever more orderly, rigidly controlled textile mills and steel plants, and faceless mobs overcrowding city streets, Whitman hailed the unpredictable and chaotic in each person. "I am large, I contain multitudes," he penned in his epic poem, "Song of Myself." The original edition of *Leaves of Grass* contained just an 18-page preface and a dozen poems, but Whitman continually revised and expanded the work. Whitman often juxtaposed various types of freedom—emotional, sexual, and political—with the harshness of American slavery. The loss of identity, hypocritical Victorianism, sexual oppression, and actual slavery lay along one continuum, according to him. "I wince at the bite of dogs," he writes. "Hell and despair are upon me/crack and again crack the marksmen/I clutch the rails of the fence, my gore/dribs/thinn'd with the ooze of my/skin/I fall on the weeds and the stones/The riders . . . Taunt my dizzy ears and beat me/violently over the head with whipstocks."

Leaves also served as a frank paean to the male body and homoerotic love. Whitman continually blended the gorgeous vistas of the American landscape with allusions to the masculine form, such as in "Song of Myself."

By the late 1850s, Whitman became a regular at a Brooklyn saloon, Pfaff's, where he joined an informal group of young gay men who called themselves the "Fred Gray Association." These relationships inspired the most explicitly homoerotic writings of Whitman's career, later known as the "Calamus" poems, named after a type of grass that grows in phallic-like spears. In the Calamus poems, he intertwined the personal again with the political. Concerned about how emerging American capitalism provoked men to see each other as rivals in an earnest struggle for economic survival, Whitman's verse offered an alternative reality in which men comforted, soothed, and healed each other in loving embrace.

Edward Prime-Stevenson

Words coined in the late nineteenth century to describe gays and lesbians such as "homosexual" or "invert" (indicating gay men were supposedly women trapped in male bodies and lesbians the opposite) were meant to separate non-heterosexuals from the rest of the population and to identify them as sufferers of a mental disease who should be treated or quarantined. Ironically, the new vocabulary also made it easier for gay men and women to organize as a community, to engage collectively in politics, and to create a separate culture. These labels meant to stigmatize gay men and women instead gave them an identity around which they could rally.

In 1906, Edward Prime-Stevenson, writing under the pen name Xavier Mayne, published the novel *Imre: A Memorandum*, a landmark of gay fiction. Born to a family of writers in 1868, Prime-Stevenson earned a law license but never practiced, instead choosing to write poetry, short stories, and music criticism for periodicals such as *Harper's*. Hoping to avoid the destruction of his literary career, he used an English-language publisher in Italy to print his homosexually-themed work. *Imre* centered on a romance between a Hungarian military officer and a British civil servant, and projected boldness in a way many later gay fiction works would not: the couple finds love and happiness and does not meet a tragic end, a cliché that frequently marks later fiction involving gay couples. In other ways, the book's pre-occupations foreshadow attitudes held by members of the first major gay American civil rights group, the Mattachine Society, during the 1950s. The book's narrator, Oswald, recalls growing up with a sense of being different. "I found myself un-like other boys in one element of my nature," he declares. "That one matter was my special sense, my passion, for the beauty, the dignity, the charm, what shall I say, the loveableness of my sex." Yet, like many later conservatives who joined the Mattachine Society, he argued that love between men could be healthy and normal, but he could accept only certain types of homosexuals. With disgust, Oswald rattles off a catalog of gay archetypes that he has no use for: "effeminate artists, the sugary and fibreless musicians, the Lady Nancyish, rich young men, the second rate poets . . .the cynical debauchers of little boys . . . the white-haired satyrs of clubs and latrines."

Prime-Stevenson thus produced a revolutionary novel that nevertheless rein-forced an ugly slander associating gay men with child molestation. He poured contempt on homosexual men whose outward personalities fell short of mainstream standards of masculinity. At the same time, he aggressively countered the stereotype of gay men as inherently feminine. If anything, he suggested, the ideal homosexual was more manly than his heterosexual peers: "We plough the world's roughest seas as men, we rule its states; direct its finances and commerce; we forge its steel; we fill its gravest professions, fight in the bravest ranks of its armies as men, so super-male, so utterly unreceptive to what is not manly, so aloof from feminine essences, that we cannot tolerate women at all as a sexual factor."

Two years later, in his 641-page *The Intersexes: A History of Similisexualism as a Problem in Social Life*, Prime-Stevenson, again using his *nom de plume* Xavier Mayne, examined the history and literature of homosexual (or as he terms them, intersexual) men and women, and the biographies of notable men and women in the community. At one point, he argued "the [homosexual] instinct is inborn" and widespread and has existed throughout history. What he called "similisexualism" was not a disease needing to be cured. He also critiqued the concept of gender, suggesting that humans did not belong in two distinct, clearly defined male and female categories, but along a spectrum from most masculine to most feminine, with most falling at intermediate points between the extremes. Even though less than two hundred copies of either of his two most important books were printed, Prime-Stevenson at the turn of the twentieth century reflected a more assertive attitude that would increasingly characterize the politics of homosexual men and women in the twentieth century.

Tennessee Williams

Until the rise of the gay civil rights movement after World War II, a tone of victimization frequently appeared in homosexual works. Gay men often appear as wounded ghosts in the works of playwright Tennessee Williams of the 1940s and 1950s. In *Cat on a Hot Tin Roof* and *Suddenly Last Summer*, homosexuality is obliquely referred to and usually associated with disease and early, tragic death. Critics would later complain that self-hatred and guilt overwhelmed Williams's treatment of sexuality, chiding him for not coming out of the closet until several years after the Stonewall Uprising in 1969.

Williams's approach to the subject of sexual orientation was no doubt shaped by his tortured childhood in which his father bullied him, mocking him as "Miss Nancy." After World War II, Williams wrote a string of critically acclaimed plays including *A Streetcar Named Desire* (1947), and openly broached the subject of homosexuality in a pair of short stories, "Hard Candy" and "The Mysteries of Joy Rio," both published in 1954. The sleazy characters in these stories led to the charge that Williams had internalized homophobia. The decaying Joy Rio, once a stately opera house, had declined, exhibiting run-of-the-mill heroic movies filled with cowboys and war heroes while physically decrepit patrons sought desperate, pain-killing sex in the balcony. One moviegoer, a pedophile named Mr. Krupper, tries to entice boys to perform sexual acts by offering hard rock candy before he suffers a heart attack.

Homosexuality forms a much more central theme in one of Williams's most famous plays, *Cat on a Hot Tin Roof* (1955). The dying patriarch of a Southern family called Big Daddy must decide whether to leave his estate to the overly dutiful, financially successful conformist son, Gooper, or the more beloved but sexually confused Brick, a one-time athlete destroying himself with drink. The drama unfolds at a former plantation home once owned by two men, presumably lovers, who died and left the property to Big Daddy. Gooper has done everything that he assumes Big Daddy wanted him to do, including siring a brood of grand-children that Brick's wife, Maggie, disdains as a group of "no-neck monsters." Gooper's devotion to Big Daddy, however, is motivated by nothing but greed. Brick, meanwhile, has been a disappointment. He mourns a friend that he met while playing football, Skipper, who has already committed suicide when the play begins. Maggie accused Skipper of having romantic feelings toward Brick. He slept with Maggie to prove her wrong but could not achieve arousal. This failure, and Brick's rejection when he confesses his attraction, apparently led Skipper to take his life. Brick drowns his sorrow in alcohol over the loss of a dear friend and also, perhaps, because he cannot accept his own inner sexual drives. In the end, the play concerns living a lie, with everyone but Brick deceiving Big Daddy about the terminal nature of his cancer. "There ain't nothin' more powerful than the odor of mendacity," Big Daddy laments at one point. "You can smell it. It smells like death."

The decaying odor of hypocrisy lingered as well over the lives of gay men and women forced to live in the closet in 1950s America. Williams would again, meta-phorically, portray gay identity in the mid-twentieth century as a kind of death in *Suddenly Last Summer*, a one-act play first staged in 1958, which takes place after a character named Sebastian has been murdered and cannibalized by enraged vil-lagers for attempting to seduce local youths. But even as Williams seemed in the 1950s to employ harmful anti-gay imagery, a new age of bolder gay self-assertion was dawning, with the rise of the first gay civil rights organizations, the Matta-chine Society for homosexual men and the Daughters of Bilitis for lesbians, and a new literary movement that wore outlaw sexuality and non-conformism as heroic badges.

Gore Vidal

After the fall of Nazi Germany at the end of World War II, Europe became an inviting home for artists of all sorts, and some of the most prominent gay writers of the 1940s, 1950s, and 1960s, such as Tennessee Williams, James Baldwin, and Gore Vidal, called Paris or Rome home. They found life in the French and Italian capitals more open-minded and less sexually suffocating than their homeland. So many gay writers joined the American expatriate community beginning in 1948 that Vidal would snort "a pack of queens . . . was on the move that summer in Europe." There, they socialized, enjoyed the continent's art and drew inspiration from it, plunged into sexual affairs, read each others' works, and reinforced their identities as gay men and women. The intense competition and camaraderie among this generation of artists spurred them to new heights of creativity. The stupendous output of gay literature after World War II led one exasperated *New York Times* book critic to lament the "groaning shelf" of homosexual-themed literature being produced each year.

Tennessee Williams's style of evasions on the topic of sexuality became more rare. Increasingly, characters in the novels of post-war writers were openly gay. Meanwhile, the themes of writers like Gore Vidal often reflected the political sen-sibilities of the era's civil rights organizations like the Mattachine Society. Born in 1925, Vidal (the grandson of Senator T.P. Gore and distant relative of Vice President Al Gore) enjoyed success as playwright, novelist, screenwriter, and social commentator. He started life at the United States Military Academy at West Point, where his father served as an officer who taught aeronautics. With little formal education, Gore Vidal enlisted in the Army during World War II and achieved the rank of sergeant although his novels and other works showed vast historical and literary erudition.

Vidal dealt with sexual issues with far greater bluntness than his authorial predecessors and many of his peers. In his third novel, *The City and the Pillar* (1948), Vidal insisted that masculinity and homosexuality were not mutually exclusive. His book aimed to convince audiences, historian Byrne Fone suggested, "that homosexuality can—almost—be as normal and ordinarily American as football." This stance is ironic given the book's violent ending. The protagonist, Jim Willard, remains haunted by a boyhood crush, Bob Ford. In making an athlete his main gay character, Vidal stays faithful to his aim of "normalizing" homosexuality, but that intent is undermined when, responding to the publisher's pressure, the author concludes the book with Willard murdering Ford. Perhaps this ending altered the tradition of gay literature up to that point in that such books usually ended with the gay hero committing suicide rather than homicide. The climax, however, underscored the old homophobic idea of gay men and women as unstable and amoral. In 1968, Vidal released a new version of the book, *The City and the Pillar Revised*, which the author thought better fit his original artistic intentions, but which hardly presented a more affirming image of gay men. In the new ending, Ford calls Willard a "queer" and violently attacks him, prompting the tennis player to sodomize him in retaliation.

Most of Vidal's works featured important gay characters and often addressed issues directly concerning gay men in the second half of the twentieth century, such as the plot of his play *The Best Man* (1960), which centers on a hapless victim whose identity is primarily heterosexual who gets blackmailed after a homosexual tryst. Vidal, however, never shied from broad satire and relished his role as a provocateur. His novel *Myra Breckinridge* (1968) undoubtedly represents his most outrageous (and infamous) work. The novel centers on the adventures of the title character, a teacher of a "Posture and Empathy" course discovered after a car crash to be a transgendered female still in transition. She reverts back to her previous identity as Myron when she can no longer obtain the hormones needed to maintain her female identity. The novel also includes an orgy, and scenes of sadism and rape, as when Myra (still a female) sodomizes a straight male character with a dildo. Condemned by many as pornographic, *Myra Breckinridge* is thought to be the first mainstream American novel with a transgendered central character, and Vidal implodes the notion of maleness and femaleness as concrete realities even as he savagely mocks traditional gender roles and the notion of "normal" sexuality.

Allen Ginsberg

The 1950s counterculture of the Beats celebrated sexual rebellion, admired black culture (sometimes in a condescending way), experimented with drugs, and rejected the bland materialism that marked the decade. Some of the leading Beats were gay, with Allen Ginsberg often described as the United States' first openly homosexual poet. Ginsberg did not shy away from describing his love and lust for the male body in poetry collections like *Howl*, a book that sparked a landmark obscenity case.

The Beat writers celebrated brutal self-honesty, merging the personal and the political even as they painfully confessed sexual anxiety and self-doubt, politically incorrect thoughts, homosexual crushes, and moments of petty violence and criminality. In the process, they began shattering the closet for millions of gay men and women who felt compelled to live their sexual affairs in secret shame. No homosexual writer before Ginsberg had written, under his own name, so openly of his hunger and desires.

Edward Albee

As previously stated, literary critics in the early 1960s began to complain about the "groaning shelf" of postwar gay literature, often suggesting the alleged outsized influence of gay and lesbian authors subverted American values and cheapened the arts. After Tennessee Williams's last great play *The Night of the Iguana* premiered in 1961, the *New York Times* ran an essay by the newspaper's new drama critic, Howard Taubman, titled, "Not What It Seems." Taubman insisted, "It is time to speak openly and candidly about the increased incidence and influence of homosexuality on New York's stage." Modern plays, he lamented, were filled with characters who were basically gay men thinly disguised as heterosexual men and women. "Characters represent something different from what they purport to be," he wrote. "It's no wonder they seem sicker than necessary." Taubman clearly had Williams in mind, among other gifted playwrights.

One of the biggest targets of the journalistic anti-homosexual backlash would be one of the most talented of the new dramatists of the early 1960s, Edward Albee. An adopted child of wealth who grew up on Long Island, Albee spent his childhood as an indifferent student who became aware of his homosexuality at an early age, leaving his parents after a heated argument when he was 19. Earning a living at odd jobs such as serving as a Western Union delivery man and with a small weekly stipend from a trust fund set up by his grandmother, Albee poured himself into his writing, "Why do homosexuals always write rotten love poetry to each other?" a character in an early Albee one-act play, *Ye Watchers and Ye Lonely Ones*, asks, before bitterly answering himself: "Because homosexual love is rotten too."

He penned his first hit, *The Zoo Story*, in 1958. The play depicts two men, Peter and Jerry, in an animated conversation while sitting on a bench in Central Park. Peter wants a quiet moment, but Jerry will not let him have it. Jerry needles his unwitting companion with a series of personal questions while sharing tales from his own chaotic life. When Peter tries to leave, Jerry pulls a knife and drops it, challenging his startled companion to use it. Frightened, Peter picks up the weapon, prompting Jerry to run towards the blade and stab himself. Terrified, Peter runs away as Jerry dies. The play addresses sexuality only once when Jerry confesses that for 11 days, at the age of 15, he was "a h-o-m-o-s-e-x-u-a-l."

In 1960, Albee authored his most controversial, most reviled, and most acclaimed, full-length play, *Who's Afraid of Virginia Woolf?* As the play unfolds, a married couple, George and Martha, have brought a much younger couple, Nick and Honey, to their home for drinks and conversation. The guests watch in horror as their hosts torment each other with insults and accusations as they relive their disappointments and argue about their child, who later turns out to be imaginary. The play opened to mostly positive reviews in 1963, winning a Tony Award and the New York Drama Critics Circle Award for best play, but afterwards critics perceived a gay subtext in the work, charging that Albee's characters were stand-ins for bickering gay couples. The onslaught began with an article in the 1963 *Tulane Drama Review* where editor Richard Schechner complained, "The American theater, our theater, is so hungry, so voracious, so corrupt, so morally blind, so perverse that *Virginia Woolf* is a success . . . I'm tired of morbidity and sexual perversity which are there only to titillate an impotent and homosexual theater and audience. I'm tired of Albee."

Albee followed up with a surreal drama, *Tiny Alice*. The idea that this play too was part of some hidden literary gay agenda again inflamed critics, including future novelist Philip Roth who, in an essay for the *New York Review of Books*, complained that *Tiny Alice* was a "homosexual daydream" and mocked its "ghastly pansy rhetoric and repartee." Other theater critics blasted the "infantile sexuality" of gay-authored plays while the English-born American novelist and critic Wilfrid Sheed in *Commentary* insisted he wanted "the homosexual sensibility asserted openly in one play rather than sneaked into twenty. It would, if nothing else, leave a cleaner smell."

Matt Crowley

The American political mood changed in an era that saw the rise of the civil rights movement and the tragedy of the Vietnam War. This new sensibility, emphasizing candid speech and sexual freedom, filled the 1968 play *The Boys in the Band*. Matt Crowley said that when he wrote the play he was responding to what one writer called "closeted drama," in which authors kept gay themes submerged. As Crowley recalled, "This critic wondered why America's leading playwrights didn't really write what they were really writing about." He had time on his hands, having washed out as a Hollywood screenwriter, and decided to answer this artistic challenge. Crowley came up with the idea of focusing a play on the relationships that might evolve and the revelations that might unfold as eight gay friends and one straight onlooker gather for a birthday party.

The Boys in the Band became the first mainstream play set in a gay household and a box office hit. The eccentric list of party guests drew laughter from straight and gay audiences. One character, Emory, bravely battles multiple levels of bigotry in his relationship with an African-American boyfriend. Another character, Larry, revels in his promiscuity. Michael, meanwhile, is tormented by his alcoholism and the guilt he feels about his homosexuality because of his religious beliefs.

Producers originally planned for the play to run for one week off-Broadway, but it turned into a Broadway smash that drew lines of theater-goers circling the block. After the Stonewall Riot in 1969, the work drew greater attention, inspiring the production, in 1970, of a popular film. Never had such a wide audience been treated to such a detailed exploration of gay life and never had gay characters been fleshed out in such rich detail. As *New York Times* theater critic Clive Barnes put it, *Boys* was "by far the frankest treatment of homosexuality I have ever seen on stage."

Gay activists, however, would later see many of *Boys'* main characters as demeaning caricatures and complained about the "internalized homophobia" so in evidence in the script. Later, skeptics asked why Crowley did not devote more of his script to addressing the source of several characters' self-hatred: the larger society's hostility to homosexuality. The Gay Liberation Front picketed the Los Angeles premiere of the film version, attacking what it saw as a demeaning depiction of gay men as weak and hyperemotional. Nevertheless, *Boys* would be a source of inspiration, positively and negatively, for gay playwrights into the twenty-first century, such as Tony Kushner (author of *Angels in America*) and Jeff Whitty (who wrote the satirical musical *Avenue Q*). "I was watching television, maybe an awards telecast, and I saw the scene [from the film version] where the men were dancing together," Kushner remembered. "I was 10 or 11. I was already aware I had different feelings from all the other boys my age, and there was this movie with men dancing with each other and looking kind of sexy. And I thought: 'That's interesting. What is that?' It frightened me and disturbed me and excited me. It was really my first intimation that there was a world beyond Lake Charles, La."

Tony Kushner's Angels in America

By embracing multiculturalism, some American gay, lesbian, and bisexual authors during the late twentieth and early twenty-first centuries hoped to save their country from its sometimes destructive strife. They also continued to battle for tolerance from the straight majority. From the age of Edward Prime-Stevenson to the post-World War II era, these gay and lesbian authors often tried to demonstrate that, outside of their choice of sexual partners, they were just like their straight peers. Frequently, homosexual writers aimed to depict the "normality" of gay men and women by creating characters who conformed to mainstream norms of masculinity and femininity. The shortcoming of such an approach became obvious: it kept heterosexual men and women in place as the standard by which all others must be judged. The characters who did not conform to these norms often were portrayed as depressed, chemically dependent, childish, impulsive, and bitchy. By the 1980s, works like *Torch Song Trilogy*, centering on the loves and life of a drag queen, marked a paradigm shift. Homosexual people, the play loudly announced, need not be embarrassed by what was unique and beautiful about gay culture. Flamboyant "queens" could be heroes.

This transformation happened in the hardest of circumstances: as the AIDS epidemic created a gay holocaust in America and instigated a new wave of fearful homophobia, with the ill hounded out of schools, neighborhoods, and even entire communities, and the most hysterical in the straight community calling for concentration camp-like quarantines of the infected. The disease, many straights said, reflected God's judgment on an immoral lifestyle. The genius of Tony Kushner's *Angels in America: A Gay Fantasia on National Themes* derives from flipping this perspective on its head. In his epic stage production, gay men stand in judgment of a morally bankrupt nation ruled by straight men and those who collaborate with the oppression of gay people. In the full play's two parts, consisting of *Millennium Approaches* and *Perestroika*, the loves, heartbreaks, acts of kindness, and those of betrayal within the gay community are used to define life in the United States from the time of McCarthyism in the 1950s to the resurrection of extreme conservatism during the Reagan era of the 1980s.

Angels in America focuses on the AIDS epidemic, struggles over gay identity post-Stonewall, the fear of emerging from the closet, and the guilt that religious communities impose on gay men and women. The ambitious script also tackles much broader themes such as immigration, the dynamic between leftist politics and political conservatism in the late twentieth century, paranoid anti-communism, and the Jewish experience in America. A dream in which an angel crashed through the ceiling of a sick friend's home provided the first inspiration for Kushner to write *Angels*. He eventually conceived of a story centering on five gay central characters: two men struggling with AIDS; a closeted, married homosexual man; and Roy Cohn, the real-life attorney who helped craft Senatpr Joseph McCarthy's infamous witch hunt of the early 1950s—a cruel dragnet that destroyed many gay lives along the way. One of the central characters, Prior, has been diagnosed with AIDS and fears that he has gone insane when the spirits of his ancestors, and angels who proclaim him to be a prophet, begin to haunt him. Prior's diagnosis frightens his boyfriend, a liberal lawyer named Louis, who leaves him and begins a relationship with the unhappily married and confused conservative attorney named Joe, a Mormon who is torn between the demands of his heart and that of his church, which sees homosexuality as a grave sin. Joe is cheating on his wife, the drug-addicted Harper. Roy Cohn, also dying of AIDS, courts Joe to do work for his conservative political causes even as the attorney battles his disbarment on ethics charges. Cohn is also haunted by the ghost of Ethel Rosenberg, another real-life figure who the New York attorney helped send to the electric chair for supposedly sending atomic weapons secrets to the Soviet Union. The compassionate heart of the play is provided by Belize (who in his off-hours dresses in drag). Belize ends up working as Cohn's nurse. When Cohn dies, Belize steals the infamous man's remaining AZT, a drug used to slow the progress of the disease, to relive Prior's suffering.

While angels are used to fill Prior's hallucinations, Cohn serves as the script's devil—a bitter sociopathic liar who insists to the end that he cannot be a homosexual because to him gay men are, by definition, losers. "Homosexuals are not men who sleep with other men," he insists to his incredulous doctor. "Homosexuals are men who in fifteen years of trying can't get a pissant anti-discrimination bill through City Council. Homosexuals are men who know nobody and who nobody knows. Who have zero clout. Does that sound like me, Henry?" Throughout, Prior shows not just humor, but abounding courage. At one point, he has a vision of heaven, which has been abandoned by God. Angels offer the gift of an eternity frozen in time, an existence of unchanging sameness, a temptation for a man ravaged by an infection altering his body in lethal ways. Prior will have none of it. Even if the changes in his body are, for the moment, killing him, Prior knows that an existence without change is only a living death. "I want more of life," he says. "I can't help myself. I do. I've lived through such terrible times, and there are people who live through much worse, but . . . I want more life."

Cohn, Prior, and Belize each provide the gay and straight communities with moral lessons: Cohn displays the moral costs of untrammeled ambition and self-deceit; Prior provides the gifts that flow from forgiveness; and Belize offers the centrality of compassion in becoming fully human. Regardless of the secular grounding within twentieth century gay and lesbian literature, many audience members found *Angels* to be a religious experience. Most of the play unfolds in the year 1985, but the story ends five years later on a note of cautious optimism, with Harper, after being tormented by delusions, thinking clearly again, and Prior hinting that he might indeed survive to see a better world.

Part One of *Angels* debuted in 1991 in Los Angeles, with Part Two reaching the stage the following year, eventually winning a Pulitzer Prize. The HBO cable network adapted it as a mini-series in 2003. At times confusing and chaotic, the work nevertheless stands as one of the masterpieces of twentieth-century literature, gay or straight and was oddly prophetic. At the conclusion of Part Two, Prior speaks of the future of gay men. "We won't die secret deaths anymore," he predicts. "The world only spins forward. We will be citizens. The time has come . . . More Life. The Great Work Begins." Kushner could never have known that the next two decades would see the development of treatments that would mean AIDS was no longer a death sentence, at least in the West where the drugs were more widely available. He could not have anticipated the dramatic legal reforms coming after the turn of the century in which anti-discrimination laws would be adopted across the country and marriage equality for gay men and women starting to become a reality for all. The great work had indeed begun.

NOTEWORTHY WHITE LESBIAN AUTHORS

Emily Dickinson

The challenges facing gay male authors in the nineteenth and twentieth centuries were in some ways magnified for lesbians. Society persecuted gay men more ruthlessly, but women, gay or straight, had a harder time being heard and restrictions on what women could say about sexuality was even more tightly restricted than for their male peers. For writers like Emily Dickinson, sexual feelings could not be addressed directly as they were by authors like Whitman.

One of the most famous recluses in American literary history, Dickinson once admitted that she fled when she saw guests arriving and even forced her doctor to examine her by asking her questions from another room. She hid from company to the point that even her family called her "The Myth," because they so rarely saw her. Her relationships with both men and women were often from a distance, and she directed much of her intense private feelings most often towards other women, particularly her sister-in-law Susan Gilbert Dickinson. From her writings, it is clear that Dickinson burned with a decades-long obsessive passion for Susan. These works remained hidden from the public for decades because of Dickinson's extreme shyness until they were discovered by her youngest sister upon her death and published posthumously.

Susan Dickinson, married to Emily's brother Austin, became a neighbor in 1857. In spite of their close proximity, Emily continued her voluminous correspondence to Susan, sending her 267 poems and gazing at her through the windows of her home. She was inspired and tantalized by the haunting nearness of Susan, separated from her by panes of glass. Emily tormented herself, imagining what secrets lay in Susan's heart and soul.

Dickinson was underappreciated for the most part of her life. The first volume of her work was published posthumously in 1890, and a collection of her poetry became available for the first time in 1955, when scholar Thomas H. Johnson published *The Poems of Emily Dickinson*. Nevertheless, she helped to establish an American voice in literature and would unintentionally serve as an inspiration for later generations of lesbian writers.

Gertrude Stein

While the early twentieth century remained an era marked by a hypocritical double standard that allowed men more avenues to express themselves sexually than women,throughout her career, Gertrude Stein shattered the walls built by strict nineteenth-century American culture. Refusing to be confined by either literary or gender conventions, her unconventionality led to wide speculation about her love life.

Born to wealthy parents in Allegheny, Pennsylvania, in 1874, Stein grew up in Oakland, California, but lost her mother at age 14 and her father by age 17. At Radcliffe College, Harvard University's school for women, she began to study under psychology professor William James, the brother of Henry James. There, she fell in love with a fellow student, May Bookstaver, who was already in a relationship with another woman. The romantic triangle proved distracting to Stein, whose grades suffered, leading her to drop out of school. Traveling to New York and Europe in 1903, she wrote her first novel with an unambiguous lesbian storyline, *Q.E.D.* (from the Latin phrase *quad erat demonstrandum*, or "what is to be proved" in English), but this work would see the light of day only posthumously. Published in 1950 under the title *Things As They Are*, *Q.E.D.* centered on a lesbian triad similar to the one that Stein had recently experienced. Her next work, *Three Lives* (published in 1909), marked the launch of her more mature, abstract writing style. Both lesbianism and an interracial romance shape "Melanctha," one of the stories in this collection.

Stein gained personal and artistic confidence with the budding of her long-term romance with Alice B. Toklas, who Stein met in Paris around the time that she was writing *Three Lives*. Toklas would appear in fictional form in several of Stein's books. After an already long career, Stein did not produce a bestseller until her ironic *The Autobiography of Alice B. Toklas* (1933), in which she assumed the voice of her lover and wrote in an accessible style with titillating descriptions of her encounters with the great and infamous American and European artists of the day—novelist Ernest Hemingway, the poets Ezra Pound and T.S. Eliot, and painters like Paul Cézanne and Pablo Picasso. This work made Stein a celebrity with a lucrative career as a public speaker. Her sexuality would become an open secret for the rest of her life.

Ann Bannon and the Rise of Lesbian Pulp

Changes in American publishing practices during the early twentieth century allowed more openly homosexual writers to reach a broader audience. Just before World War II, publishers experimented with reaching a mass readership with what were originally called "pocket books," printed with cheap paper covers and which sold in drugstore bins and newsstands rather than traditional bookstores. Companies like Dell and Avon published what were called Armed Services Editions to an even larger audience—soldiers who passed them from hand-to-hand while fighting in Europe and Asia. By the 1950s, these evolved into the post-war "paperbacks," which featured often-sensationalistic content: crime stories, violent westerns, war tales, and science fiction. Sometimes the books included racier content that book companies took chances on because of the potential for high sales. With covers adorned with pictures of busty women in various states of undress, some of the stories included explicit lesbian themes. One fan, Lee Lynch, recalled her nervousness as she browsed the lesbian pulps in drugstores. "[R]egular vigilance turned up books I was petrified to take to the cashier," she wrote. ". . . Valerie Taylor's *The Girls in 3-B* and Randy Salem's *Man Among Women*: these books I would savor alone, heart pounding from both lust and terror of discovery, poised to plunge the tainted tome into hiding."

Books like Ann Bannon's *Odd Girl Out*, empowering in their time, have not aged well. The prose is overwrought, the bedroom tensions are drawn out over too many pages, the characters are shallow, and the lovers in such books too often fall into easy "butch" (masculine) and "femme" (more conventionally feminine) archetypes. Yet, Bannon (born Ann Weldy in 1932) and other lesbian pulp writers opened their readers to a world where educated women did not shy away from newly discovered sexual identities and found pleasure and love with other women, free of shame. To many readers, such stories must have seemed like a fantasy escape from the tight strictures of their hometowns and inspired their search for community.

Bannon was a 22-year-old housewife struggling with her own identity when she began her writing career. Her novel *Odd Girl Out* (1957) featured a character, Laura Landon, who awakens to her long-suppressed sexual desires when she encounters a flirtatious, bisexual beauty named Beth as she is accepted into the Alpha Beta sorority house her first year in a small liberal arts college. As Beth arouses passions in Laura's heart, Laura struggles with the lesbian stereotypes she harbors:

> She thought that homosexual women were great strong creatures in slacks with brush cuts and deep voices; unhappy things, standouts in a crowd. . . .
> [S]he thought, "I don't want to be a boy. I don't want to be like them. I'm a girl. I am a girl. That's what I want to be. But if I'm a girl why do I love a girl? What's wrong with me?

Beth has to correct Laura's shallow focus on outward appearances. "Laura, we're just as queer as the ones who look queer," she tells her younger, less experienced friend. Beth eventually realizes that though she does care deeply for Laura and finds comfort in her arms, she is in love with a man, Charlie. Laura has plotted for the two to drop out of college and begin a life together in another city, but Beth tells her female lover at a train station that her heart belongs to her boyfriend. In an earlier era, a lesbian in a novel most likely would have met a tragic end, committing suicide. Instead, Laura, while hurt, does not hate Beth for the rejection. She leaves for a new life of integrity, abandoning a dishonest past in which she pretended to be straight.

Bannon's novels at times reiterated lesbian stereotypes, but for all their defects, her books helped a post-World War II generation of lesbians feel like they were not alone. Another lesbian author, Katherine V. Forrest, said the Bannon books saved some gay women from suicide. "I found Ann Bannon's *Odd Girl Out* the year it was published, 1957, in Detroit. I was eighteen years old, isolated in my queerness, filled with self-loathing," said Forrest, author of the 1983 novel *Curious Wine*. ". . . Ann Bannon helped to save our lives."

Patricia Highsmith

Ann Bannon became a beloved figure in the American lesbian community. However, there have been few lesbian writers as brilliant as Patricia Highsmith. The moody, often unpleasant, and bigoted writer of such classic psychological thrillers as *Strangers on a Train* (later adapted into a powerful Alfred Hitchcock movie) and *The Talented Mr. Ripley* (the source material for a gripping film of the same name starring Matt Damon) made a hobby of emotionally wounding the people in her life. As her biographer Joan Schenkar observed, "She wasn't nice. She was rarely polite. And no one who knew her well would have called her a generous woman."

Born in Fort Worth, Texas, in 1921, Highsmith often seemed more drawn to the sociopaths who peopled her fiction than the living, breathing human beings in her real life. Her tales, filled with false identities and inscrutable motives, reflect an author whose true feelings and motives remained hidden in shadows. Her first novel, *Strangers on a Train*, sold modestly when published in 1950 until the following year when it was adapted for the screen by Alfred Hitchcock. The book centers on the encounter between an architect, Guy Haines, who wants to divorce his wife, Miriam, who has cheated on him, and Charles Anthony Bruno, a sociopath who wants to kill his father. Bruno makes a sinister offer: he will kill Guy's wife in return for Guy murdering Bruno's father. He suggests that it will be a perfect pair of murders since neither man will have a clear motive for the homicide. Bruno later kills Guy's wife and spends much of the rest of the novel pressuring Guy to live up to his end of the pact that the killer believes has been made.

Bruno is an irredeemably evil villain, unlike the anti-hero whose dark adventures would enliven five of Highsmith's novels, Tom Ripley. In *The Talented Mr. Ripley* (1955), we are introduced to Tom, a low-rent con artist with a knack for forging signatures, imitating voices, and mimicking personalities. Ripley convinces a shipping magnate, Herbert Greenleaf, that he is a close friend of the wealthy man's son,

Dickie, who is whiling away his youth and fortune in Italy. The elder Greenleaf hires Ripley to travel to Europe to convince Dickie to return to the United States and take his rightful place in the family business. Ripley finds Dickie, convincing him they were old school friends. Dickie tells his girlfriend that Ripley is such a non-entity that he must have forgotten the relationship. Ripley becomes friends with the wealthy Dickie's inner circle, the heir providing the con artist an expense account sufficient to live the high life. The relationship turns chilly, however, when Dickie discovers Tom dressed in his clothes and imitating him. Dickie tries to rid himself of the interloper who, sensing he is about to lose his meal ticket, murders his benefactor. Through fraud, he accesses Dickie's considerable fortune and steals his late benefactor's identity. Much of the rest of the novel depicts his numerous near-escapes from detection. Highsmith's genius is her ability to make the reader identify with so evil a man and feel dread when his crime is almost detected. The Ripley character proved so fascinating that he became the central figure in five novels that became known to fans as the "Ripliad" (in honor of Homer's "Iliad")—the original book and *Ripley Underground* (1970), *Ripley's Game* (1974), *The Boy Who Followed Ripley* (1980) and *Ripley Under Water* (1991).

Highsmith implies that Dickie and Ripley feel a homosexual attraction towards each other. In 1952, she wrote her sole explicitly gay-themed novel under the pseudonym Claire Morgan titled *The Price of Salt* (1952). In a break from the past, the lesbian characters, Therese and Carol, do not meet tragic ends, but surrender to intense, fierce emotional and physical passion. Therese is smitten by Carol, a customer she serves at a department store. A romance blossoms when she delivers the purchases to Carol's home. Carol's marriage is crumbling, and her bitter, estranged husband, Harge, has taken away the couple's daughter after discovering a previous lesbian affair. Carol's love affair with Therese offers emotional salvation for the elegant women, but they are being spied on by a private investigator hired by Harge. The gumshoe records the women having sex, which gives Harge the evidence that he needs to win custody of the daughter. Harge forces her to break off her relationship in return for allowing the mother only supervised visits with her child. This resolution pains Therese, but the ending is ambiguous, with the possibility open that love might still triumph in the end. The novel sold approximately one million copies in the United States the year after its release. By the 1950s, not all gay and lesbian characters in American literature were doomed to be murdered or commit suicide.

Susan Sontag's Critique of Camp

Public intellectual, essayist, and political activist, Susan Sontag published her first major work, "Notes on Camp," in 1964. (Camp derives from the French term *se camper*, meaning "to pose in an exaggerated fashion.") As gay novelist Christopher

Bram wrote, there are two meanings to the word "camp": "a deliberate style of gay behavior, the nelly variations of talk and movement that include female pronouns and limp wrists" and "an approach to art best summed up in the phrase, 'So bad it's good.'" It was made mainstream by Susan Sontag, herself a lesbian, who argued that the camp style was a major force in American culture. As Sontag wrote, "The hallmark of Camp is the spirit of extravagance . . . It incarnates a victory of 'style' over 'content,' 'aesthetics' over 'morality,' of irony over tragedy . . . The whole point of Camp is to dethrone the serious . . . More precisely, Camp involves a new, more complex relation to 'the serious.' One can be serious about the frivolous, frivolous about the serious." Camp art could include anything from the music of flamboyant pianist Liberace to Tiffany lamps, from cheaply-made and badly-acted Japanese horror films from the 1950s to tongue-in-cheek 1960s TV shows like *Batman*.

In her essay, Sontag meant to argue that gays, like Jews, represented a socially stigmatized group that played an unacknowledged, profound role in reshaping American art. (Sontag's parents were Jews of Lithuanian and Polish descent.) Her seriously flawed essay, however, led some readers to an unfortunate conclusion. By arguing that camp was pervasive, she led those hostile to homosexual men and women to find a sinister or disabling gay message in art even when none was intended.

She wrote extensively about photography, culture and media, AIDS and illness, and human rights. Her books include four novels: *The Benefactor* (1963), *Death Kit* (1967), *The Volcano Lover* (1992), and *In America* (1999); a collection of short stories; several plays; and nine works of nonfiction, one of which was *Illness as Metaphor* (1978) a monograph written after she was diagnosed with an aggressive form of breast cancer in 1975 but lived for another three decades, detailing how myths around the disease can derail effective treatment. She also wrote *Against Interpretation and Other Essays* (1966), *On Photography* (1976), *AIDS and Its Metaphors* (1989), *Where the Stress Falls* (2001), *Regarding the Pain of Others* (2002), and *At the Same Time* (2007).

She was a human rights activist for more than two decades, serving from 1987 to 1989 as president of the American Center of PEN, the international writers' organization dedicated to freedom of expression and the advancement of literature. She led campaigns on behalf of persecuted and imprisoned writers. Her stories and essays appeared in newspapers, magazines, and literary publications all over the world.

Rita Mae Brown

The most prominent of the post-Stonewall generation writers placed lesbian pride and the unmasking of heterosexual privilege at the forefront of their work. Rita Mae Brow stands as a notable example of such writers. Born in 1944 in Pennsylvania to a single, teenaged mother who left Rita in an orphanage because she felt unfit to be a parent, Brown devoted herself to shattering stereotypes of lesbians and bisexuals. She showed brilliance as a student early on. She won a scholarship to the University of Florida, which she later claimed was revoked in 1964 because of her involvement in the civil rights movement. The revocation may have had more to do with her comment to an officer in her sorority that she did not particularly care if she had a romantic relationship with a man or a woman. Upon her expulsion, Brown was broke and living in a car. She hitchhiked to New York and joined an early chapter of the National Organization for Women, only to be kicked out by NOW due to her repeated criticism that the feminist organization was indifferent to the unique issues faced by lesbians. She received a Ph.D. from the Institute for Policy Studies in Washington, D.C., in 1973, and first gained attention from a national audience with the publication of two feminist poetry collections titled *The Hand That Cradles the Rock* (1971) and *Songs to a Handsome Woman* (1973). "The male party line concerning lesbians is that women become lesbians out of reaction to men," Brown wrote in "Take a Lesbian to Lunch," a provocative 1972 essay.

> This is a pathetic illustration of the male ego's inflated proportions. I became a lesbian because of women, because women are beautiful, strong, and compassionate. Secondarily, I became a lesbian because the culture that I live in is violently anti-woman. How could I, a woman, participate in a culture that denies me my humanity? . . . To give a man support and love before giving it to a sister is to support that culture, that power system, for men receive the benefits of sexism regardless of race or social position.

Her most important work, the novel *Rubyfruit Jungle*, was published in 1973. Like Brown herself, the protagonist named Bolt is a "bastard" child booted out of college for her sexuality before moving to New York. With a steely nerve, she never apologizes for her lesbianism and her individualism. Brown received rejection notices from numerous major publishers before signing a contract with a small feminist outfit, Daughters Press. The work electrified lesbian audiences, eventually selling millions of copies and becoming one of the most popular lesbian-themed novels of all time.

Revolutionary in its time, *Rubyfruit* nevertheless has not aged well. In her rejection of traditional masculinity, Brown displayed condescension toward so-called "butch" lesbians. One character, Molly, turns down a "dyke" in a bar and then exclaims, "What's the point of being a lesbian if a woman is going to look and act like an imitation of a man? Hell, if I want a man, I'll get the real thing not one of these chippies. I mean [...] the whole point of being gay is because you love women. You don't like men that look like women, do you?" Brown, however, grew as an artist over time and concluded that heterosexuality was largely a social myth, not grounded in real people's lives. "I don't believe in straight or gay," she said in a 2008 interview. "I really don't. I think we're all degrees of bisexual."

VOICES OF COLOR: LESBIAN, GAY, AND BISEXUAL

Although sexuality can be concealed at great emotional cost to the individual, there are no closets that can offer a black man or woman refuge. Black gay men historically faced double challenges to their full humanity from a dominant society that devalued their color and their romantic choices while black lesbians faced a third barrier to equality from a culture that often also demeaned women. The usual dangers faced by African Americans—lynching, beatings, terrorist threats, discrimination, and poverty—magnified exponentially for lesbian, gay, and bisexual blacks. Lesbian Latino, Hispanic, and Native Americans faced not just prejudice about their sexual identities, but also bore the painful legacy of conquest and genocide, and assumptions of racial and cultural inferiority by Anglos. Simultaneously, lesbian, gay, and bisexual people of color had to battle homophobia within their own racial groups and struggled to find a welcoming and safe place to call home. African American, Latino, Hispanic, and Native American lesbian writers did not have the luxury of being apolitical. The very existence of their art challenged the concept of white supremacy. Such writers faced conflicting and at times overwhelming political demands while facing confusion and pain, not only when they discovered their sexuality, but also when they became conscious about white racism and racial oppression.

Countee Cullen, Langston Hughes, and the Harlem Renaissance

For one homosexual African-American writer central to the Harlem Renaissance, Countee Cullen, an early experience of white racism proved unforgettably painful and inspired one of his most memorable poems, "Incident." Orphaned at an early age and raised by a grandmother, Cullen related how he was "riding in old Baltimore" as a child in a state of glee until he noticed a white child staring at him. "Though he was no whit bigger," he related how the boy responded to his innocent smile by sticking out his tongue "and called me 'Nigger.'"

Cullen burned brightly before his brief life ended in 1946 due to high blood pressure and kidney-related blood poisoning when he had reached only his 43rd year. He wrote like a man in a hurry, cranking out five volumes of poetry, a novel, and two children's books, as well as editing a poetry anthology. Cullen married the daughter of the African-American scholar W.E.B. DuBois, Yolanda, and later another woman, Ida Roberson, although he had a number of romances with men throughout his life. Despite insisting at one point that he was "a poet, not a Negro poet," race formed a central theme in much of his verse. The topic of racial oppression also allowed him to discuss sexual orientation in a more coded way. In the poem "Tableau" (1925), readers understood that Cullen mourned how the color line divided whites and African Americans. A more aware audience also understood that the poet mourned the way in which a homophobic culture prevented men who loved each other and women who loved other women from openly celebrating their feelings.

Cullen and other gay and bisexual Harlem Renaissance writers such as Richard Bruce Nugent, Wallace Thurman, and Langston Hughes faced a more difficult challenge in addressing their sexual longings and identities in their writings than even their white peers. As the literary scholar Emmanuel S. Nelson noted, "Both black and white readers expected the writers [of the Harlem Renaissance] to foreground the race-specific aspects of the African American experience. And the economics of the literary marketplace and the tenuousness of the black writers' position in the United States during the 1920s denied them the level of artistic freedom and personal autonomy necessary for forthright explorations of unconventional sexualities."

Langston Hughes's sexuality remained so deeply buried that his orientation remains a subject of fierce debate among scholars today. One biographer, Arnold Rampersad, uncovered evidence that Hughes had confessed to a sexual tryst with a sailor. However, Rampersad insisted that there was not enough evidence based on this known instance to suggest that Hughes was a homosexual. Sexuality certainly was not a central topic in the poet's writings. Like Countee Cullen, Hughes focused on capturing the black experience. Envisioning himself as a voice for black people, he wrote in accessible language for a broad audience and sought to capture in verse some of exciting pulse of the jazz, blues, and gospel music that he deeply loved.

Some of his poems can be read both as pleas for justice for African Americans, and, less obviously, a plea for gay men like himself to have their deepest personal desires respected. Readers, however, have to sift closely for clues regarding his love life. His most famous poem, "A Dream Deferred," compares the black freedom struggle to a raisin withering in the sun, a festering sore, rotting meat, or a heavy load that suddenly, under relentless pressure, explodes. In a lesser-known coda, "Tell Me," Hughes bitterly laments that his loneliness, his personal dream, is also deferred, hidden so deeply it dare not be expressed. He never identifies the object of his private desires, but the tone is that of the lovelorn.

"Tell Me" became the subject of fierce controversy in 1991 when words from the poem were used on a poster advertising Gay and Lesbian History Month. Some African Americans expressed homophobic outrage that a man widely regarded as a literary hero, perhaps the Harlem Renaissance's most acclaimed genius and a spokesman for black rights, was being smeared as a supposed deviant. Nevertheless, literary critics found even more hints regarding Hughes's subterranean identity in works such as "Young Sailor" and "Submerged Streets." The closet society imposed on even such distinguished figures, however, meant that even Hughes could not be both a "race man," as defenders of black dignity were once called, and an openly gay man at the same time.

James Baldwin

James Baldwin did as much as any African American writer to expand the boundaries of what could be discussed sexually and romantically in black literature. The child of an unmarried woman, Baldwin spent his childhood being physically brutalized by his father and taunted and bullied by his peers who mocked the small-statured boy's effeminate speech and body language. Linguistically gifted at an early age, he sought escape from his suffering through the church and became a minister at the tender age of fourteen, honing his eloquence for a future life as a wordsmith.

The endless pressures of American anti-black racism and homophobia left Baldwin wondering if he could hold onto his sanity and prompted his decision in 1948 to leave his native New York for Paris with only $40 in his pocket. He devoted much of his literary life to exposing the illogic of white supremacist thinking and warning of its danger to the country's survival in works such as *Notes of a Native Son* (1955), *Nobody Knows My Name* (1961) and *The Fire Next Time* (1963).

Not as well-known were Baldwin's examinations of sexual awakening and the roots of homophobia. His essay, "The Preservation of Innocence," written just one year after his escape to Europe, and published in the little-known Moroccan journal *Zero*, provocatively links the heterosexual fear and hatred of homosexuals to men's contempt for women. Society's "debasement of and . . . obsession with [homosexual men] corresponds to the debasement of the relations between the sexes," Baldwin suggested. He believed that heterosexual men in the mid-twentieth century often defined themselves by their sexual and social subordination of women. Such heterosexuals despised their male homosexual peers because they saw gay men as traitors to their gender who chose to be parodies of women. Gay men were inferior and despised, in this mindset, because of their proximity to women.

Baldwin produced numerous classics of the gay canon, including a 1951 short story, "Outing," which centers on two teenage boys spending a day together at a church picnic and the terror one boy feels as he becomes aware of his attraction to his companion. His 1956 novel *Giovanni's Room* became a landmark in gay arts and letters even though it featured some of the old effect of portraying gay men as prone to criminality and promiscuity. Written in flashback form, *Giovanni* concerns the doomed romance between an American, David, and Giovanni, an Italian. David canot cope with his homosexuality and breaks off the relationship, reducing Giovanni to despair and a seedy sexual existence in Paris that eventually leads to him committing murder. *Another Country* (1962), a more sophisticated novel less obsessed with gay guilt, explores love among a cast of eight racially diverse homosexual men in New York City. The characters at times suffer doubt about the meaning of their homosexuality and long for belonging in the larger world, but they also find kindness and a home in each others' arms.

John Rechy

No refuge from the stresses of society awaited the characters in Mexican-American author John Rechy's gritty fictional world of drag queens, pimps, drug addicts, hustlers, and desperate "johns" looking for hookups with male prostitutes. If Baldwin's characters yearned, sometimes desperately, for love, Rechy's creations, in books such as *City of Night* (1963), stalked the dark urban landscape for sexual pleasures of all varieties.

Rechy came from aristocratic parents who fled to America to escape the violence of Pancho Villa's militia after the 1910 Mexican Revolution. Even though he grew up in humble circumstances, Rechy studied journalism at Texas Western College and served a stint in the U.S. Army before producing a controversial literary sensation, *City of Night*. With the dialogue written in realistic street slang, the book follows the travels of an unnamed man as he offers sex for cash from New York to the West Coast and describes his tormented customers, including a lonely old man, a sadomasochist, and another male prostitute. Rechy describes a sordid world, but he does not condescend or judge. His gift derives from lending dignity to even the most broken-down human wrecks. The seediest sex in *City of Night* still retains an elegance and humanity. The theme of authenticity in an age that imposed fake public images on gay men figures prominently in the novel. "[W]hatever a guy does with other guys, if he does it for money, that don't make him queer," insists one male prostitute named Pete. "You're still straight." With its cast of confused social rejects, *City of Night* captures the degree to which later twentieth-century LGBT writers had freed themselves from the need to meet the social expectations of the heterosexual majority. Reader reactions ranged from morbid fascination to deep admiration. Among the book's many fans would be Jim Morrison of the legendary California rock band The Doors, who would reference the title of the book in the hit song "L.A. Woman."

In spite of his themes, or maybe because of them in the anti-authoritarian climate of the 1960s and 1970s, Rechy's stature rose. Two of his other books focused on gay themes, *This Day's Death* (1969) and *Rushes* (1979). The first of these novels details the suffering of a man trapped in a police crackdown on gays in Griffith Park in Los Angeles while the second focuses on marginal men seeking pleasure in a leather bar. If an earlier generation of gay activists sought respectability by adopting middle-class styles and manners, Rechy achieved the same objective by mocking bourgeois morality, his gritty works winning him a National Endowment for the Arts fellowship.

Audre Lorde

After Baldwin, many writers also appreciated the interlinking of racism, sexism, and homophobia. Audre Lorde was such an artist. Born in New York City in 1934, the child of immigrants from Grenada, Lorde knew the experience of being an unwanted stranger in a strange land—the sense of being seen as alien in her home country.

So nearsighted that she was classified as legally blind, at an early age she sometimes answered questions by speaking in rhymes. She saw language itself as expressing the multicultural reality of her world. "Words had an energy and power and I came to respect that power early," she said. "Pronouns, nouns, and verbs were citizens of different countries, who really got together to make a new world." After graduating from Hunter College, Lorde published her first collection of poetry, *The First City*, in 1968.

Lesbianism became a central theme of works such as *Zami: A New Spelling of My Name* (1982). She sought to create a more inclusive concept of lesbianism to include all women who felt strong emotional ties to other women, whether these relationships were ever consummated in the bedroom. She also connected lesbianism to her blackness, suggesting in *Zami* that she and all black women in the Americas shared a mystic bond with their ancestral mothers in the African homeland. Lorde joyfully celebrated the beauty and poetry of the black womanly form, rapturously contemplating "sweat-slippery dark bodies, sacred as the ocean at high tide." Lorde's works blended eroticism with blazing hot political outrage, as in the poem "Power" in the 1976 collection *Between Ourselves* where she simmered with moral outrage as she reflected on the fate of a white police officer who was acquitted of heartlessly gunning down an African-American child by a jury of eleven white men and one black woman who had been metaphorically dragged "over the hot coals of four centuries of white male approval" and by whose complicity "lined her own womb with cement to make a graveyard for our children."

Paula Gunn Allen

The work of lesbian, gay, and bisexual writers of color in the late twentieth century, such as Paula Gunn Allen, reflected a basic truth in American history: that the United States never had a single culture or language, and that black slaves and sharecroppers, Mexican farm workers, and eastern and southern European immigrant factory laborers were as responsible for creating the United States as any collection of white "Founding Fathers." The United States and its citizens had always been a place where cultures and peoples collided and sometimes blended, with the country's core identity transforming with the birth of each new child and its culture morphing with each social encounter across color lines.

Allen's very existence reflected the hybridity of American culture. With a Laguna-Sioux-Scottish mother and a Lebanese American father, Allen grew up in New Mexico, a state with a sizeable Mexican American and Mexican community. Heavily inspired by female-centered myths shared by Native American peoples in the southwestern United States, such as the tales of Grandmother Spider and the Corn Maiden, Gunn's poetry and short stories suggested a vital connection between these feminine supernatural figures and the transformative bonds engendered in the lesbian community. Central to such myths, she suggested, was the idea of the interconnectedness of all living beings, an idea in direct opposition to the worldview of white racists. Both Native Americans and lesbians had endured centuries of sometimes homicidal cruelty, but their bonds and their ties to nature, nevertheless, ensure both groups a type of immortality. Gunn expressed this concept powerfully in her poem "Some Like Indians Endure," where she praises the resilience of lesbians and Indians alike, enduring as the sun, the stars, and "the persistent stubborn grass of the earth."

Gloria Anzaldúa

Born in South Texas, Gloria Anzaldúa saw no need to prioritize any element of her complex identity as a woman, a bisexual, and a Latina—a blended personal history that she has expressed by writing poems that freely switched from English to Spanish to the hybridized "Spanglish" often spoken on the U.S.-Mexican border. Coming of age during the rise of Chicano nationalism, which argued that Mexican Americans enjoyed a unique heritage and history and should separate from corrupting and racist Anglo culture, Anzaldúa argued for what she called *mestizaje*, which in Spanish literally means the process of racial mixing. In Anzaldúa's works, however, the term refers to the embracing as well of languages, nationalities, sexualities, religions, foods, and music styles.

To Anzaldúa, *mestizaje* represented not only a prophetic plan for saving the world from the destructive horrors of greed, racism, and ever-deadlier wars but also reflected current reality. In books such as *Borderlands/La Frontera: The New Mestiza*, Anzaldúa made clear that racial categories, the concept of gender, and neatly demarcated categories of sexuality are lies, illusions that fragment peoples and open the door to conquest and exploitation of the many by the privileged few. No one lived in the easily defined racial categories like "Mexican," "black," or "Anglo," or "straight" and "gay" in the complex meeting ground that she called home.

TRANSGENDER LITERARY ACTIVISM

While the most revolutionary of the lesbian and gay authors such as Gloria Anzaldúa directly questioned traditional notions of gender, transgendered authors in the early twenty-first century (whether they identified as male, female, or felt comfortable assigned to neither category) challenged old ideas of gender with their very existence. Many of the published works by transgender authors deal with explicitly political topics and personal experiences, though traditional novels, plays, poetry and even comic books and graphic novels are now part of a growing transgender literary genre.

Kate Bornstein

Performance artist Kate Bornstein blazed a trail as a transgender writer with her 2012 memoir *A Queer and Pleasant Danger*, which described the spiritual and philosophical journey that author took with her fellow Baby Boomers after World War II. The subtitle of *Queer* hits the highlights of Bornstein's convulsive, startling life: "*The True Story of a Nice Jewish Boy Who Joins the Church of Scientology and Leaves Twelve Years Later to Become the Lovely Lady She Is Today.*" In her memoir, Bornstein recalled her feelings, even as a small child, of being an alien in her own body. Born Al Bornstein, she remembered: "Whatever it was that boys did, I couldn't do naturally. I *learned* how to act. . . . I wanted to grow up to be Audrey Hepburn: skinny, graceful, charming, delightful, smart, talented, a star and a lady." She recalled being drawn to the Church of Scientology, widely regarded to be an eccentric, mind-controlling cult, because of its teachings that humans are occupied by "Thetans," bodiless and genderless beings who occupy different bodies over countless lifetimes. Bornstein believed the Church of Scientology's unconventional beliefs explained her own confusion over identity. She poured herself into the group, even working on founder L. Ron Hubbard's yacht. Still known as Al Bornstein, she married a female church member and fathered a daughter, but after twelve years of activism within Scientology, the church—which has a history of homophobia—excommunicated her and cut her off from her ex-wife and daughter.

While a practicing Scientologist, Bornstein continued to wrestle with her gender identity. Upon leaving the church, she began receiving psychological therapy before finally deciding to undergo reassignment surgery. As a woman, Bornstein discovered that she was a lesbian, and in *Queer and Pleasant Danger* she relates her experiences with a sadomasochistic lesbian couple. Her memoir proved to be a classic autobiography, with topics ranging from explicit details on the experience of surgical gender reassignment to confessions about her struggles with eating disorders while dealing with a borderline personality disorder, to simple fashion tips. A major focus, however, remained challenging the very idea of gender as a product of nature, as opposed to being a product of the social imagination.

Bornstein insists "the culture may not simply be creating roles for naturally-gendered people, the culture may in fact be creating the gendered people." In short, Bornstein says, no one is born "male" or "female" as we commonly understand the terms. They learn in the mainstream culture that "men" and "women" look and act certain ways, have certain ways of expressing themselves, and certain innate desires. Writers like Bornstein suggest that absent this indoctrination, each person represents a spectrum of identities that do not fit in any conventional gender categories. During her career as a performance artist, Bornstein also explored the issues treated in her memoirs in stage works such as *The Opposite Sex Is Neither* (1993).

Matt Kailey

The late Matt Kailey (one of the co-authors of this volume) underwent a similar, if slightly less complicated, transformation, inspiring others to face identity issues and not accept unhappiness simply in the interest of avoiding society's disapproval. Born Jennifer Kathleen Kailey in 1955, he did not begin his transition from being a woman until he reached the age of forty-two. An activist at heart, he quickly became a leader of the Trans Man Support Group for the Gender Identity Center of Colorado. For eighteen years, he reached out to other transgender men and women as a social caseworker before becoming one of the first high-profile journalists for *Out Front*, one of the first LGBT journals published in the western United States.

While working at *Out Front*, Kailey rose from staff writer to managing editor in 2007, and thus became the highest-ranking transgender man in the world of American journalism. Having earned a master's in education, he was not just a journalist, but an author of books such as his autobiographical *Just Add Hormones: An Insider's Guide to the Transsexual Experience* (2005), and *My Child is Transgender: 10 Tips for Parents of Adult Trans Children* (2012). Identifying as a gay trans man, Kailey also taught psychology and human sexuality courses at Red Rock Community College and Metropolitan State University of Denver.

Kailey, who died in 2014, believed that transsexuals bore a lesson for the entire human race. "Transsexuals are the ones who can change gender as we know it," he wrote in *Just Add Hormones*.

> We are the ones who can liberate not only ourselves but the rest of society from the strict cultural standards that are almost impossible for anyone to meet. For women who have tried and failed to measure up to the airbrushed fantasies in glossy men's magazines, for men who measure "success" by both muscular bodies and muscular bank accounts and fail to "succeed" at

either one, wouldn't it be nice to take a deep breath and just say, "Forget it." Transsexual people have little choice and so, eventually many of us do just that. And in the midst of that overwhelming freedom, we forge ahead and form our lives—the lives that we were meant to live.

Max Wolf Valerio

As with Bornstein and Kailey, a complex interplay between gender and sexuality defined Max Wolf Valerio, born in 1957 of Native American, Spanish Jewish, and Northern European descent. Valerio spent much of his life as a lesbian. The concept of being transsexual was completely alien to him in his early years. "I was dyke-identified for fourteen years, and more, if you count my adolescence," he said in a 2006 interview. "Early on, I realized I was attracted to women, and so, a lesbian identity made the most sense to me. It was all I knew to name myself. The idea of transitioning in 1975 and before, when I was a teen, was completely off the map."

Valerio considered himself a radical leftist feminist during his time as a woman and rejected the idea that gender roles stemmed from biology rather than strict and disempowering rules imposed by a male-run, sexist society. He said that his views on the role of biology in shaping gender identity changed, however, when he began to take testosterone during his transition from female to male. "I came into transition feeling very strongly that I was not going to 'buy' into what I thought were 'masculine' or male behaviors, many of which I found repugnant," he said. "I had that feminist background you know! I also just thought that so many of these feelings or behaviors were caused only by socialization. The revelation of the testosterone for me, was that the truth was so much more complex . . . I had to find that I was wrong, and that many of these feelings are fed by testosterone and not simply by socialization as I had thought."

That biochemical transformation may have influenced Valerio's politics as well, as the author of works such as *The Testosterone Files: My Hormonal and Social Transformation from Female to Male* (2006) transitioned from being a leftist to a libertarian-style Republican. Valerio even ended up defending the strict voter ID laws that the Republican Party supports, laws that often impose barriers to the ballot for transgender men and women who have adopted new names as well as new genders. "Trans people are not hothouse flowers who wilt at the slightest obstacle or pressure," he said, dismissing the difficulties such laws pose for trans voters whose new identities might not match their public records. "We're resourceful, resilient, and, often, extraordinarily strong people."

Janet Mock

Trans writers often complain that even sympathetic cisgender people persist in forcing transgender men and women into clear-cut "male" and "female" categories. Janet Mock, a trans author and activist, took offense at the headline of a generally glowing portrait of her life co-written by Kierna Mayo and published in the May 18, 2011, edition of *Marie Claire* magazine under the headline, "I Was Born a Boy." These were words that Janet (born Charles) Mock never would have used. "I do wish I could change one thing about the piece: the use of the term 'boy' which is used a few times," she said of the article. ". . . I was born in what doctors proclaim is a boy's body. I had no choice in the assignment of my sex at birth . . . My genital reconstructive surgery did not make me a girl. I was *always* a girl."

Born of Hawaiian and African-American heritage, Mock recalled her first painful awareness that the male identity society imposed on her did not match how she saw herself. "Once, when I was five-years-old, a little girl who lived next door to my grandmother dared me to put on a muumuu and run across a nearby parking lot. So I did . . ." She said, "It felt amazing to be in a dress. But suddenly my grandmother appeared, a look of horror on her face. I knew immediately that I had crossed some kind of line . . . It didn't take very long before the social cues got louder and clearer. My parents started scolding me over the way I walked and held my hands. I learned to hide aspects of my personality. Playing with girls was fine, for example, but playing with their Barbies was something I could do only behind closed doors."

After an excruciating, emotionally uncomfortable sexual encounter with a boy at age seventeen, Mock decided that she would need complete sexual reassignment surgery in order to be happy. She heard the surgery was available for $7,000 in Thailand, a much lower cost than in the United States, and she went there for the operation at age eighteen. She began attending the University of Hawaii just two weeks after the operation, able to think about something other than her gender for the first time. Later earning a master's degree in journalism from New York University, she became an editor of *People* magazine and has designed educational programs for LGBT youth.

On CNN's *Piers Morgan Live* show to promote her book *Redefining Realness: My Path to Womanhood, Identity, Love, and So Much More* (2014), Mock created a media sensation when she sharply criticized Morgan after the host asked her about telling her boyfriend about her past, which he said might be uncomfortable because "you used to be yourself a man." During the interview, she was identified on-screen as someone who "was a boy until she was 18," and the show's Twitter feed asked readers, "How would you feel if you found out the woman you are dating was formerly a man?" Mock, of course, never considered herself a man. Essentially, she ran into the transphobic assumption on the Piers Morgan show that led to the headline in the *Marie Claire* profile: that one's gender is more shaped by external genitalia than by one's consciousness. "What they're saying is, 'Only until I got the surgery, then I was a woman,'" Mock said. Her complaints only inspired a bitter rejoinder from Morgan that his trans critics were "dimwits" for not realizing the TV host was on their side.

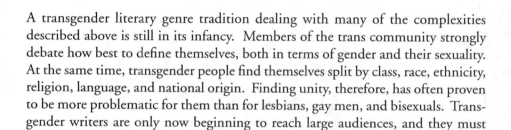

A transgender literary genre tradition dealing with many of the complexities described above is still in its infancy. Members of the trans community strongly debate how best to define themselves, both in terms of gender and their sexuality. At the same time, transgender people find themselves split by class, race, ethnicity, religion, language, and national origin. Finding unity, therefore, has often proven to be more problematic for them than for lesbians, gay men, and bisexuals. Transgender writers are only now beginning to reach large audiences, and they must overcome these internal divisions as they describe the joys and difficulties of being a trans man or woman to the larger world.

Chapter 10

LGBT CHARACTERS AND CULTURE IN FILM AND TELEVISION

The LGBT community and its allies have come to be incredibly savvy makers and manipulators of film and television imagery. These images have a good deal of power in defining queer culture for the heteronormative lawmakers and social arbiters as well as for LGBT people themselves. Whether working from motion pictures, video, or the digital format that today encompasses them all, LGBT models, actors, writers, directors, and myriad other workers in these industries have shown talent, courage, and perseverance in creating and influencing the visibility and status of LGBT people on the media. Their ability to do so in defiance of obscurity, censorship, and offensive stereotypes is also an important part of this chapter. While the worthiness of these artists should be acknowledged, a good deal of these changes must also be attributed to the bottom line. The LGBT community has become part of a highly desirable demographic as well as a market force in its own right.

LGBT CHARACTERS IN AMERICAN MOVIES

Cinema is arguably the most popular art form of the twentieth century. Developing in the late 1800s, the modern American film industry soon emerged as the world leader, and its productions are still a financially and culturally significant national export. Movies can represent expressions of popular culture or great art; they can be a frivolous waste of time or trigger a life-changing experience; they can promote communal identity or provide a unique interpretation of the world. Most of the films with LGBT-related themes or characters discussed will be those achieving acclaim and that were widely seen by the American public rather than more obscure works.

Much can be gained from exploring the interaction between American society and its film industry. Though often following general trends in society, and

163

sometimes lagging behind, there are many examples worth noting when film and television actors and executives "pushed the envelope" in their depiction of LGBT themes and characters. It would be nice to attribute philanthropic motivations to the movie stars and film studios who challenged LGBT stereotypes. However, film scholarship shows little evidence of the triumph of the common good unless it leads to increased profits. The good news is that showing LGBT themes and characters with more realism and complexity did become more profitable over the years, at first because controversy itself sells and later because the films interacted powerfully with the changing opinions of the target audiences.

Gay, Lesbian, and Bisexual Significance in Early Film, 1895-1933

The coding for sexual identity in early film differs considerably from the way we read sexuality in film today. There are a number of very early films where people embrace, caress, and dance with others of the same sex. However, in the late nineteenth and early twentieth centuries, people expressed this kind of physical closeness with others of the same sex without necessarily expressing homosexual undertones. For example, *The Dickson Experimental Sound Film* (1894/5), showing two men waltzing together, has been called one of the earliest American LGBT films. The men are dancing to "*Song of the Cabin Boy,*" a bit of light opera melody about life at sea without women. Because of these details, today the film is often dubbed *The Gay Brothers*. However, there is no evidence that the dancing men are gay (or brothers). At the time that the film was made, their "masculine" posture, haircuts, and clothing would count for more about their gender than the fact that they danced together. Other nineteenth-century films that suggest LGBT meaning include *Sandow*, an 1894 film with a bodybuilder showing his muscles in various poses and *Princess Ali*, an 1895 film in which a circus "bearded lady" dances. Interpretation is also limited by these films' simplicity: these early films were each less than a few minutes long and meant to be seen in a nickelodeon, a kind of arcade with one-person viewing machines.

The first same-sex American film kiss occurs in the 1927 feature (full-length) film *Wings*, which was also the first film to win the Best Picture Oscar. In *Wings*, Jack and David are friends who compete for the affection of Mary, the "girl next door." They become combat pilots for France in World War I, but David crashes behind enemy lines and is presumed dead. However, he manages to steal a German plane and is soon on his way back to the Allies. Tragically, Jack shoots down David's "enemy plane" in an attempt to even the score for his friend. Landing to inspect the wrecked German biplane and take a souvenir, Jack realizes he has inadvertently shot down the man he was trying to avenge. As David lies dying, he and Jack speak movingly of their love for each other, and Jack kisses David on the corner of his mouth. After David dies, Jack returns to America and is reunited with Mary. Whether the kiss is an expression of homosexual love, the profound connection between two young men bonded by combat, or both, is impossible to tell. Certainly the kiss between Jack and David is the emotional climax of the film.

Though not limited to the gay community, cross-dressing was also used in early American film comedy. Performances with men dressing as women—and less often, women dressing as men—draws from roots found in theater from Shakespeare to vaudeville. Some of the earliest American films with cross-dressing include the performances of Gilbert Saroney, who dressed up as a woman for comic effect in nickelodeon films such as *Old Maid Having Her Picture Taken* (1901). But Saroney was only one of many: Charlie Chaplin, Buster Keaton, Fatty Arbuckle, Stan Laurel, Wallace Beery, and many others employed this classic bit. Whether these performers were expressing a part of their personal gender identity is difficult to say and perhaps not as important as the ideas that they expressed in their performances. The comedy comes both from reinforcing and from blurring the lines between the genders. For example, in one scene from *A Woman* (1915), Charlie Chaplin's character dresses as a woman in order to fool a pretty young woman's father. The humor derives from watching Chaplin struggle to get into women's clothing, pad his chest with a handbag, and stumble in his oversized shoes as he attempts a hip-swinging walk. But after he borrows the right shoes, shaves off his mustache, and applies some makeup, his behavior matches his appearance as "feminine." A gifted actor, Chaplin is quite convincing as a woman, and Chaplin-in-drag becomes funny because his sweetheart's philandering father, entranced by this performance of femininity, flirts aggressively with "the new girl."

In the early 1900s, the American film industry was relatively free to depict characters and plot lines that explore ideas outside of the heteronormative standard. *A Florida Enchantment* (1915) has the main characters taking magic seeds that change women into men and vice versa. The two guard characters in *Salome* (1923) are played as flagrantly gay stereotypes (in keeping with the over-the-top setting) as is the set designer character in *The Broadway Melody* (1929). In her Oscar-nominated American film debut, Marlene Dietrich wears a tuxedo as the nightclub singer Amy Jolly in *Morocco* (1930). Moving through the audience and playfully interacting with them is practically *de rigueur* for female nightclub singers in movies of this era. In such movies, a lovely, provocatively dressed young woman might teasingly dally with various men in the audience as she sings, caressing one in passing, briefly sitting in the lap of another, and kissing a wealthy old fellow before flitting back to the stage. In *Morocco*, Dietrich reverses this familiar pattern by appearing in men's clothes and kissing a woman in the audience as she sings "Give Me the Man Who Does Things" in French. Dietrich stated, "I'm sincere in my preference for men's clothes—I do not wear them to be sensational." However, this tuxedoed image of Dietrich is sensational, and it becomes the trademark look of her celebrity. In *Queen Christina* (1933), another film of the thirties noted for its daring sexual ideas, Greta Garbo plays the famed bisexual seventeenth-century monarch with aplomb, dressing (and passing) as a man, taking a male lover, and maintaining a long-standing and jealousy-ridden affair with Countess Ebba Sparre. The ideas about sexual identity in films like *Morocco* and *Queen Christina* are not just sexually unfettered but exquisitely designed and beautifully lit and shot. They are icons of the glamour of early Hollywood not just because of the performances of Dietrich and Garbo but also because of the talent of directors, designers, and countless others. This period of creative freedom, however, was not to last.

The Censorship Era, 1908-1956

As the motion pictures grew into a very popular and profitable industry in Hollywood, the moral content of the movies came to worry some government and religious leaders. Groups such as the New York Board of Motion Picture Censorship and the Women's Christian Temperance Union objected to Hollywood's celebration of glamour, wealth, and sensual pleasures. These and other civic organizations convinced their members to avoid certain films on moral grounds. In response, American film industry leaders made several attempts at self-regulation. In 1908 they created the mostly ineffectual National Board of Censorship. Then the 1915 Supreme Court case *Mutual Film Corporation v. Industrial Commission of Ohio* found that movies are a business, not an art form, and are therefore not protected by the First Amendment right to free speech. This encouraged state and local groups in their quest to censor films.

Knowing their business was in jeopardy, film industry leaders made another, more successful attempt, at self-regulation. The Motion Picture Producers and Distributors of America (MPPDA) was formed in 1922. Although this trade association was a private-sector entity rather than a government agency, it grew to wield considerable power. A 1927, MPPDA document advised care in dealing with any suggestion of "sex perversion" (the term used by the MPPDA for any sexual expression outside the heteronormative standard). However, the greatest power of this censorship body came in 1934, when the Motion Picture Production Code ("the Code") was instituted, requiring producers to submit their films to the MPPDA office for approval. The MPPDA Purity Seal, shown immediately after the film's main title, became vital to the film's profit in an era where local groups might picket and boycott a film deemed immoral. In addition, those filmmakers who stepped outside the Code were charged a fine. Overtly queer characters and plots were forbidden during this heyday of the MPPDA (changed to the Motion Picture Association of America, or MPAA, in 1945). The Code stated that "sex perversion or any inference to it is forbidden." This became the standard in American film until 1956, when the Supreme Court ruled in *Burstyn v. Wilson* that movies are an art form, thus restoring First Amendment rights to motion pictures.

There were several reasons for the concern over morality in American film. Prohibition, the other great moral concern of this period, was flouted on the movie screen. (Of course, it was flouted off the screen as well, but not with millions of people watching.) In addition, the popularity of Hollywood films made the personal lives of its movie stars national news, and the early 1920s saw several serious Hollywood scandals. The director William Desmond Taylor's death was linked to drug abuse. Actress Mary Pickford, dubbed "America's sweetheart" for her many movie roles that emphasized purity and innocence, divorced her husband to marry her lover, actor Douglas Fairbanks, who was the masculine ideal of the time—"America's hero." Comedian Fatty Arbuckle threw some very wild parties, and, in a devastating turn of events, a young woman was found dead after one of them. Another factor was the prejudice against immigrants, many of whom fled the film industries of Europe for Hollywood with the outbreak of World War I. The belief that Europeans, particularly Jews, did not adhere to American (meaning "Christian") moral standards was the true anti-Semitic drive behind some of the organizations that pushed to censor film.

Some of the shifts in American gender culture also contributed to moral scrutiny of the movie business. Traditional roles for men and women had changed. The industrial revolution meant that more men had office jobs, and the decrease in manual labor devalued men's physical prowess, a traditional marker of "masculinity." Women gained the right to vote in 1920, and increasing numbers of women worked outside the home, no longer defining their "femininity" solely through housework and child care. Gays, lesbians, bisexuals, and trans people, once isolated in small towns, came to America's growing cities and found each other, creating romantic and social bonds that merged into communities. These new freedoms were threatening to those who wished to conserve the older, more conservative power structures, and so the expression of these freedoms came to be censored in the movies as well.

Pansies and Mannish Women, 1934-1956

Depictions of gay men and lesbians did not disappear from Hollywood film during the censorship era. However, gay men and lesbians appeared mainly in supporting roles and cameos rather than leading roles, and even these smaller roles were caricatures rather than true characters. The "Pansy Craze," a surge of popularity for effeminate male performers in the speakeasy circuit of the twenties and thirties, laid the groundwork for the Hollywood version of this stereotype. The high, sometimes lisping voice of these characters played well in the new talkies, and their silly, fussy demeanor was popular in comedies. One classic example of the pansy character is Egbert Fitzgerald in the first Fred Astaire/Ginger Rogers vehicle, *The Gay Divorcee* (1934). Egbert was played with flair by Edward Everett Horton. Called "Aunt

Egbert" by his friends and "Pinky" by his family, Egbert enjoys toy dolls when not timidly practicing the law. He serves as a perfect foil for the straightforward masculinity of Guy Holden, the Astaire character.

Another prominent stereotype of the era was the mannish woman, a character whose short or severely dressed hair, tailored clothing, assertive opinions, and career outside the home is seen as unfeminine. A prime example of the mannish woman can be seen in *Woman of the Year* (1942), in which Katherine Hepburn plays Tess Harding, a brilliant journalist writing about international politics. Tess's devotion to her work and her lack of concern for feminine charm, keeping house, and having children threatens her marriage to the sportswriter Sam Craig, played by Spencer Tracy.

The ability of these proto-queer characters to slide past the MPPDA censors might surprise present-day audiences. Fortunately for film art, the censors were ignorant of many cues of gay culture. The Code forbade certain words, such as "pansy," from being spoken and certain actions (same-sex romantic interludes, for example), but the censors could not see or control the way in which actors used their voices and bodies to suggest the homosexual characters snuck into subversive scripts.

Certain low-budget horror films of this time also contained homosexual undertones, with the monster or alien expressing the power and loneliness of the queer social outsider. One example is *Dracula's Daughter* (1936), in which the title character, Countess Marya Zaleska, longs to free herself of the vampire nature that she inherited from her father. She tries to end her curse by destroying her father's body. When that attempt fails, she turns to a psychiatrist for help, but he cannot free her either. With all options gone, she kidnaps the psychiatrist's girlfriend and flees with her to Transylvania. Analyzing this film closely from a gay perspective leads one to note that like homosexuality, vampirism cannot be destroyed or cured, and that eventually one's inborn desires take over.

Silly, "Sick," and "Criminal" Homosexual Characters in 1940s, 1950s, and 1960s

World War II brought a return and celebration of the intense same-sex friendships that made *Wings* (1927) such a moving film. While men forged powerful relationships in the armed services, women did the same while serving as nurses and factory workers. While such relationships in these films are not explicitly gay or lesbian, they did provide the premises for same-sex intimacy that peacetime, heterosexual stories did not. The war-time separation of men and women also opened up the possibility of men playing at being women and women playing at being men. Again, this is not so much an explicitly gay or lesbian expression as it is a license to stretch and bend conventional ideas about how to perform gender. For example, in a number of wartime comedies and musicals, cross-dressing is used as a comic device, as when a group of actors dress up in drag for a number in *Star Spangled Rhythm* (1942). These well-known actors—Fred MacMurray, Franchot Tone, Ray Milland, and Lynne Overman—are movie stars playing movie stars in this Paramount vehicle, doing a favor for a studio security guard so he can look good for his sailor son who is home on leave. Other wartime comedies and musicals feature seemingly gay and lesbian situations and dialogue, which appear only to be laughed off as mistaken assumptions. In *Up In Arms* (1944), couples on a double date, all in uniform, sit back to back on a crowded streetcar with the women together on one side and the men together on the other. Each person is talking to his or her date but appears to be talking to his or her seatmate. When one woman says, "I'm so glad you didn't grow a mustache," she appears to be talking to the woman beside her. The same thing occurs when one of the men say, "You look great in a uniform," and the other folks on the streetcar assume he is talking to the fellow beside him. These lighthearted movies always undercut any homosexual meaning—the characters are presented as heterosexual after all, with "proper" romantic interests in the opposite sex. In these films, gay or bisexual identity is put on as a kind of comic mask, only to be removed when the joke is over.

In the post-war period, gay and lesbian figures re-emerged as true characters rather than momentary masks "put on" by heterosexual characters for comic relief. However, these new roles appear in thrillers and dramas rather than comedies and musicals, and they are almost always either murderers or victims. This shift can be attributed to a number of factors. As the somber atmosphere of the Cold War began to infiltrate the culture, the dangers of being different began to be expressed in the movies. LGBT people were shown to be social misfits, strange beings whose "weakness" made them victims or whose "unnatural" appetites made them predators. American film also began to emphasize a greater sense of social realism, partly influenced by the growing availability of international films that explored a world outside of the heteronormative standard. In addition, the competition from family-friendly television meant that film began to be targeted to a more grown-up audience.

Two examples of gay men as murderers come from celebrated filmmaker Alfred Hitchcock, a British director who had a long career in Hollywood. In *Rope* (1948), an actual murder (the famous Leopold and Loeb case) was used as the basis of the script. Two young gay men commit a murder simply as an exciting exercise of Nietzschian *übermensch* philosophy. Both the case itself and the film depiction blended many elements that became conflated in the suspicious Cold War mentality of the time, where the political tensions between the USA and the USSR extended into concerns about communists hidden in American communities. In *Rope*, the young men playing the Leopold and Loeb characters are homosexual, associated with the arts, students of German philosophy, privileged elitists, and murderers.

Each quality—not just the willingness to murder—is seen as contributing to a lack of sane, healthy, moral "masculinity."

In *Strangers on a Train* (1951), Hitchcock presents another arrogant homosexual murderer. The charming, intelligent, and psychopathic playboy Bruno Anthony flirtatiously scrapes up an acquaintance with Guy Haines, a tennis player with political ambitions, during a train journey. Bruno half-jokingly suggests that he and Guy exchange murders, each ridding the other of an unwanted person in their lives. Later, Bruno murders Guy's trashy and troublesome wife, then attempts to blackmail Guy into keeping his part of the "bargain." Guy is half-beguiled and half-repulsed by Bruno, and Guy must become more active and determined (more "masculine") to defeat Bruno, the homosexual villain. In this whole endeavor, Guy is perhaps psychologically defeating the despised part of himself. The film is based on a Patricia Highsmith novel of the same title, and although the film and the book have some important differences, the relationship between the two men is fundamentally the same and serves as the engine that drives the narrative. Highsmith, who was a lesbian, wrote, "Each was what the other had not chosen to be, the cast off self, what he thought he hated, but perhaps in reality loved."

Homosexual film characters were also presented as victims during the postwar period. One notable example is *The Children's Hour* (1961). Originally a successful Broadway play written by Lillian Hellman (premiering in 1934), the story was first brought to film in 1936 under the title *These Three*. Under the terms of the existing MPPDA censorship code, however, the original lesbian storyline was forbidden. This hardly mattered to producer Sam Goldwyn. When told he could not make a film about lesbians, he replied, "That's okay! We'll make them Americans!" The change from forbidden lesbian love to a heterosexual love triangle, however, did not make for a great film. The 1961 remake under the original title, *The Children's Hour*, was released only months after an amendment to the Production Code allowed "sex aberration" in films as long as it was presented with "care, discretion, and restraint." The idea was that since film was an art form enjoying First Amendment rights, it should be allowed to address the same range of subject matter addressed by plays and novels. Working under the newer, more tolerant MPAA code, this 1961 version remained fairly true to Hellman's original play and was a better film for it. The story has a number of roles for strong female characters. Karen Wright and Martha Dobie are good friends who run a private school for girls. A spiteful little girl named Mary, who is the school bully, tells her grandmother Amelia that she saw Karen and Martha kissing. As Amelia spreads the rumor that Karen and Martha are lesbians, Martha acknowledges her romantic feelings for Karen. Eventually, the school loses all its pupils because of the scandal, and the teachers unsuccessfully sue Amelia for slander. Karen breaks off her engagement to a young doctor but does not commit to Martha. In the end, Martha, who thinks her romantic feelings for Karen are "wrong" and "sick," commits suicide.

Midnight Cowboy (1969) presents another example of the gay victim, along with another aspect to the changing production code. Supreme Court decisions in 1968 found that obscenity could be defined differently for children than for adults and that a classification system could be used to indicate appropriate audiences for motion pictures. That same year, the MPAA instituted the first movie rating system: G for general audiences, M for mature audiences, R for restricted audiences (children under sixteen must be accompanied by an adult), and X for films where no one under sixteen is admitted. The X rating meant that films that did not meet the MPAA's standards for "decency" could still be distributed and shown. *Midnight Cowboy*, which includes depictions of male homosexuality, nudity, drug use, physical violence, and prostitution that might seem unremarkable to many viewers today, received an X rating from the MPAA. It is the first and only X-rated film to receive an Academy Award—and, in fact, it won three. (Two years after its release, the rating for *Midnight Cowboy* was revised to R.)

In *Midnight Cowboy*, the gay characters are lonely, depressed, and afraid. The tender friendship between the two main characters, Joe Buck and Ratso Rizzo (played by Jon Voight and Dustin Hoffman), is a small redemption of this dismal existence. Joe is a small-town Texan whose past, revealed in flashbacks, includes child abandonment, child abuse, and rape. Ratso, the child of poor Italian immigrants, is a physically fragile but mentally tough street hustler. He dreams of a better life in Miami while he ekes out a marginal existence in New York City through petty theft. Joe naively travels to New York to "make it" as a gigolo, but he lacks the complex and subtle communication skills necessary to negotiate paying sexual encounters with women or men in the city. When Joe meets Ratso, they follow a traditional narrative path of male bonding: the two conflict before becoming business partners and ultimately friends. Although their relationship does not become sexual, their love for each other is powerful and indeed the only solace in the ugly world they inhabit. As Ratso's health worsens, Joe manages to get some money from a violent and abortive sexual encounter with a man he picks up in a bar. He buys bus tickets to Miami for himself and Ratso, but Ratso dies just as the bus reaches their destination. In this powerful film, Joe's love and care for Ratso "makes him a man" in ways that all his ambition for money and sexual prowess could not.

Elevated LGBT Characters in the 1970s, 1980s, and 1990s

During the seventies, eighties, and nineties, some LGBT film characters came to be presented in a sympathetic and even admiring light. Various films from this period portray them facing difficult situations with courage and wit. LGBT characters formerly seen as duplicitous and dangerous were now sometimes portrayed as clever or hip. This change both reflects and fuels the changing attitudes toward LGBT people in America. The seventies in particular was a transitional decade for the LGBT community, triggered by the Stonewall riots of 1969 and galvanized by the election and subsequent murder of San Francisco City Supervisor Harvey Milk in 1978. The decade culminated with 75,000 people taking part in the 1979 National March on Washington for Gay and Lesbian Rights. Accordingly, a number of seventies films celebrated the courage and integrity displayed by the LGBT human rights movement. In the eighties and nineties, the growing AIDS crisis focused attention and sympathy on the gay community, and some films of that period explored the tragedy of this epidemic. Of course, some Americans responded to the AIDS crisis by committing hate crimes against LGBT Americans, and some films explored those stories as well.

A number of these new, "elevated" LGBT characters began to appear in films based on popular European plays or movies. An especially important example of this kind of film is the UK-USA film co-production of *The Rocky Horror Picture Show* (1975), based on a theatrical musical of the same title by Richard O'Brien. A British actor and writer with a love of low-budget horror and science-fiction films, O'Brien worked with Australian director Jim Sharman in developing the play, which premiered in London in 1973 and in Los Angeles in 1975. Twentieth Century Fox gained the filming rights. Upon release, it was initially ignored by most theatergoers. Only through its growing cult status as a midnight movie with audience participation did the film garner success. Starting in 1976 at the Waverly Theater in New York City, audience members began attending midnight screenings dressed as film characters and talking back at the screen. These lines, as well as the rice, toast, and other things thrown at the screen, became ritualized and synced with certain moments in the film. Soon, groups in other cities began doing the same thing. The film continues to run midnight screenings to this day: *The Rocky Horror Picture Show* has the longest continuous film release in history.

The story involves a cross-dressing bisexual, Dr. Frank N. Furter, who seduces both members of a heterosexual couple, Brad and Janet. A hodgepodge of other complications ensue, and like the musicals that it vamps, *The Rocky Horror Picture Show* uses a loose narrative structure as an excuse to string together a series of song-and-dance numbers. The brilliance of the film lies in its clever network of playfully theatrical references to horror movies, science fiction movies, and musicals. The film is also revolutionary in communicating LGBT-friendly messages: all sexual pleasure is good, and embracing queer identity is liberating and transformative. It is these messages that made attending audience-participation screenings of *The Rocky Horror Picture Show* a rite of passage for LGBT teens in the seventies and eighties.

Another classic example of this new genre of LGBT-friendly films based on a European work is *Victor/Victoria* (1982), in which Victoria Grant (played by Julie Andrews), a talented but impoverished soprano in 1934 Paris, impersonates a drag queen with the help of a gay impresario. Her new show as Victor, a man impersonating a woman, is a hit seen by visiting Chicago nightclub owner King and his secretly gay bodyguard, Squash. King is smitten with "Victor" and determined to prove he/she is a woman. The film, a terrific exploration of gender as performance, is based on the 1933 German comedy film *Viktor und Viktoria*.

Finally, *The Birdcage* (1996) based on the 1978 French-Italian film *La Cage aux Folles* was an important box-office winner in this category. In this film, Albert and Armand Goldman (played by Nathan Lane and Robin Williams), a gay couple, own The Birdcage, a nightclub in the South Beach area of Miami, Florida, where Albert performs as a drag queen. Armand's son Val is engaged to Barbara, the daughter of Kevin Keeley, a conservative Republican senator. Fearing her father's disapproval, Barbara tells Senator Keeley that Val's parents are a distinguished and traditional heterosexual couple. When Keeley's family-values re-election campaign is damaged by news of the homosexual affair of a close family-values colleague, he decides to visit Arnold and Armand as a photo op to distract from the scandal, only to find the Goldmans' establishment is a gay hangout. Tipped off that paparazzi are waiting outside, the senator agrees to let Val's parents help him escape detection by walking out the entrance dressed as a woman. This wildly entertaining film was a hit with audiences, who appreciated the scathing indictment of sexual hypocrisy regardless of the genders involved.

The devastation of the 1980s and 1990s AIDS crisis became the subject of American films that portrayed gay, lesbian, and bisexual characters depicted in a positive light. *Longtime Companion* (1989), one of the first Hollywood feature films to deal with AIDS, focuses on eight central characters, and it highlights one different date per year for nine years, running from 1981 to 1989. This allows the filmmakers to show how AIDS and fear run through the group, affecting careers and personal relationships. The scene from 1981, the first year, shows friends in the gay community calling each other in response to a *New York Times* article about a new "gay cancer." In the scene from 1989, the final year, half of the group is dead. The title of the film comes from the term used in *New York Times* obituaries to refer to a gay or lesbian individual's surviving lover. The movie succeeds in humanizing the AIDS crisis for the broader heterosexual audience; the various effects of the disease and the efforts to fight it are presented with compassion and interest. After the film won the Audience Award at the U.S. Film Festival and actor Bruce Davidson was nominated for Best Supporting Actor for his work in the film, the film reached a population slightly beyond its art-house distribution. However, the film was also criticized for focusing on wealthy, white, male victims when the disease was affecting so many outside that demographic.

Philadelphia (1993) was a more high-profile film that dealt with AIDS. The film aimed at box-office success and achieved it, casting popular actors Tom Hanks as Andrew Beckett, a productive lawyer fired from a corporate firm for having AIDS, and Denzel Washington as Joe Miller, Beckett's initially homophobic attorney. After a very cautious premiere at just four theaters, *Philadelphia* was allowed expanded distribution and eventually became one of the highest-grossing films of the year. Like *Longtime Companion*, the film was structured to be more palatable to mainstream heterosexual audiences than to express the experience of the gay community for the gay community. Though director Jonathan Demme made a special effort to hire local people actually suffering from AIDS as extras in the film, Hanks and Washington, along with soundtrack musician Bruce Springsteen (all known heterosexuals), were the celebrities most associated with the film. In addition, the protagonist in the film, once again, was a white, wealthy, educated man. That being said, the story of Andrew Beckett was sympathetically told and beautifully acted. Hanks won a Best Actor Oscar for his performance, and Washington's performance was praised by critics as well.

Other elevated LGBT characters from the eighties and nineties include those who are the target of hate crimes, as in the *Torch Song Trilogy* (1988), a movie based on the play by Harvey Fierstein. In the film, Fierstein plays Arnold, a gay female impersonator who meets the right man only to see him murdered in a homophobic attack. Another example is *Boys Don't Cry* (1999), a feature film based on the actual murder of Brandon Teena, a trans man whose female anatomy was discovered by a group of men who beat, raped, and murdered him. LGBT characters are also shown sympathetically in some noteworthy movies dealing with physical and psychological exile. The bisexual character Shug Avery in *The Color Purple* (1985) is banished from her church and community by her preacher father; the homeless gay street hustler Mikey Waters in *My Own Private Idaho* (1991) wanders from rural Idaho to Portland, Oregon, to Italy in search of his mother. These characters from the films of the seventies, eighties and nineties are victims, to be sure—victims of disease, of bigotry, and of rejection. Yet, unlike their counterparts from the forties, fifties, and sixties, the more modern LGBT characters are seen as brave, tragic, and even noble. Their queerness is no longer the root of these characters' suffering. Instead the problem is ignorance and fear of a terrifying epidemic, or mistreatment by their heterosexual colleagues, or rejection and abandonment by their families.

Characters in Early Twenty-first Century Movies

The paths explored by LGBT characters have moved from near invisibility to demonization to heroism. The trajectory of this interest has led to the full flowering of LGBT characters as flawed, real, complex human beings. At the same time, LGBT rights, particularly the fight for marriage rights, have become a kind of *cause celebre* of the early twenty-first century. Consequently, there has been an explosion of LGBT films in the early twenty-first century. Though the vast majority of green-lighted LGBT stories still feature white men, that continues to be true of the film industry in general. As a result, there are many more films about gay men than about lesbians, bisexuals, and transgendered people. On the other hand, there are new and positive developments to report. In response to demands from the LGBT community, LGBT characters are now frequently being portrayed by LGBT actors. The days of the "pansies" and "mannish women" seem to be gone, and LGBT characters are rarely portrayed as murderers whose "evil" comes from their gender identity. The enlightened consciousness of some audiences and film-makers have turned away from these ugly stereotypes much as they did from Uncle Toms and dumb blondes now largely seen as racist and sexist.

Some earlier themes discussed above, however, have been continued. Films with LGBT characters as tragic victims continue to draw in twenty-first century audiences. The *Dallas Buyers Club* (2013) tells the story of Ron Woodroof, a het-erosexual and homophobic Dallas electrician who is diagnosed with AIDS after he has unprotected sex with a drug-using prostitute. Unhappy with the harsh and ineffective drug he has been prescribed in the U.S., Woodroof goes to Mexico to get drugs that do help him. He decides to smuggle these drugs from Mexico and sell them to other AIDS sufferers in the U.S. Eventually, Woodroof comes to accept and help his ailing friends in the LGBT community for love rather than profit.

One of the most celebrated LGBT films of the new era deals with a hate crime. *Milk* (2008) is a biopic of Harvey Milk, the first openly gay politician elected in California. The film draws from the 1984 documentary titled *The Times of Harvey Milk*, which is well worth watching in its own right. *Milk* is a very different kind of film given that it had a $20 million budget and Sean Penn, a bankable star, in the lead role. In the movie, *Milk* becomes a gay activist in 1970s San Francisco who successfully runs for a position on the San Francisco Board of Supervisors. He develops a complex and troubled relationship with conservative fellow Supervi-sor Dan White, who eventually shoots and kills Milk at City Hall after murdering Mayor George Moscone [see Chapter 4]. Milk's activism and sacrifice made him a venerated figure in the gay community, and Penn's Oscar-winning portrayal made the production an important film for audiences who care about equal rights for all.

A different kind of tragic victim can be seen in *Brokeback Mountain* (2005). The main characters, cowboys Ennis and Jack (played by Heath Ledger and Jake Gyllenhaal), meet and fall in love in 1963 while working a cold mountain sum-mer on a Wyoming sheep ranch. While their sexual encounters are passionate and honest, the men's psychological relationship is more tangled. Ennis does not want to believe that he is gay. When the summer ends, the men part, go on to marry women, and father children. However, their deep connection draws them back together on several occasions over the years, and their marriages fail because of it. Ultimately, Ennis and Jack are tragic victims because their upbringing and the times and places where they lived killed the relationship they should have built their lives on. The film is important in showing the cost of socially-enforced closeting on the men and their families and also for revealing an under-represented face of the gay community: rural, blue-collar characters.

LGBT camp—the kind of playful, hyperbolic theatricality that characterized *The Rocky Horror Picture Show*—continues to thrive in the twenty-first century. *Hedwig and the Angry Inch* (2001) based on a play of the same title, tells the heart-breaks of a transgendered East German rocker who endures a botched sex-change operation, abandonment by her lover, the fall of the Berlin Wall, theft of her music, and abandonment by another lover. The film juxtaposes the high culture of Aristotelian arguments embedded in Hedwig's songs with the low culture of a gig played behind the salad bar in a chain restaurant. It communicates genuine personal tragedy via the patently artificial trappings of glam rock. It is histrionic and absurd but also sad, a tragic life wailed directly to the audience with an ironic wink.

Hairspray, a film about a plump teenager named Tracy Turnblad (and her mother, played by a man in drag) provides a good example of the continuation of the LGBT camp genre. Tracy gets a job as a dancer on a local *American Bandstand*-type program, partners with her long-time crush, and (in her spare time) racially integrates Baltimore. This film is rife with references to sixties movies of the "Gidget" and "Tammy" variety—sweet, wholesome, fun girls who have adventures and make their dreams come true. This 2007 film is a remake of the original 1988 production directed by John Waters, who has made a career out of making low-budget, camp films starring his cross-dressing childhood friend, Divine (Harris Glenn Milstead). His 1988 version of *Hairspray* with Divine as Tracy's mother was Waters's attempt to enter mainstream cinema. The film gathered a cult following that led to a wildly successful Broadway play, running for over 2500 performances, winning eight Tonys, and generating national tours and a London production. The 2007 remake, based on this play, was also a success, both critically and at the box office.

One of the best-received films of the new millennium featuring lesbian characters in feature roles is *The Kids Are All Right* (2010), a family drama involving Jules and Nic (played by Julianne Moore and Annette Bening)—a married lesbian couple with two children, Joni and Lasar, conceived by a sperm donor named Paul. The children, now teenagers, decide to find their father. They track him down, and he begins interacting with the family. When Paul and Jules work closely together on a landscaping project, they have an affair, which Nic ultimately discovers. The family ousts Paul from their lives and eventually come to forgive each other. One of the film's messages is that parenting and family are a matter of action rather than biology. Just as important, however, are the complex, fully realized, flawed characters of the two lesbian parents. While it is clear that Nic and Jules are lesbians, that fact is integrated naturally into their lives rather than being the crux of the story. The couple is not demonized or hallowed for their gender, and their problems are not unique to the LGBT community—no AIDS, no hate crimes, no social stigma, and no anguished guilt.

This well-acted, engaging, ordinary family drama is, in a sense, a film that took over a hundred years to make. The history of LGBT film reflects the struggle in

America to recognize, understand, accept, celebrate, and integrate LGBT culture and identity as part of the whole. Although the films discussed in this chapter are mainly fictional, they do reflect history, and films can change the way the LGBT community is viewed by the general public. Ideally, LGBT social mores and identity can be influenced for the better by the power of such films.

LGBT ISSUES AND CHARACTERS IN TELEVISION

Perhaps more than any other medium, television is an important contributor to the creation of identity, especially gender and sexual identity. This influence is largely due to television's pervasiveness—Americans watch an average of five hours per day. The characters and stories we see on television are enormously influential on what we perceive as normal and acceptable. In this large and diverse nation that celebrates its diversity, the "American character" has always been difficult to define. Television programming and advertising, like popular literature and brand names in the national marketplace, can be a unifying experience for very different Americans, thus establishing a foundation of shared awareness and identity.

This common American experience of television viewing essentially started in the mid-twentieth century. Although CBS and NBC began experimental television programming in the early 1930s, the Federal Communications Commission did not license commercial television broadcasting until 1941. Even then, there were only about 7,000 television sets in the U.S., or approximately one for every 20,000 Americans. By 1950, there were 10 million households with televisions in the U.S., and by the mid-fifties, about half of American homes contained a television set.

Until the 1990s, the presence of openly LGBT characters on American television shows was rare. Instead, viewers were offered only heteronormative models of heroism, nurturing, patriotism, ambition, humor, workplace relationships, competitiveness, neighborliness, and romance. However, the appearances of LGBT characters before the 1990s are all the more interesting because of their scarceness.

Homosexuality Issues on News Programs of the 1950s and 1960s

Television and the Cold War came of age together. Very few clear references to homosexuality appeared in American television series of the 1950s. One of the first widely viewed references to homosexuality during this decade occurred during the televised congressional hearings chaired by fervently anti-communist U.S. Senator Joseph McCarthy of Wisconsin. Senator McCarthy, who was made head of the Permanent Subcommittee on Investigations (PSI) in 1953, claimed that American society was infiltrated by communists. The PSI and its counterpart in the House of Representatives, the House Un-American Activities Committee (HUAC), were particularly concerned with the alleged presence of communists in the federal government and in the powerful American mass media. Homosexuality and communism were linked in the 1950s. Both were seen as secret subgroups, consisting of people deviant from "regular" (heteronormative/loyal) Americans.

The HUAC was the main governmental body addressing communism and homosexuality in the mass media, first citing for contempt of Congress the famous "Hollywood Ten" —a group of film professionals who refused to inform the HUAC about any former or present communist beliefs or to inform on their colleagues. As a result, the Hollywood Ten and others were blacklisted from working in their profession for years. The HUAC and government communist hunters also alleged that television talent was communist and/or homosexual. The HUAC, along with the FBI, the Veterans of Foreign Wars, and other groups, put pressure on network executives and program sponsors to blacklist suspected employees. *Counterattack*, a publication run by ex-FBI agents, issued "Red Channels," a report that listed radio and television actors, writers, set designers, musicians, journalists, and others as communists or communist sympathizers. Some of those who were on the list and subsequently lost their jobs, almost certainly did so because of suspected homosexuality.

Local news shows during the fifties and sixties occasionally ran episodes dealing with homosexuality. This programming often identified homosexuals as criminals and problematic social outsiders. *Confidential File*, a documentary/interview format news program produced by KVVT, an independent Los Angeles television station, aired an episode titled "Homosexuals and the Problem They Present" in 1954, "Homosexuals Who Stalk and Molest Our Children" in 1955, and a third (mercifully untitled) program in 1962 dealing with lesbians. *The Open Mind* was a high-concept news interview program originally broadcast from WRCA-TV, the flagship station for NBC in New York City. In 1956, the show broadcast an episode titled "Introduction to the Problem of Homosexuality," and despite the title, the program dealt thoughtfully with its subject, acknowledging the role that society plays in creating gender roles, considering whether homosexuality is inborn, and questioning whether it should be a criminal matter. According to Richard Heffner, the show's host, after this broadcast Cardinal Spellman threatened to have the station's license revoked. Nevertheless, *The Open Mind* also aired the episode "Homosexuality: A Psychological Approach" and, in 1957, "Male and Female in American Society." *Showcase*, a news program that originally aired on WABD, broadcast a discussion on homosexuality in 1958. Host Fannie Hurst was ordered by station management not to continue her shows on homosexual topics. Nevertheless, three more episodes of *Showcase* continued the discussion in 1959. Hurst ultimately moved the program to WNTA, an independent channel in Newark, New Jersey, in response to WABD's attempts at censorship. Various other local news programs in Detroit, Chicago, Dallas, and Miami, as well as some syndicated news programs, devoted single episodes to gay and lesbian concerns between 1957 and 1967. *The Rejected*, the first television documentary about homosexuality, was broadcast on KQED, a San Francisco PBS station, in 1961. The first national network news program on the topic was *CBS Reports: The Homosexual* in 1967.

Gay and Lesbian Characters in Television Drama of the 1960s

Prime-time network television dramas of the 1960s occasionally included homosexual characters for a single episode, and these characters were almost always disturbed and destructive. In a 1961 episode of *The Asphalt Jungle*, a police drama set in New York City, titled "The Sniper," a lesbian shoots girls she catches necking with boys. In *The Eleventh Hour*, a 1962 psychiatry drama, a high-strung actress is "diagnosed" with "lesbian tendencies." Buddy, a boy taunted by his peers for being "different," drowns in a 1963 episode of the college-setting drama *Channing*. (Buddy's homosexuality is implicit in the script.) A cross dresser strangles some nurses in a 1965 episode of *Alfred Hitchcock Presents*. *N.Y.P.D.* has two episodes dealing with closeted gay men, one in 1967 involving blackmailers and another in 1969 with a murderous gay elevator operator. In *Secrets*, a 1968 CBS Playhouse episode, a woman is on trial for having murdered her gay son. Also in 1968, an episode of *Judd, for the Defense* deals with a father's fears that his son's friend intends "gay recruitment." Finally, in 1969, a gay campaign worker murders the gubernatorial candidate who learns his secret in an episode of *The Bold Ones: The Lawyers*.

The negative portrayal of homosexual characters in television dramas of the 1960s reflected the American social attitudes of the decade. In spite of the social changes that occurred for women and people of color in the sixties, attitudes toward lesbians and gays remained unaccepting. In addition, since television is watched in people's homes, it is a more intimate medium than film. While liberal adults might choose to watch *The Children's Hour* or *Midnight Cowboy* in the cinema, television programming in this decade was meant to be "safe for children." Most Americans considered any kind of sexual content or identity outside of the heteronormative standard to be inappropriate for children. These early homosexual characters in 1960s television dramas were portrayed with restraint; they could be explained as "misfits" to children who watched these programs.

Integration of Homosexual Characters, 1970-1990

After a decade of brief appearances by homosexuals as neurotics and criminals, the world of television dramas and comedies began to offer more balanced characters. Since visibility, even if it is negative, is often the first step toward social change, we can argue that the negative homosexual characters in sixties American television series set the stage for the more positive characters that followed them. The change can also be seen as a response to institutional policy and gay and lesbian social activism: during the sixties, Illinois repealed its anti-sodomy law and activists demonstrated in New York, Philadelphia, and San Francisco. During the seventies, nineteen more states repealed their sodomy laws, and the American Psychiatric Association removed homosexuality from its list of mental illnesses.

Accordingly, important television firsts in the seventies and eighties include an episode of *All in the Family*, the first U.S. sitcom to deal with homosexuality. *All in the Family* was a ground-breaking series based on the British sitcom *Till Death Do Us Part*, which also inspired German, Dutch, and Brazilian versions. The U.S. program revolved around the frustrations of Archie Bunker, a prejudiced working-class man, and his more liberal family. In a 1971 episode titled "Judging Books by Covers," Archie wrongly suspects Roger, a new acquaintance, of being gay and discovers instead that Steve, one of his "manly" best friends, is gay. This first-season episode was praised for upending traditional gender expectations and for countering the idea that people can discern gender from simple external cues. The short-lived series *The Corner Bar* (1972-73) was the first American television show with a regular gay character. This ABC summer-replacement program had a Cheers-like set-up, and one of the regular patrons was set designer Peter Panama (played by Vincent Schiavelli). In 1983, the medical drama *St. Elsewhere* became the first American television show to devote an episode to AIDS. *Heartbeat* (1988), another short-lived series, was the first prime-time American television drama with a regular lesbian character.

Starting in the mid-nineties, however, American television positively embraced gay and lesbian characters and storylines. In fact, some film and television critics call this period "the Gay Nineties." Some of the forces converging to produce this change include the spread of AIDS to the heterosexual population, particularly in Africa, which somewhat diminished the homophobia attached to the epidemic. Another force is more nebulous but also more significant: the nineties is the decade when homosexual culture came of age. Gay and lesbian studies emerged as a distinct academic field in this decade, institutionalizing the thinking that emerged from decades of social activism. The first American generation of young adults who grew up with the gay and lesbian rights movement became the darling consumer group of the 1990s. Competition for this demographic was fierce, and network and cable television created increasingly focused programming to gain access to this prime market: liberal, urban, young, and professional. Correspondingly, characters shifted from being merely visible to familiar in the programming devised to capture this market. Forty percent of prime-time television programming between 1994 and 1997 included at least one episode with LGBT content, and there were recurring LGBT characters on nineteen television series in this four-year period.

Some highlights of this period include *Tales of the City*, a mini-series aired on PBS over three nights in 1994. The series and its sequels are based on a series of novels set in 1970s San Francisco by Armistead Maupin. The stories deal with the romantic pursuits of a variety of gay and straight characters. Originally optioned by HBO in 1982, the mini-series project was deemed too controversial because of the portrayal of homosexuality, nudity, and drug use. The project was then picked up and produced by the United Kingdom's Channel 4 in conjunction with PBS. Although PBS received the highest ratings ever to that time for the *Tales of the City* broadcast, the network was threatened with cuts to its federal funding, and the sequels—*More Tales of the City* (1998) and *Further Tales of the City* (2001)—moved to Showtime.

Another highlight of the homosexual-accepting nineties is a 1996 episode of the phenomenally popular sitcom *Friends* titled "The One with the Lesbian Wedding." In this episode, Ross, a central character and the ex-husband of one of the brides, gradually comes to support the marriage. Even though neither of the lesbian brides is a central character on the series and the brides do not kiss in the wedding ceremony, NBC expected a widespread protest from the program's many viewers. In fact, the network received only four complaining phone calls, and "The One With the Lesbian Wedding" became the highest-rated television episode of that week.

One of the most significant, publicized, and anticipated moments in LGBT television history occurred in 1997. After a long build-up and many positive and negative comments from sponsors, gay rights activists, and religious leaders, Ellen DeGeneres' character Ellen Morgan comes out of the closet on "The Puppy Episode" of the sitcom *Ellen*. This episode was the highest-rated of the entire series, winning two Emmys, a Peabody Award for outstanding comedy writing, and a GLAAD (Gay and Lesbian Alliance Against Defamation) Award. DeGeneres herself had come out two months earlier, an act that put her on the cover of *Time* magazine.

Mainstreaming LGBT Television in the Twenty-first Century

The twenty-first century has brought an improved standing for the American LGBT community. The social atmosphere, while not by any means free of bigotry, is more accepting. More effective treatment, as well as education, has lessened the transmission rates of AIDS and increased the lifespans of its victims. "AIDS panic" in the heterosexual community subsided. The growing LGBT leadership role in American institutional life has also contributed to the normalization and assimilation of the LGBT community into the larger social fabric. As LGBT people begin to make their way into the hierarchy of religious groups and the government, the LGBT community has moved toward assimilating into the dominant culture. The largely successful push for gay marriage is one indicator that the LGBT community is being integrated into the traditional American ideas about happiness and family life.

Twenty-first century television characters and plotlines reflect the assimilated status of the LGBT community. As LGBT people have become a target market for advertisers, a growing number of heterosexual viewers have become more accepting of LGBT presence on television. As a result, program sponsors and network executives have grown increasingly supportive of queer characters and storylines on network and cable television. The influx of queer characters has been integrated into a more diverse array of programming, including animation, talk shows, soap operas, and reality television as well as news, sitcoms, and dramas. There are even designated LGBT channels such as Here! and Logo.

LGBT Presence in Animated Series

The late twentieth and early twenty-first centuries have seen an uptick in LGBT characters and stories on animated television series. However, a quick review of Warner Brothers cartoons will show that animation has long been a home to gender-bending, anarchist humor. For example, Bugs Bunny has been "female" in over 45 cartoons; the first time was in Bugs' third cartoon appearance. The creators of *The Simpsons*, *Futurama*, *The Family Guy*, *South Park*, *Archer*, *Chozen*, and other series have developed their characters and humor out of this subversive tradition. Animation is a world where anything can happen: bodies and worlds are completely malleable and the transformations are endless. Applying these ideas to gender is a license to create some creative and provocative animated stories.

The creation and development of LGBT characters in animation derives from a base pattern of reliable heteronormative gender signifiers. Comic male characters like Fred Flintstone are overweight, clumsy, and aggressive, with "masculine" faces: small eyes, big noses, and big mouths. Female characters like Wilma Flintstone are slim and graceful, with more constricted movements and "feminine" faces: large eyes with long eyelashes, small noses, and small mouths. Female characters also tend to wear dresses, high heels, and jewelry—even if they are portraying housewives where such things might be impractical for everyday life. These female emblems are easy to see when dealing with animal characters: Minnie Mouse is just Mickey Mouse with long eyelashes, a bow in her hair, a dress, pumps, and frequently glimpsed panties. To create LGBT characters in twenty-first century animation, the creators can mix the male and female signifiers in the design of the character. For example, SpongeBob SquarePants has long eyelashes, but he also has a big mouth. Animators can also make the character's gender clear through dialogue and interaction with other characters: SpongeBob and Patrick (a starfish) adopt a baby scallop, and SpongeBob stays at home to take care of it while Patrick goes off to work.

The Simpsons, originally broadcast on Fox, is a popular animated family sitcom that has been on the air since 1989. The main characters, especially Homer and

Marge Simpson, the mother and father, follow heteronormative, "Flintstone-style" design. Important LGBT character development in the series began around 2002. One of Marge's twin sisters, Patty Bouvier, is a lesbian. Patty is designed with a bell-shaped torso (no waistline), slightly thick legs and body, lavender-grey hair (from chain smoking cigarettes), and drooping eyelids. Patty's storylines include coming out and an aborted lesbian wedding (Patty's beloved turns out to be a man in disguise). Selma, Patty's heterosexual twin, is nearly identical in design, but she has been a "spinster" for much of the series. (Perhaps Patty and Selma's design conflates "lesbian" with "unattractive woman.") A myriad of other lesbian, gay, bisexual, and transgendered minor characters have been depicted on *The Simpsons* as well.

South Park, a critically-acclaimed and controversial series that premiered in 1997 on Comedy Central, centers around a nucleus of fourth-grade boys in fictional South Park, Colorado. Stan, Kyle, Eric, and Kenny are foul-mouthed, obsessed with bathroom humor, and prone to involvement in bizarre escapades. (Typical little boys? That's what creator Matt Stone claims.) Recurring *South Park* characters include Big Gay Al and Mr. Slave; various gay and lesbian celebrities, including Rosie O'Donnell, also sometimes make animated guest appearances as "themselves." The program is offensive to both extremes of the political spectrum. Various episodes include "The Cissy," in which the bigoted character Eric Cartman claims to be transgender in order to use the girls' bathroom; "The F-Word," in which the boys decide to use the word "fag" (162 times) to refer to rude motor-cyclists; and "South Park is Gay!," in which Crab People attempt to take over the world by changing men into metrosexuals.

Other major animated series with LGBT characters were developed for Fox and the FX network. Seth MacFarlane has three such animated series and all fol-low the family sitcom model although they do sometimes deal with the genre in creative and controversial ways. *Family Guy*, premiering in 1999, is centered on a working-class father's family life. The breakout character is Stewie, the maniacal time-traveling baby genius who is sexually attracted to Brian, the family dog, as well as various other characters. The FX network has invested in animated series with *Archer*, premiering in 2009, and *Chozen*, which was cancelled after a few months' run in 2014. *Archer* deals with a group of selfish, back-stabbing, inept private international spies; Ray Gillette, the gay member of the group, is a little more competent and ethical than the others. The title character in *Chozen* is a gay ex-con with ambitions to be a rapper.

LGBT Characters in Television Comedies and Dramas

Many twenty-first century series have LGBT leading, supporting, and recurring characters on network and cable dramas and comedies. A few of them have had an especially noteworthy impact on the LGBT community as well as on the thinking of the heterosexual/cisgender audience.

Running from 1998 to 2006, *Will and Grace* was a groundbreaking and celebrated sitcom involving best friends who share an apartment in New York. Will is gay, and Grace is heterosexual. The series uses the contrast between Will, a rather straight-laced but well-adjusted lawyer, and Grace, a sometimes frivolous and neurotic interior designer, to create comic situations that reverse the relationship of Felix and Oscar in *The Odd Couple*, a sitcom that ran from 1970 to 1975. The familiarity of this comic pattern doubtless made some viewers more comfortable with the gay-friendly content. *Will and Grace* also excelled in exploring and deconstructing stereotypes, often through the supporting characters of Jack, an effeminate, narcissistic gay actor and Karen, a bisexual, manipulative gold-digger. Will and Jack's kiss in 2000 provided a first between two prime-time gay characters, and it was accepted with very little objection from its audience. This is especially significant since the series was the top sitcom in Nielson ratings from 2001 to 2005. The viewers for *Will and Grace* were the most desirable group for sponsors: adults between the ages 18 and 49. For this and other reasons, *Will and Grace* is a frequent shared reference point in the national conversation about LGBT rights and social acceptance.

Glee has been a LGBT cultural phenomenon to rival *Will and Grace*. The series, which ran from 2009 to 2015 on Fox, began in a Lima, Ohio, high school glee club and progresses in later seasons to include the fledgling New York music and theater careers of select characters. Each episode is presented like a musical, with dialogue and plot development interspersed with song-and-dance numbers. Members of the glee club are lesbian, gay, bisexual, and trans as well as straight and cisgender. *Glee* has been celebrated for dealing with a myriad of issues important to all young people: bullying, coming out and family acceptance, coming out and family rejection, sexual diseases, loss of virginity, and gay-straight crushes. The romances of the gay couple Kurt and Blaine as well as the lesbian couple Santana and Brittany have caught the imagination of a generation of teenagers who have not seen such things previously modeled on network television. Adult viewers are affected as well. A poll published in *The Hollywood Reporter* shows that about a quarter of the people polled who watch *Glee*, *Modern Family*, and *The New Normal* have been influenced in favor of gay marriage. (*Modern Family* and *The New Normal* are network family dramas that have gay couples as central characters.)

On cable, two programs are particularly noteworthy: *Queer as Folk* (2000-2005) and *The L Word* (2004-2009). Produced for Showtime, both series are American-Canadian versions of British miniseries originals. *Queer as Folk* uses the "group of friends" framework, allowing the series to follow multiple intersecting storylines dealing with young, attractive, gay men, each a different "type." The acting and storylines were well handled, but what was groundbreaking about the series is its frank portrayal of nudity and gay sex. Showtime, concerned about low ratings in the LGBT demographic, selected and promoted *Queer as Folk* aggressively to secure a lucrative place in that market. A new Showtime subscriber number of 1-800-COMINGOUT and the upcoming series were advertised in New York, Los Angeles, and San Francisco through websites, direct mail, gay magazines, and gay clubs. Showtime also sponsored gay pride parades and gay film festivals. The campaign worked, and *Queer as Folk* became the highest rated series on the channel. *The L Word*, following the same "group of friends" set up, had greater appreciation from its viewers than *Queer as Folk* simply because lesbians had been conspicuously absent from film and television. *The L Word* was also glamorous; it defies the stereotype of lesbian as unattractive or mannish. In fact, it was so glamorous that it has been criticized for depicting women in a way designed more to please heterosexual men than to please a lesbian audience. Be that as it may, *The L Word* was important as a rare representation of attractive, successful lesbians who are part of an integrated community.

The LGBT presence in daytime soap operas is worth mentioning as well. Originally written as radio dramas to entertain housewives in the thirties and forties, soap operas were often sponsored by housecleaning products—thus the name. Soap operas today are followed by a more diverse audience who, because of DVRs, need not be at home during the day to follow the stories. Soaps continue to be appealing to the networks because they are inexpensive to produce and intensively sponsored; a soap opera has about 24 minutes of commercials per hour versus roughly sixteen minutes of commercials per hour in typical prime-time programming.

With their settings in tightknit communities and plots involving many domestic secrets, soaps have also appealed to LGBT audiences. A number of American soap operas began broadcasting in the fifties and sixties, and their long-time viewers tend to be somewhat conservative. However, when *One Life to Live* and *All My Children* began LGBT storylines in the nineties, the response of the LGBT audience was strong, and soaps jumped at the chance to gain the loyalty of a younger audience with a disposable income. In the twenty-first century, *As the World Turns*, *General Hospital*, *The Young and the Restless*, and *Days of Our Lives* followed the trend of LGBT storylines. A good deal of drama is generated through the gay characters' coming out, family reactions, and love interests. However, much like prime-time programming, the sex scenes in these soaps are more subdued and constrained for LGBT characters than the ones for the straight characters. In addition, few LGBT soap characters are people of color, and gay characters vastly outnumber the other queer characters.

LGBT Figures on Talk Shows and Reality Programs

Some of the most influential LGBT people on television have appeared as themselves rather than as fictional characters. In contrast to the largely pathologized view of LGBT people that local news magazines took in the fifties and sixties, the view on nationally broadcast talk shows and reality programs since the nineties has been more even-handed. In some cases, what that means is that the treatment of LGBT and heterosexual/cisgender people is equally exploitative. In other cases, LGBT people have used talk and reality shows to make themselves known as attractive, successful, friendly, and non-threatening members of their communities.

The talk show is a curious animal. Neither strictly news nor strictly entertainment, the talk show is a hybrid that encourages conversation between a host, selected guests, and audience members. Talk show topics can vary from the serious to the silly. The hosts, who may or may not be trained as professional journalists, have a great deal of power in how the discussion unfolds. Their personalities, especially their on-screen likability, are a crucial factor in the success of the show.

Talk shows have gone through a series of transformations since their beginnings in the 1950s, and LGBT guests and hosts have been an important part of that metamorphosis. In the fifties and sixties, the popular variety talk show featured celebrity guests and gracious hosts like Dinah Shore who gave viewers the sense of a personal visit with pleasant, accomplished people. The rules of polite conversation applied, so host and guests behaved with decorum and did not discuss controversial issues such as homosexuality. At least during the talk show, they were the sort of people that middle-class ladies and gentlemen would be happy to have in their homes. *Open End*, a show hosted by David Susskind, which started in the late 1950s, was an exception to this. Broadcast late at night for no set length of time (until Susskind and his guests were ready to stop), *Open End* had a wide variety of guests, including gays and lesbians who used masks or lighting to obscure their faces. Susskind practiced hard-hitting journalism; he interviewed Nikita Khrushchev in 1960, one of the most intense years of the Cold War. However, this hard-hitting approach sometimes meant that his LGBT guests were asked insensitive questions or set up in opposition to anti-LGBT "expert" guests.

The Phil Donahue Show, broadcast from 1968 until 1996, was a better venue for LGBT guests. Not only did Donahue regularly include such guests, he also stressed tolerance, acceptance, and the rejection of stereotypes in his interactions with them. For the most part, Donahue avoided sensationalism, talking respectfully with LGBT guests chosen for their ability to articulate the experiences of different members of the LGBT community.

Starting in the eighties, talk shows such as *The Morton Downey, Jr. Show* turned toward selecting flashier LGBT guests and nudging shocked audience responses toward hostility. Other talk shows such as *Sally Jessy Raphael* and *Geraldo* followed suit, and some of them even scripted lines for the LGBT guests in order to foment the controversy that got high ratings. *The Jenny Jones Show* and *The Jerry Springer Show* continued this exploitative approach in the nineties. One such program led to tragic consequences. In a 1995 episode of *The Jenny Jones Show,* a gay guest surprised a male heterosexual acquaintance with the confession of a romantic crush. Three days later, the heterosexual man murdered the gay man in retaliation for what he saw as a public humiliation.

Notably, some LGBT celebrities have hosted their own talk shows. *The RuPaul Show* ran from 1996 to 1998 on VH1 and featured a variety of LGBT, straight, and cisgender guests. RuPaul, a flamboyant gay drag queen, proved to be a playful, candid, and witty host. His most autobiographical episode won a GLAAD Award. *The Rosie O'Donnell Show* ran in syndication from 1996 to 2002. O'Donnell did not officially come out as a lesbian until 2002, but she was followed by a significant LGBT audience who knew her as one of their own. Funny and well-informed, O'Donnell had a high likability factor on her talk show, which won ten Emmys in its six-year run. *The Ellen DeGeneres Show,* which premiered in 2003, can be seen as a modernization of the sort of show Dinah Shore hosted, relying on the considerable charm of its host and on pleasant celebrity interviews. The show won an Emmy in its first season and continues to earn solid ratings.

LGBT people have been in reality television since its inception with the PBS series *An American Family.* First broadcast in 1973, the program broadcast the real-life interactions and activities of the Loud family of Santa Clara, California. The oldest son, Lance Loud, came out as gay on the program. Lance startled PBS audiences from the beginning with his make-up and crimson hair, and his eventual revelation, though surely not unexpected, drew an audience of ten million. The series was re-broadcast in 1991 as part of a new wave of programming called reality television, featuring "real" people in artificial situations. Viewers seem to enjoy the voyeuristic aspect of having televised access to other people's private lives. They also enjoy the opportunity to compare themselves to the programs' contestants and to fantasize about gaining the instant fame that the contestants enjoy. Finally, reality television is popular because it is aggressively marketed and promoted by networks, which enjoy enormous profits on these relatively inexpensive programs. Unlike expensive, scripted television programs, reality programs are often watched live so that viewers can participate via voting, Twitter feeds, and other social media. Because of this, advertisers know that their commercials are more likely to be seen on reality programs than those programs recorded on DVRs.

Almost every reality television program from the nineties on has a contestant, subject, or host who is a member of the LGBT community, who welcome the opportunity to see themselves represented. But what is the appeal for the larger straight and cisgender audience? Some curious viewers probably perceive LGBT participants as interesting simply because of their gender or sexual orientation. Others enjoy seeing an LGBT person as the sort of larger-than-life personality that works in reality programming because that fits with their preconception of what LGBT people should be like.

Some of the new reality programs make the participants' personal lives into orchestrated, public entertainment. Examples include *Gays Weddings* (2002), *Boy Meets Boy* (2003), and *Playing It Straight* (2004). *Gay Weddings* illustrated in some detail the desires of LGBT couples for acceptance and validation of their union from society. *Playing It Straight* and *Boy Meets Boy* were dating series that involved participants' abilities to discern gay from straight men. Although these programs demonstrated that a false gender can be convincingly performed, the games involved were often insensitive to the participants' romantic hopes. Other programs involve participants living under continuous recorded observation while competing for a prize, such as *Survivor* (2000-), *The Real World* (1992-), and *The Amazing Race* (2001-). A gay man named Richard Hatch won on the first season of *Survivor*, and an HIV-positive Pedro Zamora used his time on screen in the 1994 season of *The Real World* to further the cause of AIDS activism. (Zamora died later that same year.) In 2003, Reichen Lehmkuhl and Chip Arndt won *The Amazing Race* while competing on the show as a "married" couple. Meanwhile, *Queer Eye For a Straight Guy* (2003-2007) relied on a team of gay men—The "Fab Five"—who gave straight men complete lifestyle makeovers. The friendships that developed between the Fab Five and their straight clients made clear to viewers that such gay-straight relationships were enjoyable and beneficial rather than threatening. *Project Runway*, broadcast since 2004, also deals with fashion, but in a competitive, runway format. The program has had numerous LGBT contestants and is co-hosted by Tim Gunn, an accomplished and openly gay designer.

Ultimately, the LGBT presence in film and television has been beneficial to heterosexual culture as well as to the LGBT community. LGBT performance of gender has illustrated a wider range of personal style: this has already transformed fashion and personal appearance for the population at large. The capacity to have cross-gender friendships unthreatened by gender difference is good for the social contract that binds diverse Americans into a community. The role that media has played in the acceptance of LGBT people as loving partners and parents also benefits society as a whole. Coming out of the closet is unique to the LGBT community, but claiming one's own sexual identity, especially in the face of parental and/or societal disapproval, is universal. The ideas expressed by LGBT artists about the right to embrace one's preferred number and nature of sexual partners and proclivities, while frightening to many, can also apply to the sexual freedom of straight and cisgender people. Finally, coming as they do from a heritage of Puritanism, Americans in general can benefit from LGBT messages that pleasure is good and that self-acceptance is liberating.

Chapter 11

CONTEMPORARY EXPERIENCES OF LGBT PEOPLE: Health Disparities, Adolescence, and the Queer Movement

The world has changed rapidly for LGBT people since the beginning of the twenty-first century. In April 2000, Vermont became the first state in the U.S. to legalize civil unions and register partnerships between same-sex couples. This achievement was followed in 2004 by the first legalization of gay marriage in Massachusetts. In June 2013 the Supreme Court dismissed California's Proposition 8, which sought to prevent same-sex marriage in the state and ruled against the constitutionality of the federal Defense of Marriage Act (DOMA). Finally, the June 26, 2015, *Obergefell v. Hodges* decision struck down all state bans on same sex marriage and ruled that marriage was a constitutional right for gays and lesbians protected by the Fourteenth Amendment to the United States Constitution.

But how do these and other important changes at the federal, state, and local level impact the lives, health, and well being of LGBT people? What are the new and emerging issues that LGBT individuals will face as they move into the new century? The following pages will describe a number of important historical events for LGBT people that have occurred in the early twenty-first century. Current psychosocial issues facing LGBT people will also be described, focusing specifi-cally on adolescence along with their developmental milestones, with two leading theories offered that enhance the understanding of LGBT health. Some factors that support healthy development for LGBT youths as they enter adulthood will be identified, followed by discussion of queer theory, which emerged during the early 1990s out of the fields of women's studies and queer studies.

IMPORTANT HISTORICAL EVENTS OF
THE TWENTY-FIRST CENTURY

Don't Ask, Don't Tell

In 1994, the Clinton administration created the "Don't Ask, Don't Tell" (DADT) policy, specifying the official federal government position on military service by gays and lesbians. The executive action both prohibited LGBT individuals from disclosing their sexual orientation to another service member while prohibiting superiors from initiating an investigation on a service member's orientation without "witnessing disallowed behaviors," though credible evidence of such behavior could be used to initiate an investigation.

The first step in the process to repeal DADT began in late 2010, with the passage of legislation requiring the president, Secretary of Defense, and Chairman of the Joints Chiefs of Staff to certify that the repeal would not harm military readiness, followed by a 60-day waiting period. In July 2011, a federal appeals court ruled against further enforcement of the military's ban on openly gay service members, leading the way to the required certification and DADT officially ending in September 2011.

By this time, national polling suggested that between 58 percent and 77 percent of Americans favored allowing gays and lesbians to serve openly in the military, with less than 27 percent being strongly opposed. At the time of its repeal, 13,650 discharges had been completed on service members in the five branches of the military (Coast Guard, Marines, Navy, Army, Air Force).

Hate Crimes Legislation

Bias-motivated crimes, more commonly known as "hate crimes," occur when victims of a crime are targeted because of their perceived membership in a social group. Race, sexual orientation, ethnicity, religious affiliation, and gender are all examples of social groups who are targets of hate crimes. Although minority groups in a society are often the target of hate crimes (i.e., gay men, African Americans), anyone can be victimized, including members of the perceived majority (i.e., Caucasian men) because of their supposed association with a social group.

What Exactly is a Hate Crime?

In 2009, Congress defined hate crimes as:

offenses involving actual or perceived race, color, religion, or national origin—whoever, whether or not acting under color of law willfully causes bodily injury to any person or, through the use of fire, a firearm, a dangerous weapon, or an explosive or incendiary device, attempts to cause bodily injury to any person, because of actual or perceived race, color, religion, or national origin of any person…

As evident in this definition, the distinction between hate crimes and other criminal behaviors lies in the intent of the perpetrator.

Some define hate crimes as divergences from traditional crimes. First, there is naturally a negative impact on the individual who is victimized. Most crimes affect an individual physically, psychologically, and emotionally; however, hate crimes add repercussions related to self-worth and identity. Notably, though a person may never have been the victim of a hate crime, the person may have increased feelings of victimization and loss of self-worth as a result.

Similarly, other vulnerable populations may feel the impact of hate crimes on individuals. As hate crimes are often directed toward an ideology or belief system, many outside the target group may find themselves victimized. For example, a hate crime against a Jewish woman may also impact a woman of Muslim background, and so on. Further, in addition to the effects upon the individual, hate crimes also terrorize the social group to which the victim belongs, such as when the genocide committed against the Tutsi people in Rwanda was meant to inform the entire community of what was and was not acceptable. Because of this "messaging" aspect, bills that include crimes against sexual minorities are crucial.

To address ongoing concerns of hate crimes against LGBT individuals, the Matthew Shepard and James Byrd, Jr. Hate Crimes Prevention Act (known as the Matthew Shepard Act) was signed into law in late 2009 as part of the National Defense Authorization Act of 2010. Both Matthew Shepard and James Byrd, Jr. were brutally murdered because of their perceived sexual orientation and race, respectively. The Matthew Shepard Act expanded the 1969 federal hate crime statutes to include crimes motivated by a victim's perceived or actual gender, sexual orientation, gender identity, or disability.

Advancing Definitions of Gender

In addition to an expanding understanding of sexuality, during the past decade our understanding of gender has changed accordingly. The University of California at Berkeley Gender Equity Resource Center defines gender as a socially constructed system of classification that ascribes qualities of masculinity and femininity to people. Gender is a socially constructed, emotional, expressed, and internal experience of masculinity and/or femininity along the spectrum that can be inclusive or exclusive of both male and female. Gender can include expression, identity, behavior, role, and feelings.

Russell B. Toomey and his research colleagues have stated that gender-nonconforming individuals (such as boys who are more feminine than other boys or girls who are more masculine than other girls) can be described as those who transgress social gender norms. These social norms are often dominant societal expectations passed down over time and often oppress those who may not ascribe to such expectations. However, recent advances have been made in gender equality. For example, in 2014, Facebook, the leading social network web site, added an additional 51 new gender options for users to choose from. The diversity of gender options, including terms such as "genderqueer" (the rejection of binary gender options) are a direct result of the advocacy from scholars in queer theory (described in further detail near the end of this chapter).

Although progress has been made toward equality for LGBT individuals living in the United States, disparities still exist. In each of these key legislative changes, opposition continues. A number of organizations rejected the similarities of LGBT people to other minority categories (such as racial or ethnic) based on the premise that identifying as LGBT was a "behavioral choice," unlike the other statuses that place an individual at risk for hate crimes.

Marriage Equality

In the past fifty years, the institution of marriage has undergone a significant revolution in the United States. Interracial marriage was legalized, and the roles of husband and wife have been redefined, with more women working and increasing numbers of men staying home. In a Pew Research Center study conducted in 2014, almost 2 million fathers stay at home, nearly doubling from 1.1 million in 1989. Divorce has also become more common today, changing the landscape of marriage.

By 2014, gay marriage had gained wider acceptance, not just in the United States but in many parts of the globe. In 1996, no country had legalized same-sex marriage; by 2014, sixteen countries had done so: Argentina, Belgium, Brazil, Canada, Denmark, France, Iceland, Netherlands, New Zealand, Norway, Portugal, South Africa, Spain, Sweden, the United Kingdom, and Uruguay. Polls in countries across the world find rising support for same-sex marriage across race, ethnicity, age, religion, political affiliation, and socioeconomic status.

Within the United States, support for marriage equality has risen dramatically in the early twenty-first century. The marriage equality revolution started with the Vermont's Supreme Court's 1999 *Baker v. State of Vermont* ruling that "civil unions" were constitutional. In 2004, Massachusetts became the first state to allow marriage for same-sex couples when the state supreme court overturned a band on such unions. Marriages and civil unions became legal in a handful of other states. In 2013, the United States Supreme Court had overturned the federal Defense of Marriage Act, passed by Congress in 1996, which had defined marriage as solely between one man and one women for all federal purposes and which allowed states to not recognize same sex marriages allowed by other states. As of March 4, 2015, through litigation or legislation, marriage equality had been achieved in 36 states, plus the District of Columbia. Approximately 72 percent of Americans lived in states in which the legislatures or the courts had provided for marriage equality. On April 28, 2015, the United States Supreme Court heard oral arguments on the constitutionality of state laws limiting marriage to one man and one woman in Kentucky, Michigan, Ohio, and Tennessee. The decision in *Obergefell v. Hodges*, the name given the four consolidated cases, extended marriage rights to same sex couples to all fifty states. In some states, such as Alabama, Louisiana and Texas, the state governments tried to delay implementation of the decision. Some county clerks announced they would resign rather than marry same sex couples, they would ignore the Supreme Court's decision, or they would refuse to issue marriage licenses to any couples, gay or straight.

It should also be noted that all of the developments described above occurred after public opinion had changed dramatically, largely occurring after a number of "normalizing" experiences transpired in the late 1990s and into the early twenty-first century. As described in chapter 10, the LGBT movement's use of the media to help heterosexual individuals to see their frequent similarities helped bring attention to the issues facing this community. Additionally, gay rights leaders discovered that framing the concept of gay marriage and other equality debates as "rights" was not an effective approach. Rather, taking a humanitarian stance (that gay people may simply want their love for each other to result in commitment just like anyone else) was a more effective message to use in branding the social movement. While a majority of Americans have moved toward equality in a number of areas, large parts of the United States have not. When cities are not included in the analysis, nearly 60 percent of citizens believe homosexuality is a sin. As described in the following section, the stress associated with perceived rejection may impact the behavioral health of LGBT people even today in this era of increasing acceptance.

CONTEMPORARY BEHAVIORAL HEALTH ISSUES FACING LGBT PEOPLE

Although significant advances have been made toward equality, mental and be-havioral health, disparities still exist within the LGBT community. These include health care disparities, alcohol, tobacco and other drug use, depression, anxiety, and suicide risk. A longer discussion of the impact that HIV/AIDS has had upon the LGBT community is also included in Chapter 6 of this volume.

Mental Health & Substance Use Disparities

A number of behavioral health disparities exist among LGBT individuals. These include suicide, emotional problems, major depression, anxiety disorders, and substance abuse. Evidence also indicates that lesbian and bisexual women are more likely than heterosexual women to experience traumatic events, such as child abuse and neglect, and have higher rates of alcohol use and partaking in controlled substances. Although most studies have collapsed lesbian and bisexual women into a single category, recent research has found that bisexual women are at especially high risk of both substance abuse and mental health problems.

In light of a number of suicides across the country, more attention has been paid to the substance use and mental health patterns of LGBT adolescents. These rates are alarming, with studies indicating suicide attempts as high as 53 percent among LGBT youth, contrasted with 7.1 percent of all American youths. LGBT youth face the conventional challenges of adolescence along with increased stress of being LGBT, which often includes questioning their sexuality or gender identity. Sexual minority youth report high rates of discrimination, verbal and physical abuse, and negative social consequences for revealing their sexuality. Adolescents who identify as gay or lesbian report nearly three times the rate of controlled substance use compared to their heterosexual peers and are more likely to use multiple substances. Extensive research literature has also linked experiences of loss of peer relationships and victimization in school (e.g., bullying, violence) to negative mental health and suicidal behavior.

A Framework for Understanding Disparities

While recognizing that the mental and behavioral health outcomes described above do not apply to all LGBT individuals, these disparities should not go unnoticed. These poor outcomes are commonly attributed to the presence of intensely stressful circumstances.

Stress Theory

Stress theory posits that as major life events and chronic circumstances accumulate, an individual becomes less equipped to adapt, adjust, and tolerate continued life stress experiences. Like the experiences that increase stress, other experiences can buffer against negative outcomes, such as the perception of strong social support. In practice, stress theory is often extended to include individuals who are part of disadvantaged groups (for example, women and ethnic minorities) because they repeatedly show increased psychological vulnerability when compared to their majority group peers. An expansive literature, focusing particularly on racial and ethnic minority groups, finds minority-specific stress experiences lead to increases in suicidal ideation and behavior.

Sexual Minority Stress

More recently, the tenets of stress theory have been applied to sexual minorities. As Ilan H. Meyer has explained, there is an association between an array of social and psychological stressors related to being part of a sexual minority group (i.e., minority stress theory, or MST). Tonda Hughes and Michele Eliason describe these as experiences of stigmatization from being a sexual minority, along with their influence on behavioral health. MST suggests that the mental health outcomes of sexual minorities are impacted by a number of distal and proximal stress experiences, with each serving as a possible focus of intervention. Distal stressors are those that occur in the environment in the form of negative experiences such as discrimination, homophobic events, and victimization because of sexual orientation. Proximal stressors occur within the individual and include internalized negative attitudes towards homosexuality, internalization of discomfort with sexuality, and emotional distress related to concealment, rejection, and acceptance by others. Proximal and distal stressors are interrelated. For example, when internalized, minority stress can encourage negative societal attitudes in individuals, as well as pressure to hide their feelings of sexuality and strongly discordant belief systems (e.g., adopting strong religious convictions against homosexuality).

The minority stress theory helps us to understand how the life of an LGBT person, even in the current age of advanced equality and human rights, is unique. The experience of coming out to family can be especially stressful with research suggesting two-thirds of youths finding the process *somewhat* or *extremely troubling*. Families appear to be primary influencers of mental health outcomes for youth. A number of studies have found an association between parental rejection and suicide attempts. Further, sexual minority adolescents are disproportionately represented among homeless youth across the United States, suggestive of the frequent occurrence of family rejection. So, while life may be better for LGBT individuals in the twenty-first century compared to the past, we still have much more work to do before equality in both the legal and emotional sense is finally realized.

THE QUEER MOVEMENT

The current queer movement finds its roots largely with the emergence of AIDS. The late 1980s saw a resurgence of militant approaches to queer advocacy, with the formation of groups such as Queer Nation, which began in 1990, seeking to end homophobia and increase gay, lesbian and bisexual visibility through a variety of direct actions. In the 1990s, young activists who felt that the words *gay* and *lesbian* were too politically conservative, began using the word *queer* as a defiant statement and an effort of reappropriation. In sociological and cultural studies, reappropriation is a cultural process by which groups reclaim (or, reappropriate) terms that were previously used to disparage the group.

Queer Theory

At the same time that social actions in the LGBT community began to frame themselves around the queer *movement*, queer *theory* emerged. Queer theory developed from queer studies and women's studies. Heavily influenced by the work of Jacob Edwards, Eve Kosofsky Sedgwick, and Judith Butler, many gender and sexuality scholars first began to use the term in the early 1990s. Queer theory builds upon both the constructs of feminism that explore gender as an essential part of the self and the social constructivist portions of queer studies that examine identity, attraction, and sexual behavior, challenging what George Chauncey referred to as the "binary sexual regime." More existential authors in queer theory have critiqued not only heterosexual constructs but LGBT perspectives as well. For example, in Alexander Doty's *Making Things Perfectly Queer*, the author separates the reception of sexuality and identification. In this way, a heterosexual spectator may find "queer pleasures" in which they can relate and appreciate, such as homoeroticism in the arts, without identifying as LGBT themselves. Similarly, LGBT individuals can appreciate the sexual tension of heterosexual relationships.

Although originally concentrated on LGBT history and literature, queer theory has expanded into the study of a number of academic interests as they relate to LGBT life—biology, sociology, anthropology, psychology, ethics, political science, and other related fields. The field has broadly included any kind of sexual activity or identity that falls outside the traditional heterosexual, cisgendered relationship. As Annamarie Jagose (1997) has written, "For most, queer has prominently been associated with simply those who identify as lesbian or gay. Unknown to many, queer is an association with more than just gay and lesbian but also cross-dressing, hermaphroditism, gender ambiguity and gender-corrective surgery."

For others, queer theory is less about what currently exists but about what could be. As posited by David Halperin and again described by Jagose, "Queer... does not designate a class of already objectified pathologies or perversions, rather it describes a horizon of possibility whose precise extent and heterogenous scope cannot in principle be delimited in advance." In short, queer is an identity always in formation and open to interpretation and conceptualization. While the history of LGBT people can be captured, written, and understood, the future of this movement cannot, because the understanding of what it means to be queer will change with each advancing generation.

Less than fifty years ago, legal, political, and social activism efforts in support of LGBT rights were in their infancy. The twenty-first century has witnessed unprecedented advances for this community. From marriage equality advancing in both the United States and across the world, to advancing hate crime policy that protects vulnerable groups, to an evolving understanding of what sex, gender, and queer means, the future of LGBT rights appears to be moving toward equality.

In the beginning we asked, how do changes at the federal, state and local level impact the lives, health, and well being of LGBT people? And, what are the new and emerging issues that LGBT individuals will face as they move into the coming century? Despite these social advances, we sought to help the reader understand there is still work to be done. LGBT individuals continue to report disparities in a host of behavioral health outcomes, including substance use, HIV risk, anxiety, depression, self-harm, and suicide. The impact that chronic and unique environmental stressors (i.e., minority stress) may be having on LGBT people is great, and it is suggestive that the world remains a difficult place for LGBT youth, adults, and families.

Perhaps the engine that has driven much of the discussion on advancing queer rights comes from this intersection of queer and gender studies. Queer theory has pushed the boundaries of what is "right and normal" and allowed a space for queer science, including philosophy, psychology, anatomy, sociology, and other social and basic sciences to flourish. While there is much left to do in the pursuit of equality for LGBT people, the advances that have been made in the academic, political, and social spheres paint a bright picture of the future to come.

Chapter 1
Understanding Sexuality in the Nineteenth Century

Though texts depicting LGBT characters have existed from the time of the antiquities, it was in the nineteenth century that an LGBT identity, as it is known today, began to be crafted through writing in various fields from science to literature.

Important texts in the field of medical and psychological understandings of homosexuality from the nineteenth century include Richard von Krafft-Ebing's self-coined medical forensic exploration of sexually deviant behaviors titled *Psychopathia Sexualis* (1886). This volume was not only popular amongst physicians and psychiatrists for the study of transgressive sexual behaviors but was also well circulated by a larger audience as pornographic material. The more sordid pieces of the text are presented in Latin as to exclude the lay reader of the time, though unsuccessfully. The text detailed for the first time in history sadism, masochism, fetishism, and homosexuality and was very influential to many of Krafft-Ebing's contemporaries including famed psychologist Sigmund Freud, painter Gustav Klimt, and philosopher George Bataille. *Sappho and Socrates* (1896) by Magnus Hirschfeld is another example of a medical text from this period. Published in pamphlet format, this piece illustrates Hirschfeld's theory of the bisexual embryo. He posits that all fetuses have a bisexual center where attraction to both sexes exists. In his piece he theorizes that through the process of fetal development opposite sex attraction increases and same sex attraction decreases in most fetuses; for homosexuals, he posits, the opposite occurs. Hirschfeld explains that this may be due to syphilis or alcoholism of the parents. A final example of a medical text is Havelock Ellis's *Sexual Inversion* (1897 with J.A. Symonds). This first English language medical text on homosexuality details 21 case studies of homosexual relationships. Ellis wrote that homosexual relationships defy taboos on age and detailed a number of intergenerational relationships. Though Ellis argues for the decriminalization of homosexual intercourse, he did not support homosexuality to the extent for which he is today widely credited. In portions of his text he writes of queer sexuality as an abnormality and as an aberration from the usual course of nature.

Not only were there developments in the field of medical and psychological sciences on the discourse surrounding homosexuality but also in writings on law and ethics. Karl Heinrich Ulrichs was a German lawyer of the nineteenth century perhaps most well-known for the legal plea, *Araxes: A Call to Free the Nature of the Urning from Penal Law* (1870). Ulrichs presented this piece in support of LGBT rights to the imperial legislature of Northern Germany and Austria, claiming sexual orientation as a right created through nature. In the piece he urges for the end of criminalization of LGBT people. He asserts that to uproot or change someone's sexual orientation is a hopeless battle against nature. He was unsuccessful at achieving decriminalization; it was not until 1967 that homosexuality was decriminalized in Germany. Another famed gay activist of the second half of the nineteenth century was English poet and socialist writer Edward Carpenter. Carpenter was unique in his time. He was self-described as a Hindu mystic who actively promoted mystic socialism. He authored *The Intermediate Sex, a Study of Some Transitional Types of Men and Women* (1908) in that line of thought. Carpenter's piece would become foundational literature for gay activists throughout the twentieth century. In *The Intermediate Sex* Carpenter discusses same-sex love, or "homogenic" love, as a pure form of love that is transcendent of class and possessing of the qualities necessary to lead society towards a more liberated state. Carpenter discuses at some length the idea of a third sex, an individual encompassing both genders, which he explains using Native American shamans as one example.

Nineteenth century literature also contains examples of the emergent LGBT movement. Perhaps most well-known of this time was Oscar Wilde. Wilde's celebrated only book, *The Picture of Dorian Gray*, first appeared in the July 1890 issue of the British serial magazine *Lipincott's*. Wilde's piece foreshadows the authors own future forays into libertinism and hedonism, including the courting of male lovers. In Wilde's moral commentary the subject of an exquisite art piece, Dorian Gray, sells his soul to ensure that he will not age. Subsequently every immoral and hedonistic act that he engages in is transposed into his portrait along with the signs of his physical aging. Another widely known artist of the time, American-British writer Henry James's piece *The Bostonians* (1886) records a relationship of two co-habitating women, Bostonian feminists Olive Chancellor and Verena Tarrant. The novel ends with Chancellor's cousin, the politically conservative Basil Ransom, eloping with Tarrant to both Chancellor and Tarrant's dismay and tears. The novel quite clearly describes a lesbian relationship of the time.

Chapter 2
Sexuality in the Twentieth Century

The first half of the twentieth century was a time of more prolific writing on the topic of human sexuality than perhaps ever before. In this time, preeminent medical and psychological thinkers conducted rigorous and systematic examinations of human sexuality that continue to underpin our basic presumptions to this day. Furthermore, this period saw some of the first thorough examinations of LGBT history and culture that were widely published.

At the turn of the century, Sigmund Freud, famed psychologist and creator of psychoanalysis, contributed foundational pieces to the human understanding of sexuality. The first was *Three Essays on the Theory of Sexuality* (1905) in which

Freud discussed his propositions on human sexuality development. The three essays were on perverse sexuality, childhood sexuality, and on the transformations of puberty. Freud's theory built on the earlier work of Richard von Krafft-Ebing and Magnus Hirschfeld. Ultimately, in these essays it is not clear if Freud viewed homosexuality as a diagnosable illness. Three decades later, however, it was confirmed in the published *Letter to an American Mother* (1935) that he indeed did not view homosexuality as a diagnosable illness. In this letter Freud very accurately categorized homosexuality as not socially advantageous for the time, yet nothing to feel shame over.

Subsequent to Freud, Alfred Kinsey released his groundbreaking and controversial reports on human sexuality, *Sexual Behavior in the Human Male* (1948) and *Sexual Behavior in the Human Female* (1953). These pieces relied on a multitude of interviews that explored human sexuality and sexual behaviors. These reports are perhaps most famous for introducing the Kinsey scale, which categorized sexuality not in a binary homosexual-heterosexual manner but through a spectrum. This would go on to influence others to explore gender and gender identity in non-binary ways. An additional scientific piece of the time was Clellan S. Ford and Frank A. Beach's *Patterns of Sexual Behavior* (1951) published in between the release of Kinsey's two books on human sexual behavior. This piece is a statistical contribution to the knowledge of sexuality that used a "cross-cultural correlational method" to compare cultural sexual practices and behaviors in 191 places throughout the world. The book concludes that there is indeed precedence for same-sex behavior as it can be viewed throughout the world both in humans and other mammals. Of the 76 places that had relevant data on homosexual behavior, 49 of the cultures were accepting of homosexuality.

With the social backdrop of the civil rights and gay liberation movement, the mid-twentieth century was filled with publications on homosexuality. Edward Sagarin, writing under the pen name Donald Webster Cory, published *The Homosexual in America: A Subjective Approach* (1951) while professor of sociology in New York City. Sagarin's contribution is a sociological survey of gays and lesbians in the United States that called for consideration of LGBT people as a minority group whose civil rights needed acknowledgement. In his piece, Sagarin praises both Freud and Kinsey with a precise and critical discernment. This book, unlike other sociological pieces of the time, was not objective in its description; this text makes a call for activism. For this, Sagarin has been recalled as a founder of the gay liberation movement.

As gay rights were just beginning to take stage in the social dialogue on civil rights, a pioneering text of history was published by Jonathan Ned Katz, *Gay American History: Lesbians and Gay Men in the U.S.A.* (1976). This piece chronicled the emergence of gay life in the United States from the time of European settlement through the time of publications with a multitude of primary documents followed by short analysis by Katz. The book is split into six thematic sections that lead through a large swath of history. This historical text set precedence for many others to follow.

Chapter 3
The Birth of the Gay Civil Rights Movement

John D'Emilio and Estelle B. Freedmen provide the best, most comprehensive survey to cover not just homosexuality in the United States, but the history of American attitudes toward eroticism, *Intimate Matters: A History of Sexuality in America* (1988). D'Emilio and Freedmen argue that American erotic culture evolved through three distinct phases: a family-centered sexual governance in the colonial period that aimed at providing property heirs and clear lines of inheritance; a capitalist era that sought to regulate sexuality in order to ensure a steady supply of workers while not allowing vice to undermine production; and to a freer era of sexual expression in the second half of the twentieth century in which marginalized groups like gay men and lesbians challenged the old order. The authors explode multiple myths about American sexual behavior, documenting widespread experimentation, the persistence of homosexuality, pre-marital sex, group sex, and other behaviors outside of the supposed heterosexual marital norm throughout American history.

Nicholas Edsall's *Towards Stonewall: Homosexuality and Society in the Modern Western World* (2003) places developments in gay society in the United States in the nineteenth and twentieth centuries in a broad context, exploring, for instance, scientific thought on the origins of homosexuality in Britain and Germany as well as exploring themes in gay literature on both sides of the Atlantic. A solid general history of gay men and women in America is provided by Neil Miller, *Out of the Past: Gay and Lesbian History from 1869 to the Present* (1995).

Some of the most intriguing work on gay history focuses on specific localities. For instance, information on the "gay migration" to major American cities in the early twentieth century derived from a work rightly regarded as a classic, George B. Chauncey's *Gay New York: Gender, Urban Culture and the Making of the Gay Male World, 1890-1940* (New York, 1994). Chauncey innovatively uses primary sources such as police records, documents from the Society for the Suppression of Vice, and diaries to document the creation of a separate gay subculture in New York in the late nineteenth century and early twentieth century. Chauncey refutes the stereotypical view of the gay past, demonstrating that gay identity and self-awareness sprang into view only after the Stonewall Riots in New York in 1969. Chauncey uncovers the migration of gay men into New York after the Civil War, charts the rise of gay neighborhoods such as in Greenwich Village, talks about the divide between "masculine" gay men and "sissies" within gay culture, documents the porous boundaries between the gay and straight worlds, and reveals the parallels between the straight world's fascination with drag shows and the racial tourism whites engaged in at black night spots like the Cotton Club. A student interested in gay history in the United States would do well to begin with this work. Meanwhile, Lillian Faderman and Stuart Timmons accomplish for Los Angeles much of what Chauncey did for New York in their less scholarly, more gossipy, but entertaining *Gay L.A.: A History of Sexual Outlaws, Power Politics, and Lipstick Lesbians* (2006.)

Homophobia: A History (2001) still gives readers the most sweeping, yet detailed account of anti-gay prejudice in the Western World, from the ancient Hebrews to late twentieth-century Europe and the United States. The author, Byrne Fone, a pioneer scholar in gay culture, has a lively writing style and, because of his encyclopedic knowledge of classical and modern literature, moves effortlessly across vast stretches of time.

Two works provided many of the personal stories referred to in this chapter: Eric Marcus's *Making History: The Struggle for Gay and Lesbian Equal Rights, 1945-1990* (1992) and Andrea Weiss and Greta Schiller, *Before Stonewall: The Making of a Gay and Lesbian Community* (1988). Marcus in particular assembled an impressive cast of prominent and obscure influential figures in the post-World War II gay community, drawing out frequently painful, sometimes humorous anecdotes as his often eloquent subjects discuss how they discovered their sexuality, their growing political awareness, their conflicts with family members, teachers, and the police, job discrimination, and their relationship to the larger gay community. *Before Stonewall* draws from the interviews filmed for the 1984 groundbreaking Emmy Award-winning documentary of the same name.

Important works on the "Lavender Scare" and the major figures in the panic over gays in government in the post-World War II era include David K. Johnson, *The Lavender Scare: The Cold War Persecution of Gays and Lesbians in the Federal Government* (2004); Roger McDaniel, *Dying for Joe McCarthy's Sins: The Suicide of Wyoming Senator Lester Hunt* (2013); Richard Hack, *Puppetmaster: The Secret Life of J. Edgar Hoover* (2007); and Nicholas Von Hoffman, *Citizen Cohn: The Life and Times of Roy Cohn* (1968).

Useful background on the Mattachine Society can be found in John Dececco, *Behind the Mask of the Mattachine: The Hal Call Chronicles and the Early Movement for Homosexual Emancipation* (2006) and on the Daughters of Bilitis in Marcia M. Gallo, *Different Daughters: A History of the Daughters of Bilitis and the Rise of the Lesbian Rights Movement* (2007).

Chapter 4
Gay Protest and Rebellion in the 1960s and 1970s

Much of the information for this chapter on LGBT history in the 1960s and 1970s came from previously cited books, such as D'Emilio and Freedmen's *Intimate Matters* (1988), Faderman and Timmons's *Gay L.A.* (2006), Fone's *Homophobia* (2001), Marcus's *Making History* (1992), *Miller's Out of the Past* (1995), and Weiss and Shiller's *Before Stonewall* (1988).

Michael Bronski's sweeping *A Queer History of the United States* (2011) covers more than five centuries, from Christopher Columbus to the present day, but some of his strongest chapters concern the 1960s and 1970s as the modern gay civil rights movement becomes more assertive. Bronski does a particularly brilliant job of demonstrating the degree to which gay culture in the United States is American culture. John D'Emilio's *Sexual Politics, Sexual Communities: The Making of a Homosexual Minority in the United States, 1940-1970* (1983), also admirably covers the gay and lesbian community in the time from the Kennedy to the Nixon administrations. Meanwhile, Irene Reti wrote a fascinating local history of the gay rights movement in *Out in the Redwoods: Gay, Lesbian, Bisexual, and Transgender History at UC Santa Cruz, 1965-2003* (2003).

Readers interested in the sometimes strained relationships between the gay civil rights movement and other freedom struggles should consult Maurice Isserman and Michael Kazin's *America Divided: The Civil War of the 1960s* (2000) and Todd Gitlin's *The Sixties: Years of Hope, Days of Rage* (1987) as well as works that explore the marginalized status of lesbians within the feminist movement such as Sara Evans's *Personal Politics: The Roots of Women's Liberation in the Civil Rights Movement & the New Left* (1979) and Alice Echols's *Daring to Be Bad: Radical Feminism in America, 1967-1975* (1989). These sources also cover the so-called "sexual revolution" in the 1960s and the 1970s.

Fred Fejes and Kevin Petrich provided one of the best analyses of how American television programs depicted gays and lesbians in the article "Invisibility, Homophobia, and Heterosexism: Lesbians, Gays and the Media," in the December 1993 issue of *Critical Studies in Mass Communication*. David Kopay wrote of his experiences as a gay player in the NFL in *The David Kopay Story: An Extraordinary Self-Revelation* (1977). An academic analysis of sports, homosexuality, and masculinity can be found in Brian Pronger's *The Arena of Masculinity: Sports, Homosexuality, and the Meaning of Sex* (1992).

Some of the most fascinating personal testimonies in this chapter derive from the eminent scholar Martin Duberman's innovative *Stonewall*, in which he traces the lives of six people in the years before and after the Stonewall Riot in New York to explain the larger cultural and political forces in play during that catalyzing event in gay history. The other most notable work on this historical turning point is David Carter's exquisitely detailed *Stonewall: The Riots That Sparked the Gay Revolution* (2010). The riots are also thoughtfully covered in Jonathan Katz's *Gay American History: Lesbians and Gay Men in the U.S.A.* (1976). Don Teel widens the lens and considers Stonewall in the context of the rise of radical politics in the LGBT community in *The Gay Militants: How Gay Liberation Began in America, 1969-1971* (1995).

The crusade by the LGBT community to end the psychiatric profession's diagnosis of homosexuality as a mental illness, and the motives and personalities of the key figures within the psychiatric community who battled over this issue, receive the smartest analysis in Ronald Bayer's *Homosexuality and American Psychiatry: The Politics of a Diagnosis.* (1987).

The late journalist Randy Shilts movingly tells of Sgt. Leonard Matlovich's legal battles over his dismissal from the Air Force and explores the entire history of the American military's discrimination against gay men and women, and the heroism of such soldiers, sailors, and marines, in *Conduct Unbecoming: Gays & Lesbians in the U.S. Military* (1993). This is one of several important, thoroughly researched, and well-written works by Shilts on American gay politics and life in the 1970s, which also include his groundbreaking *And the Band Played On: Politics, People, and the AIDS Epidemic* (1987) and *The Mayor of Castro Street: The Life & Times of Harvey Milk* (1982).

For more on the anti-gay backlash in the 1970s and beyond, see Didi Herman's *The Antigay Agenda: Orthodox Vision and the Christian Right* (1997), Warren Blumenfeld's *Homophobia: How We All Pay the Price* (1992) and Ruth Murray Brown's *For a Christian America: A History of the Religious Right* (2002). The social context of the Steve Dahl disco riot can be found in Jefferson R. Cowie's *Stayin' Alive: The 1970s and the Last Days of the Working Class* (2010.)

Chapters 5 and 6
HIV 101
Sociocultural and Historical Impact of HIV/AIDS in the Gay Community

Randy Shilts's *And the Band Played On: Politics, People, and the AIDS Epidemic* (1987) is the seminal work on the discovery and spread of HIV and AIDS. Critical of the response of the government, medical community, mass media, and even the gay community, Shilts tells the tale through the perspective of a professional journalist who had been reporting exclusively on the AIDS epidemic. The government, doctors, and media were afraid to show compassion for a community as stigmatized as the gay community, which was labelled as the foremost affected by the epidemic. Initially, the gay community distanced itself from the AIDS epidemic, claiming that it was not a "gay disease." After enough time and deaths, however, the gay community began raising the funds for research and treatment that was mostly unavailable from official government sources. Shilts's insider perspective, as a journalist and as a gay man, provides the perfect lens through which to view the first several years of AIDS in America.

HIV among the gay community is part of a greater health context addressed in *Unequal Opportunity: Health Disparities Affecting Gay and Bisexual Men in the United States,* by editors Richard Wolitski, Ron Stall, and Ronald Valdiserri (2008). Specifically in their chapter titled, "Interacting Epidemics and Gay Men's Health: A Theory of Syndemic Production among Urban Gay Men," Stall and colleagues highlight the many different psychosocial issues that come together and concomitantly impact gay men in the neighborhoods in which they live. These so called "gay ghettos" are neighborhoods found in all major U.S. cities where gay men congregate and are both home to protective and risk factors. Stall and colleagues highlight some of those factors and also how childhood sexual abuse, depression, substance abuse, and intimate partner violence all independently interact with each other and with HIV risk and infection among men who have sex with men. The authors further address how minority status drives gay men to these communities, which facilitate access to risk, and how the resulting syndemic is socially produced.

In addition to the gay community, HIV disproportionately affects the black community as well. Jacob Levenson, in *The Secret Epidemic: The Story of AIDS and Black America* (2005), tracks how the HIV virus spread through black communities. He notes phenomenon not unlike Shilts did in his book—inattention by the government and community at large—but also highlights the role of drug use and living situations specific to migrations and displacements of African Americans. Readers seeking more information on the impact of HIV in the Latino community are directed to Rafael Diaz' book, *Latino Gay Men and HIV: Culture, Sexuality, and Risk Behavior* (2013). Diaz addresses six sociocultural influences on sex risk behaviors among Latino men who have sex with men: homophobia, machismo, poverty, family dynamics, racism, and the tendency to not discuss sexual matters. Like Shilts and Levenson, Diaz uses accounts of actual people to highlight the impact that HIV/AIDS has on his community of study.

Chapter 7
Transgender and Beyond

There are many organizations available to help transgendered and gender-diverse people. Most of the web sites listed below have links to other sites.
Fenway Community Health—*www.fenwayhealth.org*—is a Boston-based organization that primarily works on health care issues for local LGBT groups. A long standing international group for female-born, male-identified persons is FTM International (FTMI)—*www.ftmi.org.* Gender Education and Advocacy (GEA)— *www.gender.org*—is a national organization specifically focusing on the

needs and rights of gender-variant people. The Gender Identity Center (GIC) of Colorado—*www.gicocolo.org*—supports and provides information and referrals for transgendered and transsexual people. A Washington-based political organization, Genderpac (GPAC)—www.gpac.org—focuses on gender rights. The International Foundation for Gender Education (IFGE)—*www.ifge.org*—has been a leader since 1987, in information and referral services for gender and transgender issues. The National Transgender Advocacy Coalition (NTAC)—*www.ntac.org*—is a national organization working for social and legal reform to secure rights for transgendered and other gender-diverse individuals. Parents, Family and Friends of Lesbian and Gays (PFLAG)—*www.pflag.org*—is a support organization for loved ones of LGBT people. Transgender Law and Policy Institute (TLPI)—*www.transgenderlaw.org*—is a national organization dedicated in advocacy for transgendered people.

Chapter 8
Transgender Issues

The ordeal of Maria José Martínez-Patiño during the 1988 Summer Olympics is poignantly described in Anne Fausto-Sterling, *Sexing the Body: Gender Politics and the Construction of Sexuality* (2000). Fausto-Sterling's work also brilliantly summarizes in accessible language the science behind sexual identity and the socially constructed nature of gender.

Trans Bodies, Trans Selves: A Resource for the Transgender Community (2014) edited by Laura Erickson-Schroth represents one of the most essential resources for trans men and women on topics ranging from health issues to legal rights to trans history in the United States. *Transgender 101: A Simple Guide to a Complex Issue* (2012) presents some of the same information in shorter and simpler form. Readers interested in developments in trans civil rights since the 1990s would do well to consult Susan Stryker's e-book *Transgender History* (2009). Among the best books on the experience of being a trans man or woman are Matt Kailey, *Just Add Hormones: An Insider's Guide to the Transsexual Experience* (2005), and Janet Mock's sharing of her life story as a trans woman of color in her 2014 book, *Redefining Realness: My Path to Womanhood, Identity, Love & So Much More* (2014).

Information on how American psychiatry has interpreted trans identity can be found in American Psychiatric Association (APA), *Diagnostic and Statistical Manual of Mental Disorders*, Fifth Edition, 2013; Zack Ford, "APA Revises Manual: Being Transgender is No Longer a Mental Disorder," *ThinkProgress.org*, December 3, 2012, http://thinkprogress.org/lgbt/2012/12/03/1271431/apa-revises-manual-being-transgender-is-no-longer-a-mental-disorder/; and Beth Schwartzapfel, "Transgender People Want Shrinks to Stop Calling Them Crazy," *Mother Jones.com*, December 5, 2012, http://www.motherjones.com/politics/2012/12/transgender-psychiatry-dsm-dysphoria. See also the Committee on Lesbian, Gay, Bisexual, and

Transgender Health Issues Gaps and Opportunities; Board on the Health of Select Populations; Institute of Medicine; and *The Health of Lesbian, Gay, Bisexual, and Transgender People: Building a Foundation for Better Understanding.* (2011). The statement by the APA supporting trans civil rights can be found at "APA Issues Position Statements Supporting Transgender Care and Civil Rights," *ThinkProgress. org,* August 21, 2012, http://thinkprogress.org/lgbt/2012/08/21/721441/apa-issues-position-statements-supporting-transgender-care-and-civil-rights/.

For information on new Medicare and private insurance policies covering gender-affirming surgery, see Associated Press, "Coverage for Gender Surgery Jumps; More Insurers Paying for Sex Transformation Services," *New York Daily News,* December 8, 2011, http://www.nydailynews.com/life-style/health/coverage-gender-surgery-jumps-major-insurers-paying-sex-transformation-procedures-article-1.988863; Ariana Eunjung Cha, "Ban Lifted on Medicare Coverage for Sex Change Surgery," *The Washington Post,* May 30, 2014, http://www.washingtonpost.com/national/health-science/ban-lifted-on-medicare-coverage-for-sex-change-surge ry/2014/05/30/28bcd122-e818-11e3-a86b-362fd5443d19_story.html; and Dana Dovery, "Gender Reassignment Surgery Must Be Covered By Insurance in New York State, Says Governor Cuomo," *medicaldaily.com,* December 12, 2014, http://www.medicaldaily.com/gender-reassignment-surgery-must-be-covered-insurance-new-york-state-says-governor-314092.

An explanation of informed consent clinics can be found in *Trans Bodies, Trans Selves* and *Transgender 101: A Simple Guide to a Complex Issue,* 2012. Additional information is available from "A Primer on Transition: The Basics of Changing Your Physical Sex," *Transsexual.org,* http://www.transsexual.org/index.html.

Medical neglect and abuse of trans patients is detailed in "EMS Denied Transgender Patient Care Causing Her Death, Alleges Sheepshead Bay Lawyer," *sheepsheadbites.com,* April 2, 2013, http://www.sheepsheadbites.com/2013/04/ems-denied-transgender-patient-care-causing-her-death-alleges-sheepshead-bay-lawyer/; Sarah D. Fox, "Damages Awarded After Transsexual Woman's Death: Payout to Mother of Victim of Bigoted Emergency Workers' Negligence," *www.gendercentre.org.au,* December 12, 1998, http://www.gendercentre.org.au/resources/polare-archive/archived-articles/damages-awarded-after-transsexual-womans-death.html; Fausto-Sterling describes the medical abuse of intersexual children in *Sexing the Body.*

Trans men and women face unique issues with pregnancy and aging. In addition to *Trans Bodies, Trans Selves,* readers should consult Joanne Herman, "Can Transgender People Bear Children?" *Huffington Post,* March 28, 2011, http://www.huffingtonpost.com/joanne-herman/can-transgender-people-be_b_839703. Ryan Schuessler, "For Aging Transgender Population, Retirement Can Be Bittersweet Refuge," *America.aljazeera.com,* February 20, 2014, http://america.aljazeera.com/articles/2014/2/20/for-aging-transgenderpopulationretirementcanbebittersweetrefuge.html, and "Transgender Aging," *sageusa,org*, http://www.sageusa.org/nyc/index. cfm. for more on the topic.

The law pertaining to gender identity has undergone rapid and often contradictory changes. Consult Lindsey Bever, "Utah – Yes, Utah – Passes Landmark LGBT Rights Bill," *The Washington Post*, March 12, 2015, http://www.washingtonpost. com/news/morning-mix/wp/2015/03/12/utah-legislature-passes-landmark-lgbt-anti-discrimination-bill-backed-by-mormon-church/; Crosby Burns and Jeff Krehely, "Gay and Transgender People Face High Rates of Workplace Discrimination and Harassment: Data Demonstrate Need for Federal Law," *American Progress*, June 2, 2012, americanprogress.org, https://www.americanprogress.org/issues/lgbt/news/2011/06/02/9872/gay-and-transgender-people-face-high-rates-of-workplace-discrimination-and-harassment/; Gary J. Gates and Jody L. Herman, "Transgender Military Service," The Williams Institute, (May 2014), http://williamsinstitute. law.ucla.edu/wp-content/uploads/Transgender-Military-Service-May-2014.pdf.; "Issues: Non-Discrimination Laws," *National Center for Transgender Equality, transequality.org*, http://transequality.org/issues/non-discrimination-laws; Marisa Taylor, "Study: Military Is Ready for Transgender Troops," *america.aljazeera.com*, August 26, 2014, http://america.aljazeera.com/articles/2014/8/26/transgender-militaryreport.html.

On the issue of public accommodations, read Crosby Burns and Philip Ross, "Gay and Transgender Discrimination Outside the Workplace: Why We Need Protections in Housing, Health Care, and Public Accommodations," Center for American Progress, *americanprogress.org*, July 29, 2011, https://www.american-progress.org/issues/lgbt/report/2011/07/19/9927/gay-and-transgender-discrim-ination-outside-the-workplace/; Sunnivie Brydum, "Texas Doubles Down on Transphobic Legislation, Adding $2,000 Fine for 'Wrong' Bathroom Use," *advocate. com*, March 10, 2015, http://www.advocate.com/politics/transgender/2015/03/10/texas-doubles-down-transphobic-legislation-adding-2000-fine-wrong-ba; and Edgar Walters, "'Bathroom Bills' Pit Transgender Texans Against GOP," *Texas Tribune*, April 4, 2015, http://www.texastribune.org/2015/04/04/bathroom-bills-pit-transgender-community-against-g/. Regarding marriage, see "FAQ About Transgender People and Marriage Law," *lambdalegal.org*, http://www.lambdalegal. org/know-your-rights/transgender/trans-marriage-law-faq. A valuable source on parental rights for trans men and women is Leslie Cooper, *Protecting the Rights of Transgender Parents and their Children: A Guide for Parents and Lawyers*, American Civil Liberties Union, *aclu.org*, https://www.aclu.org/sites/default/files/field_document/aclu-tg_parenting_guide.pdf

The Southern Poverty Law Center provides an excellent resource on hate groups and hate crimes at its website, *splcenter.org*. As examples, see "Assault on Maryland Transgendered Woman May Be a Hate Crime," *Hatewatch, splcenter.org*, http://www.splcenter.org/blog/2011/04/27/assault-on-maryland-transgendered-woman-may-be-a-hate-crime/ and Bob Moser, "Violence Engulfs Transgender Population in D.C.," *Intelligence Report* (Winter 2003) No. 12, *splcenter.org,* http:// www.splcenter.org/get-informed/intelligence-report/browse-all-issues/2003/win-ter/disposable-people. The reasons many hate crimes go unreported by the trans community are outlined in Daniel Gorton, "Anti-Transgender Hate Crimes: The Challenge for Law Enforcement," Gay and Lesbian Anti-Violence Fund, Inc. and The Anti-Violence Project of Massachusetts (April, 2011), http://www.masstpc. org/pubs/3party/AVP-anti_trans_hate_crimes.pdf; The suspicious death of one trans woman performer is detailed in Al Baker and Nate Schweber, "Woman Dies in a Brooklyn Fire That Is Deemed Suspicious," *New York Times,* May 12, 2012; Meredith Hoffman, "Transgender Star Lorena Escalera's Murder Still Unsolved a Year After Death," *dnainfo.com,* May 7, 2013; and "Transgender Performer Dies In Suspicious Brooklyn Fire," *gothamist.com,* May 30, 2012, http://gothamist. com/2012/05/13/transgender_performer_dies_in_suspi.php.

Evidence of changing American attitudes toward the trans community can be found in Samantha Allen and Nico Lang, "11 Ways 2014 was the Biggest Year in Transgender History," *Rolling Stone,* December 23, 2014, http://www.rollingstone. com/culture/features/11-ways-2014-was-the-biggest-year-in-transgender-history-20141223?page=2 and "Survey: Strong Majorities of Americans Favor Rights and Legal Protections for Transgender People," Public Religion Research Institute, November 3, 2011, http://publicreligion.org/research/2011/11/american-attitudes-towards-transgender-people/#.VUY6OUJJVUR; Reactions to Jared Leto's depic-tion of a trans woman in Dallas Buyers' Club are in Steve Friess's, "Don't Applaud Jared Leto's Transgender 'Mammy,'" *Time Magazine,* February 28, 2014, http:// time.com/10650/dont-applaud-jared-letos-transgender-mammy/.

The audience numbers for Bruce Jenner's 2015 interview on 20/20 are in Rick Kissell, "Bruce Jenner Interview Ratings: 17 Million Watch ABC Special," *Variety,* April 25, 2015, http://variety.com/2015/tv/news/bruce-jenner-interview-ratings-17-million-watch-abc-special-1201479968/.

Chapter 9
Creating an American LGBT Literary Tradition

Two invaluable resources for the study of the LGBT literary tradition in the United States are Claude J. Summers, ed., *The Gay and Lesbian Literary Heritage: A Reader's Companion to the Writers and their Works, from Antiquity to the Present* (2002) and the best collection of writings by gay men, *The Columbia Anthology of Gay Literature: Readings from Western Antiquity to the Present Day* (1998). Readers interested in the history of gay and lesbian arts and letters, and the portrayal of the LGBT community should also examine Michelangelo Signorile, *Queer in America: Sex, Media, and the Closets of Power* (1993).

White Gay and Bisexual Writers

Walt Whitman's standing as one of the greatest American poets of all time could rest on his collection *Leaves of Grass*, first published in 1855 but constantly revised and expanded by the author through an edition published in 1891. Other key works are his anti-alcohol novel *Franklin Evans, or The Inebriate: A Tale of the Times*, (1842) and *Democratic Vistas* (1871), which includes Whitman's thoughts on political topics such as the Louisiana Purchase and the dehumanization and alienation prompted by the nineteenth-century economy. Katherine Molinoff's *Walt Whitman at Southold* (1966) remains the most detailed examination of Whitman's alleged molestation of a student while he was a teacher, while David S. Reynolds' *Walt Whitman's America: A Cultural Biography* (1995) stands out not just as a thoughtful examination of Whitman's life but as a history of the times in which he lived.

Edward Prime Stevenson wrote two groundbreaking works under the pen name Xavier Mayne, a novel, *Imre: A Memorandum* (1906), and a nonfiction work the historian Byrne Fone calls the first major example of "gay studies," *The Intersexes: A History of Similisexualism as a Problem in Social Life* (1908). Fone examines Prime-Stevenson's career and impact in *Homophobia: A History* (2000).

Tennessee Williams became one of the most beloved, and most performed, American playwrights in the twentieth century and one whose works were frequently adapted for the movies. His more prominent works include *The Glass Menagerie* (1944), *The Rose Tattoo* (1951), *Cat On a Hot Tin Roof* (1955), *Suddenly Last Summer* (1958), *Sweet Bird of Youth* (1959) and *Night of the Iguana* (1961). One of his most explicitly gay-themed works, and one that paints an ugly portrait of gay men, can be found in a collection of short stories, *Hard Candy: A Book of Stories* (1954). The life and art of Tennessee Williams are skillfully explored in Lyle Leverich, *Tom: The Unknown Tennessee Williams* (1995) and in Donald Spoto, *The Kindness of Strangers: The Life of Tennessee Williams* (1986).

Christopher Bram provides a crisp, compelling portrait of numerous prominent gay authors in the post-World War II era, such as Gore Vidal, Truman Capote, James Baldwin, and Tony Kushner in *Imminent Outlaws: The Gay Writers Who Changed America* (2012). Gore Vidal's key novels include *The City and the Pillar* (1949) and a new version that Vidal believed better captured his original intention. His play *The Best Man* (1960) depicts a man whose world is turned upside down when a blackmailer threatens to reveal his hidden homosexuality. Vidal's most significant novels include *The City and the Pillar Revised* (1965), *Myra Breckinridge* (1968) and a series on American politics and prominent eighteenth- and nineteenth-century American political figures including *Burr* (1973), *Washington, D.C.* (1967) and *Lincoln* (1984).

Numerous Beat writers were gay or bisexual, including Jack Kerouac, Gregory Corso, William S. Burroughs, and Allen Ginsberg. There are several excellent works on the Beat Movement including Gregory Stephenson, *The Daybreak Boys:*

Essays on the Literature of the Beat Generation (1990), Edward Halsey Foster, *Understanding the Beats* (1992), and a provocative, lively recent work, Bill Morgan's *The Typewriter is Holy: The Complete, Uncensored History of the Beat Generation* (2011). Ginsberg stands out as one of the most important of the Beat writers due to his poetry collection, *Howl and Other Poems* (1956) but also because of the heartbreaking *Kaddish and Other Poems* (1961), *The Fall of America: Poems of These States* (1973) and *Mind Breaths* (1978).

Edward Albee served as a lightening rod for the critics because of the raw emotion and verbal violence of his characters as seen in one collection of his plays, *The Zoo Story; The Death of Bessie Smith; The Sandbox: Three Plays* (1960), and his standout contribution to the theater, *Who's Afraid of Virginia Woolf?* (1963). *Tiny Alice* (1964) stands as his most baffling play and one that drew fierce attacks from critics for its supposed subliminal gay content.

Openly gay men moved from being marginal characters played for comic relief to central figures in the theater with Matt Crowley's play, *The Boys in the Band* (1968). Interesting insights into this important work can be found in Ellis Nassour, "Matt Crowley Revisits The Boys in the Band," *TotalTheater.Com*, http://www.totaltheater.com/?q=node/640 (2008).

Although it was largely comic, Harvey Fierstein's *Torch Song Trilogy* (1978) marks one of the first times in theater history that a cross-dresser was presented as a well-rounded and noble character whose romantic ups and downs were not that different from most audience members' lives. Some background on the making of the play and the reaction can be found in Maddy Costa, "How We Made . . . Harvey Fierstein and Antony Sher on Torch Song Trilogy," *The Guardian;* (2012). First staged more than two decades ago, Tony Kushner's *Angels in America: A Gay Fantasia on National Themes* (1993), like *Torch Song*, was originally three separate plays. It stands as not only one of the landmarks of twentieth-century LGBT literature, but of American theater. Other Kushner works include an adaptation of an earlier Bertolt Brecht play, *The Good Person of Szechuan* (1997) and *A Dybbuk, or Between Two Worlds* (1997).

Lesbian Authors

Perhaps because of her extreme social phobia or because of the sexist attitudes prevailing toward women authors, only a dozen of Emily Dickinson's more than 1,800 poems were published in her lifetime and her genius was largely unknown. Numerous collections of her work were published after her death in 1886. Thomas H. Johnson edited *The Complete Poems of Emily Dickinson*, originally published in 1955, and reprinted in 2013, and it remains the best and most comprehensive collection of her work. Richard B. Sewell wrote an award-winning biography of the poet in 1974, *The Life of Emily Dickinson*. Dickinson's sexuality is thoughtfully explored in Lillian Faderman "Emily Dickinson's Letters to Sue Gilbert," *Massachusetts Review* 18 (Summer 1977) and Ellen Louise Hart, "The Encoding of Homoerotic Desire: Emily Dickinson's Letters and Poems to Susan Dickinson, 1850-1886," *Tulsa Studies in Women's Literature* Volume 9, No. 2 (Fall 1990).

Gertrude Stein did not deal explicitly with homosexuality in most of her works, but a lesbian love triangle is at the heart of the plot for the 1903 novel *Q.E.D.* (published posthumously as *Things As They Are* in 1950). Other significant works are *Three Lives* (1909) and *The Autobiography of Alice B. Toklas* (1933), a work unusually accessible for Stein and one that provides intriguing stories about artists such as Pablo Picasso and about her experience on an ambulance crew in Europe during World War I. Stein's experiences in the war are also detailed in Janet Malcolm, "Gertrude Stein's War: The Years in Occupied France," *The New Yorker* (June 25, 2013). A compelling personal look at two prominent LGBT authors in the early twentieth century can be found in Edward Burns, ed., *The Letters of Gertrude Stein and Carl Van Vechten, 1913-1946* (1913). Michael Gold, in "Gertrude Stein: A Literary Idiot," *The New Masses* (December 1936), harshly assesses Gertrude Stein's writing as being all style and no substance.

Standout titles in lesbian pulp fiction include Valerie Taylor, *The Girls in 3-B* (1959), and Randy Salem, *Man Among Women* (1960). Ann Bannon (Ann Weldy's *nom de plume*), however, stands as the queen of the genre. *Odd Girl Out* (1957), *I Am a Woman* (1959), *Woman in the Shadows* (1959), *Journey to a Woman* (1960), and *Beebo Brinker* (1962) number among her most popular novels.

Patricia Highsmith ranks as one of the most gifted of the twentieth-century lesbian authors and her novels certainly stand as some of the most sinister. Landmarks in her career include *Strangers on a Train* (1950; 2012), *The Price of Salt* (written under the pseudonym Claire Morgan and published in 1952), *The Talented Mr. Ripley* (1955; 2012) and the rest of the "Ripliad": *Ripley Underground* (1970), *Ripley's Game* (1974), *The Boy Who Followed Ripley* (1980), and *Ripley Underwater* (1991). A good collection of her short stories can be found with *The Selected Stories of Patricia Highsmith* (2001). Joan Schenkar penned a gripping biography of the writer, *The Talented Miss Highsmith: The Secret Life and Serious Art of Patricia Highsmith* (2009).

"Camp" refers to a central artistic style and sensibility in gay-themed art, literature, and movies. The best starting point for understanding camp is Susan Sontag, "Notes on Camp," *Partisan Review* (1964). A more extended look at the influence of camp on American culture can be found with David Van Leer, *The Queening of America: Gay Culture in Straight Society* (1995).

The post-Stonewall spirit of pride, assertion, and fierce rejection of heterosexism can be found in Rita May Brown's essay "Take a Lesbian to Lunch" in Chris Bull, ed., *Come Out Fighting: A Century of Essential Writing on Gay and Lesbian Liberation* (2001). Readers can also experience Brown's powerful declarations of lesbian liberation in poetry collections such as *The Hand That Cradles the Rock* (1971) and *Songs to a Handsome Woman* (1973). Her first novel, *Rubyfruit Jungle* (1973) remains her most important and popular work despite its sometimes dated depiction of so-called "butch" lesbians and other stereotypes.

Voices of Color

Countee Cullen and Langston Hughes are two of the important African-American writers identified as gay or bisexual by later scholars. Major Jackson edited a helpful overview of Cullen's chief creations in *The Collected Poems* (2013). Langston Hughes's most notable works include *The Ways of White Folks* (1934), and *Montage of a Dream Deferred* (1951). Readers should also consult the *Selected Poems of Langston Hughes* (1958) and *Five Plays by Langston Hughes* (1963).

James Baldwin became one of the most important African-American writers to pry open the literary closet. His innovative essay, "Preservation of Innocence," appeared in the obscure Moroccan journal *Zero* in 1949, and saw homophobia as resting on a foundation of misogyny. The essay can be found in *James Baldwin: Collected Essays* (1998). His *Notes of a Native Son* (1951), *Giovanni's Room* (1956), *Another Country* (1962), and *The Fire Next Time* (1963) sometimes explicitly deal with gay themes but almost always confront America's poisonous race relations. Randall Kenan provides an insightful biography with *James Baldwin: American Writer (Lives of Notable Gay Men and Lesbians)* (1993). Kenan also authored an excellent novel exploring the devastating impact of fundamentalist religion on gay men with *A Visitation of Spirits* (1989).

John Rechy's fascination with the urban underworld, including some of its gay denizens, fascinated a wide audience in the 1960s. Rechy rejected the idea that gay writers must apologize for their sexuality and aim for hypocritical bourgeoisie standards of morality. Along with his most famous work, *City of Night* (1963), interested readers should explore *The Day's Death* (1969) and *Rushes* (1979).

Few African-American poets were as gifted at exploring the dynamic intersections of racism, sexism, class oppression, and homophobia as Audre Lorde, a source of some of the most biting social commentary in the late twentieth century. A great overview of her career was compiled in *The Collected Poems of Audre Lorde* (1997). *Undersong: Chosen Poems Old and New—Revised* (1992) is a masterpiece while *Zami: A New Spelling of My Name* (1982) provides a fine example of her prose style. Her fascinating life is explored in Alexis De Veaux, *Warrior Poet: A Biography of Audre Lorde* (2004).

Notable works by Paula Gunn Allen include *Blind Lion Poems* (1974) and *Star Child: Poems* (1981), and two fine anthologies of her poetry can be found with *Skins and Bones: Poems 1979-1987* (1988) and *Life is a Fatal Disease: Collected Poems 1962-1995* (1997).

Meanwhile, Gloria Anzaldúa's *Borderlands/La Frontera: The New Mestiza* (1987) has long been a staple of graduate seminars and rightly so due to its explorations of the intersections of race, class, gender, sexuality, nationality, and language.

Transgender Literary Activism

Kate Bornstein, a standout among trans writers, has authored numerous nonfiction works including *Gender Outlaw: On Men, Women, and the Rest of Us* (1994), *Hello, Cruel World: 101 Alternatives to Suicide for Teens, Freaks, and Other Outlaws* (2006), and *A Queer and Pleasant Danger: A Memoir* (2012.) More biographical information can be found in Julie Gerstein, "Queer on All Sides: Kate Bornstein's Life In and Out of Scientology," *Bibliophile*, June 5, 2012, http://www.biographile.com/queer-on-all-sides-kate-bornsteins-life-in-and-out-of-scientology/3122/ and "Gender Outlaw: On Men, Women, and the Rest of Us by Kate Bornstein," *Kirkus Reviews* (June 1, 1994), https://www.kirkusreviews.com/book-reviews/kate-bornstein/gender-outlaw/.

Among Matt Kailey's standout works are *Just Add Hormones: An Insider's Guide to the Transsexual Experience* (2005), *Teeny Weenies and Other Short Subjects* (2012), and *My Child is Transgender: 10 Tips for Parents of Adult Trans Children* (2012). Biographical information can be found in Jacob Anderson-Minshall, "Op-Ed: Remembering Pioneering Trans Writer, Activist Matt Kailey," *The Advocate*, May 21, 2014, http://www.advocate.com/commentary/2014/05/21/op-ed-remembering-pioneering-trans-writer-activist-matt-kailey.

A poet and essayist, Max Wolf Valerio writes of how he has juggled multiple identities in *Male Lust* (2000), *The Bridge We Call Home* (2002), *The Phallus Palace* (2002), and *The Testosterone Files: My Social and Hormonal Transition from Female to Male* (2006). Helen Boyd's interview with him, "Five Questions With . . . Max Wolf Valerio," was published at *en/Gender: Helen Boyd's Journal of Gender and Trans Issues* (November 29, 2006), http://www.myhusbandbetty.com/2006/11/29/five-questions-with-max-wolf-valerio/. Valerio is quoted on California voter ID laws in Alex Berg, "Unique Problems for Transgender Voters," *The Daily Beast* (November 2, 2012), http://www.thedailybeast.com/articles/2012/11/02/voter-identification-laws-create-unique-problems-for-transgender-voters.html.

Janet Mock shared her life story as a trans woman of color in her 2014 book, *Redefining Realness: My Path to Womanhood, Identity, Love & So Much More* (2014). Other resources on Mock include an autobiographical article by her as told to Kierna Mayo, "I Was Born a Boy," *Marie Claire* (May 18, 2011), http://www.marieclaire.com/sex-love/advice/a6075/born-male/ and another by Mock, "'More Than a Pretty Face' Sharing My Journey to Womanhood," (May 17, 2011), *janetmock.com*, http://janetmock.com/2011/05/17/janet-mock-comes-out-transgender-marie-claire/. Details on Mock's dispute with TV host Piers Morgan can be found in

Chris Geidner, "Transgender Advocate Janet Mock: Piers Morgan 'Sensationalized' My Story," *Buzzfeed* (February 4, 2014), http://www.buzzfeed.com/chrisgeidner/transgender-advocate-janet-mock-piers-morgan-sensationalized#.siMn8VRq7.

Chapter 10
LGBT Characters and Culture in Film and Television

The Celluloid Closet (1981) by Vito Russo is a pioneering text on LGBT culture in cinema. Russo's activism and film scholarship worked in tandem throughout his professional life. A lifelong LGBT advocate, Russo co-founded the Gay & Lesbian Alliance Against Defamation (GLAAD), an organization that evaluates LGBT depictions in the media. Russo loved movies, and in the early 1970s he began a series of camp movie screenings and lectures for the Gay Activists Alliance in New York. *The Celluloid Closet*, a groundbreaking overview of the LGBT presence in film, was the culmination of his film work thoughout the seventies. The original edition of the book was released during the height of the AIDS epidemic, and some of Russo's sense of outrage about this comes through in the text. The book was made into a documentary film of the same title, released after Russo's untimely death from AIDS in 1990. The film, released in 1996, is more entertaining and less political than the book. *Vito*, a 2011 documentary of Russo's life, was well received; it is a helpful overview of this important LGBT media critic.

Queer Images: A History of Gay and Lesbian Film in America (2005) by Harry M. Benshoff and Sean Griffith is a carefully researched and well written overview of LGBT representation in American film. Both authors are academics widely published in film and media. Like Russo, Benshoff and Griffith's knowledge of the pertinent films is impressive. Unlike Russo, however, the authors are professional scholars, so their approach to the subject is more erudite and even handed. In short, *Queer Images* both updates and deepens the overview provided in *The Celluloid Closet*.

Now You See It: Studies on Lesbian and Gay Film (1990) by Richard Dyer is an overview of the same time period; however, it addresses LGBT documentary and experimental films more thoroughly than the Russo or Benshoff/Griffin texts. *New Queer Cinema: The Director's Cut* (2013) by B. Ruby Rich offers a variety of essays on LGBT cinema. The chapter on Gus Van Sant's Milk was particularly helpful. *Out Takes: Essays on Queer Theory and Film* (1999), edited by Ellis Hanson, provides a nice array of essays dealing mainly with queer readings of older Hollywood films. *Queer Popular Culture: Literature, Media, Film, and Television* (2011), edited by Thomas Peele, also addresses a variety of topics addressed in this chapter.

The Queer Encyclopedia of Film & Television (2005), edited by Claude J. Summers, is an essential reference for film and LGBTQ scholars, with over 150 well-written and informative entries. This chapter benefitted from the entries on talk shows, soap operas, sitcoms, dramas, news, and reality programming. *Gay TV and Straight America* (2005) by Ron Becker was helpful in analyzing the upsurge of LGBT American network programming in the 1990s. *Ethereal Queer: Television, Historicity, Desire* (2013) by Amy Villarejo does a fine job of examining how technical changes in television have affected its history in regards to LGBT viewership and content.

More specialized material on this subject can be found in *Queer Love in Film and Television: Critical Essays* (2013) edited by Pamela Demory and Christopher Pullen. Noteworthy essays in the collection deal with *The L Word, Will and Grace, RuPaul's Drag Race, Queer as Folk, Modern Family*, and *Brokeback Mountain. Lesbians in Television and Text after the Millenium* (2008) by Rebecca Beirne provides a much-needed lesbian perspective on some of the same programs. *Queers in American Popular Culture* (2010), edited by Jim Elledge, also has a number of illuminating essays, particularly those dealing with *Ellen, Grey's Anatomy*, and *South Park*.

Chapter 11
Contemporary Experiences of LGBT People: Health Disparities, Adolescence, and the Queer Movement

The twenty-first century has been witness to a broad discussion of LGBT rights in the realm of law and politics. This discussion ultimately resulted in the increase of legal rights and recognitions for LGBT people. Furthermore, the health and wellness of LGBT people took the stage and became a focus of the behavioral and medical sciences. Attempts were made to explain the negative health symptoms experienced by LGBT groups. These events occurred alongside intense development of LGBT studies by the intellectual writings of multiple queer theorists.

The expansion of legal protections for LGBT people occurred when the Matthew Shepard and James Byrd, Jr. Hate Crimes Prevention Act was signed in 2009. *Hate Crime: Impact, Causes and Responses,* Second Edition (2015) by Neil Chakraborti and Jon Garland offers a holistic review of the theory, research, and public policy underpinning hate crime legislation. This comprehensive textbook composed of eleven chapters examines hate crimes through various contexts including international differences, and unique social phenomena, for example through the intensification of Islamophobia in the west. Two chapters are devoted to hate crimes motivated through homophobia and transphobia respectively. This text by two leading scholars in the field of hate crimes gives thoughtful consideration to both offenders and victims and provides policy recommendations for future hate crime legislation.

The most important revelation for LGBT issues in the behavioral and medical sciences was the comprehensive application of minority stress theory to LGBT peoples. Ilan Meyer conducted a systematic meta-analysis of LGBT behavioral health research and published his findings in the piece *Prejudice, Social Stress, and Mental Health in Lesbian, Gay, and Bisexual Populations: Conceptual Issues and Research Evidence* (2003). In this foundational analysis Meyer shows through review of the existing literature of the time that lesbians, gays, and bisexuals experience mental health disorders at a higher rate than their heterosexual counterparts. Mainly, the author argues "stigma, prejudice, and discrimination create a hostile and stressful social environment that causes mental health problems." The text theorizes that the stress created from experiences of prejudice and discrimination, of being rejected for being LGBT, of hiding ones identity, and that internalizing homophobia leads to negative health outcomes for LGBT people. This piece would go on to become seminal in future research in the behavioral health sciences.

Along with the developments described above in law and the social sciences, there was an explosion of literature in the humanities that built queer theory. Perhaps the most well-known contributions are Eve Sedgwick's *Epistemology of the Closet* (1990) and Judith Butler's *Gender Trouble: Feminism and the Subversion of Identity* (1990). Sedgwick's main claim is that limitation of sexuality to a binary between homosexuality and heterosexuality is overly simplistic. She demarcates the ways in which a third sex that defies a gender and binary sexuality has existed for some time. She alludes to examples from Oscar Wilde's literature among others. Butler's piece is best known for defining a new mode of feminist, post-structural analysis. Gender, Butler describes, is not in fact an essential marker of identity but is instead constructed socially. She describes gender as a performative act, and ends by arguing that an essential feminine identity is not necessary for the feminist movement to continue towards its proclaimed objective.

A subsequent addition to queer theory is Alexander Doty's *Making Things Perfectly Queer* (1993). Doty explains that sexuality and gender are not the only realms of queer analysis. Heterosexually identified individuals can have queer moments in an otherwise heterocentric world. His book contains much less jargon than other contributors' writings on queer theory and uses many examples from popular culture and media to explain concepts. Further establishment of this theoretical tradition occurred through the appearance of the text *Queer Theory* (1996) by Annamarie Jagose. Jagose describes the emergence of queer theory from the voice of multiple authors and many social movements including the homophile movement, lesbian feminism, and gay liberation. Jagose uses the voices of her contemporaries, such as Butler, to show that there is a need to produce a new mode of thought that does not rely on constructed binary notions of identity.

Index

A

Acquired Immunodeficiency Syndrome (AIDS), 60, 65
Affordable Care Act, 121
AIDS, also see HIV
  discussion of, 66–67
  public health problem, 71
  Ryan White CARE Act, 71
  scope of the problem, 61-62
AIDS Service Organizations (ASOs), 75
Ajanaku, Maua Adele, 50
Albee, Edward, 140
Alcohol Beverages Control Department (ABC), 52
Allen, Paula Gunn, 156
All in the Family (television), 180
Amazing Race, The (reality show), 188
Amendment 956, 76
American Educational Gender Information Service, 112
American Family, An (reality show), 187
American Medical Association, 96
American Psychiatric Association (APA), 24, 96
Androgen insensitivity, 111
Androgynous, 100
And The Band Played On (Shilts), 75
Anzaldúa, Gloria, 157
Archer (animated series), 182
Araxes: A Call to Free the Nature of the Urning from Penal Law (Ulrichs), 11
Arbuckle, Fatty, 167
As the World Turns (television), 185
Asphalt Jungle, The (television), 179
Autobiography of Alice B. Toklas, The (Stein), 146
Aversion therapy, 23

B

Baker v. State of Vermont (1999), 192
Baldwin, James, 31, 32, 154
Baldwin, Tammy, 59
Barebacking, 80
Baumer, Leanna, 123
Beach, Frank, 22
Best Man, The (Vidal), 139
Between Ourselves (Lorde), 156
Bigender, 100
Binary sexuality, 21
Birdcage, The (movie), 173
Blick, Roy, 36
Bono, Chaz, 132
Borderlands/La Frontera: The New Mestiza (Anzaldúa), 157
Bornstein, Kate, 158
Bostonians, The (James), 14
Boston Marriage, 14
Boy Meets Boy (reality program), 188
Boys Don't Cry (movie), 174
Boys in the Band, The (Crowley), 141
Bradford, Judith, 123
Brandon, Teena, 94
Bridges, Style, 37
Briggs, John, 57
Broadus, Kylar, 103
Brokeback Mountain (movie), 175
Brown, Helen Gurley, 45
Brown, Rita Mae, 150
Bruce, Lenny, 45
Bryant, Anita, 57
Burns, Kenneth, 40
Burstyn v. Wilson (1956), 166
Bush, George H.W., 69

C

Calamus poems (Whitman), 135
California Penal Code, 36
Call, Hal, 40
Carlyle, Thomas, 40
Carpenter, Edward, 13
Cat on a Hot Tin Roof (Williams), 137

Centers for Disease Control (CDC), 62, 74
Chaplin, Charlie, 165
Children's Hour, The (movie), 170
Chiles, Lawton, 69, 76
Chozen (animated series), 182
Christopher, George, 52
Cisek v. Cisek (1982), 127
Cisgender, 103
City and the Pillar, The (Vidal), 139
City of Night (Rechy), 155
Cohn, Roy, 35
Color Purple, The (movie), 174
"Coming out," 44
Committee on Government Operations, 35
Comstock Act, 19
Condoms, 76
Congenital adrenal hyperplasia (CAH), 117
Convenience sampling, 88
Conversion therapy, 23, 24
Corner Bar, The (television), 180
Cory, Daniel Webster, 44
Council on Religion and the Homosexual (CRH), 52
Cox, Laverne, 132
Crossdressers, 101
Crowley, Matt, 141
Crystal, Billy, 56
Cullen, Countee, 152
Cuomo, Andrew, 123

D

Dahl, Steve, 59
Dallas Buyers Club (movie), 175
Daughters of Bilitis (DOB), 29, 41
David Kopay Story, The (Kopay), 49
Days of Our Lives (television), 185
Defense of Marriage Act (DOMA), 189, 192
DeGeneres, Ellen, 181
Diagnostic and Statistical Manual of Mental Disorders (DSM), 23, 113–114
Dickinson, Emily, 145

Dickson Experimental Sound Film, The (movie), 164
Die Conträre Sexualempfindung (Moll), 8
Dietrich, Marlene, 165
Disorders of sex development (DSD), 109
Dizygotic twins, 20
Don't Ask, Don't Tell (DADT), 190
"Double V," 29
Douglas, Alfred, 13
Down low, 85
Dracula's Daughter (movie), 168
Drag Queen/King, 101

E

East Coast Homophile Organizations (ECHO), 53
Ego-Dystonic Homosexuality (EDH), 24
Eisenhower, Dwight, 34
Eleventh Hour, The (television), 179
Ellen DeGeneres Show, 187
Ellis, Havelock, 9
Employment Non-Discrimination Act (ENDA), 103, 106, 122
Entrapment, 36
Equal Employment Opportunity Commission (EEOC), 121
Executive Order 13762, 122
Eyde, Edith, 29

F

Fabian Society, 13
Faderman, Lillian, 40
Fairbanks, Douglas, 167
Falwell, Jerry, 59, 77
Family Guy (animated series), 183
Family Research Council, 113, 123
Feinberg, Leslie, 112
Female-to-Male (FTM), 98
Feminine Mystique, The (Friedan), 46
Fierstein, Harvey, 174
First City, The (Lorde), 156
Flintstone, Fred, 182
Florida Enchantment, A (movie), 165

Flynn, Dan, 124
Ford, Clellan, 22
FORGE, 121
Fred Gray Association, 135
Freud, Sigmund, 17–18, 22
Friedan, Betty, 46, 47
Friends (television), 181
Futurama (animated series), 182

G

Gabel, Thomas James, 132
Gabrielson, Guy, 34
Garbo, Greta, 166
Gay and Lesbian Alliance Against Defamation (GLADD), 181
Gay Brothers, The (movie), 164
"Gay Cancer," 75
Gay Civil Rights,
   during World War II, 32–35
   influence of feminism, 46–47
   lavender scare, 31–36
   political activism in the 1950s, 38–42
   post World War II, 31–39
Gay Divorcee, The (movie), 167
"Gay liberation," 44
Gay Liberation Front, 54, 142
Gay Men's Health Crisis (GMHC), 75
Gay press, 29, 31–32
Gay purge,
   by police departments, 35
   in government, 34–35
   in the military, 34
Gay Related Immune Disorder (GRID), 61, 68
Gays Weddings (reality program), 188
Gender, definition of, 191
Gender dysphoria, 113
Gender fluid, 100
Gender identity, 94
Gender Identity Disorder (GID), 113
Genderqueer, 100
General Hospital (television), 185
Geolocation, 81
Geraldo (talk show), 186
Gerber, Henry, 19–21

Ginsberg, Allen, 139
Glee (television), 184
Grace, Laura Jane, 132
Greece, 5
Gunn, Tim, 188

H

Hairspray (movie), 176
Hate Crimes Legislation, 190
Hay, Henry, 38
Heartbeat (television), 180
Hedwig and the Angry Inch (movie), 176
Hellman, Lillian, 170
Helms, Jesse, 76
Hepburn, Katherine, 168
Hermaphrodite, 110
Highsmith, Patricia, 148–149, 170
Hirschfeld, Magnus, 12, 19
Hitchcock, Alfred, 169
HIV,
   clinical practice, 89–90
   communities affected by, 73
   contracted by, 63–64
   definition of, 62
   discussion of, 62–63
   federal funding, 69
   future policy, 87
   gay culture and, 74–77
   history of, 68–69
   how contracted, 63–64
   media initial messages, 74–75
   prevention of,
     abstinence model, 76–77
     harm reduction model, 76–77
   public policy development, 69
   research, 88
   risk for contracting the virus, 79–81
   risks for different subgroups,
     African-American gay men, 84
     age, 81–82
     Hispanic men, 83–84
     race, 82
     substance use, 86–87
   scope of the problem, 61–62

symptoms of the infection, 64–65
  clinical latency phase, 64
testing for, 65–66
treatment of, 66
viral load, 64
Holbrook, Hal, 55
Hollingsworth v. Perry (2013), 193
Hollywood Ten, 178
Homophile, 27, 40
Homophobia, 106
Homosexual in America: A Subjective Approach (Sagarin), 38
Homosexual in America, The (Cory), 44
Homosexuality,
  aversion therapy, 23
  biological links to, 20
  conversion and reparative therapies for, 23
  curing of, 22–23
  early understanding of, 6
  gay press, 30–31
  government sponsored research, 22
  medical model of, 11
  psychology and, 6–7
  self-awareness, 29–30
  sexology and, 7
Hooker, Evelyn, 22
Hoover, J. Edgar, 35, 40
Hössli, Heinrich, 11
House Un-American Activities Committee (HUAC), 177
Howl (Ginsberg), 140
Hudson, Rock, 69
Hughes, Langston, 152–153
Human Rights Campaign (HRC), 123
Hunt, Buddy, 37
Hunter, Tyra, 91
Hunt, Lester C., 37
Hurst, Fannie, 178

I

Imre: A Memorandum (Mayne), 135
In re Estate of Gardiner (2002), 126
Indigenous tribes, 5
Industrial Workers of the World, 39

Institute for Sexual Research, 12
Intermediate Sex, The (Carpenter), 13
International Olympic Committee (IOC), 111
Intersex, 109
Intersexes: A History of Similisexualism as a Problem in Social Life, The (Prime-Stevenson), 136
Intersexual,
  children, 116–117
  definition of, 111

J

James, Henry. 14
Jenner, Bruce, 132
Jennings, Dan, 39
Jenny Jones Show (talk show), 186
Jerry Springer Show (talk show), 186
Judd, for the Defense (television), 179
Just Add Hormones: An Insider's Guide to the Transsexual Experience (Kailey), 116, 159
"Just Say No," 69

K

Kailey, Matt, 159
Kallman, Franz, 20
Kameny, Frank, 34, 38
Kaposi Sarcoma, 68
Kertbeny, Karl-Maria, 10
Kids Are All Right, The (movie), 176
Kinsey, Alfred, 18, 20–21
  Kinsey Scale, 21
Kinsey Reports, 20–21
Kleinfelter's Syndrome, 117
Koop, C. Everett, 69, 77
Kopay, David, 49
Krafft-Ebing, Richard von, 7–8

L

Labouchere Amendment, 5
Ladder, The (magazine), 31, 41
Lambda Legal, 116
Lavender scare, 27, 31–36

Leaves of Grass (Whitman), 14, 134
Leto, Jared, 132
Libido Sexualis (Moll), 8
Lindsay, John, 51
Littleton v. Prange (1999), 126
Longtime Companion (movie), 173
Lorde, Audre, 50
L Word, The (television series), 184

M

MacFarlane, Seth, 183
Machismo, 84
Making of Gay Sensibility, The (Bronski),
 6
Male-to-Female (MTF), 98
Mallon, Denee, 123
Manchurian Candidate, The (movie), 32
Marcus Welby, M.D., 55
Marriage equality, 192–194
Martin, Del, 41
Martínez-Patiño, Maria José, 111
Matlovich, Leonard, 56
Mattachine Society, 27, 136
Matthew Shepard and James Byrd Jr. Hate
 Crimes Prevention Act of 2009,
 128, 191
May, Nancy, 53
Mayne, Xavier, 135
McCarthy, Joseph, 33–35, 177
Meagher, John F.W., 20
Men who have sex with men (MSM), 78
Mestizaje, 157
Midnight Cowboy (movie), 171
Military Code of Justice, 27
Milk (movie), 175
Milk, Harvey, 52, 58–59, 68
Misogyny, 108
Mock, Janet, 161
Modern Family (television), 184
Moll, Albert, 8
Monozygotic twins, 20
Moral Majority, 59, 77
Morocco (movie), 165
Mosaic genetics, 117

Moscone, George, 58
Motion Picture Producers and Distribu-
 tors of America (MPPDA), 166
Motion Picture Production Code
 (MPPC), 166
Movies,
 censorship era of, 166–167
 gays and lesbians in early fims, 164–166
 LBBT characters in the 70s, 80s and
  90s, 171
 LGBT characters in, 163–176
 pansies and mannish women, 167–168
M.T. v. J.T. (1976), 126
*Mutual Film Corporation v. Industrial
 Commission of Ohio* (1915), 166
*My Child is Transgender: 10 Tips for Parents
 of Adult Trans Children* (Kailey),
 159
My Life (Ellis), 9
My Own Private Idaho (movie), 174
Myra Breckinridge (Vidal), 139

N

National Institute of Mental Health
 (NIMH), 22
National Institutes of Health (NIH), 22
National Organization for Women
 (NOW), 47
Neutrois, 100
New Normal, The (drama), 184
New York City, 27
Nickelodeon, 164
Night of the Iguana, The (Williams), 140
North American Conference of Homo-
 phile Organizations (NACHO),
 53

O

Obergefell v. Hodges (2015), 2, 125, 126,
 189, 193
Odd Couple, The (television), 184
Odd Girl Out (Bannon), 147
*O'Donnabhain v. Commissioner of Internal
 Revenue* (2010), 96

Oedipus Complex, 17
Old Maid Having Her Picture Taken (movie), 165
One, Inc. v. Olesen (1958), 19
One Life to Live (television), 185
Oosterhuis, Harry, 5
Open End, 186
Opposite Sex Is Neither, The (Bornstein), 159

P

Pansy Craze, 167
Paragraph 175, 12
Parker, Annise, 124
Parker, William, 35
Patient Protection and Affordable Care Act, 65
Patterns of Sexual Behavior (Ford and Beach), 22
Pearson, Drew, 37, 56
Pelosi, Nancy, 24
Peña, Gilbert, 124
Permanent Subcommittee on Investigations (PSI), 177
Phalloplasty, 114
Philadelphia (movie), 173
Phil Donahue Show, 186
Pickford, Mary, 167
Picture of Dorian Gray, The (Wilde), 12
Plath, Bill, 52
Playing It Straight (reality program), 188
Poems of Emily Dickinson, The (Dickinson), 145
Polycystic ovary syndrome, 120
Posttraumatic stress disorder (PTSD), 82
Prime-Stevenson, Edward, 135–136
Princess Ali (movie), 164
Prohibition, 167
Project Runway, 188
Proposition 8, 189
Psychiatrists, military during WWII, 28
Psychoanalysis, 17
Psychoanalytic Theory of Male Homosexuality, The (Lewes), 18

Psycho (movie), 32
Psychopathia Sexualis (Krafft-Ebing), 7

Q

Queen Christina (movie), 165
Queer, 109
Queer and Pleasant Danger, A (Bornstein), 158
Queer as Folk (television series), 184
Queer Eye For a Straight Guy (reality program), 188
Queer movement, 195–196
Queer Nation, 195
Queer theory, 196
Questioning, 109
Quillan v. Walcott (1978), 127

R

Radke v. Miscellaneous Drivers & Helpers (2012), 126
Rado, Sandor, 23
Reagan, Nancy, 69
Reagan, Ronald, 56, 59, 68, 69
Real World, The (reality show), 188
Rebel Without a Cause (movie), 32
Rechy, John, 155
Redefining Realness: My Path to Womanhood, Identity, Love, and So Much More (Mock), 161
Red Scare, 33
Reitz, Jennifer Diane, 114
Rejected, The (documentary), 179
Reparative therapy, 23
Riddle, Debbie, 124
Ripley, Tom, 148
Robertson, Pat, 59
Rockefeller, Abby, 47
Rocky Horror Picture Show, The (movie), 172
Rodwell, Craig, 50
Rofes, Eric, 87
Rope (movie), 169
Rosenberg, Julius and Ethel, 33
Rosie O'Donnell Show, 187

RuPaul Show, 187
Rushes (Rechy), 155
Ryan White CARE Act (RWCA), 69
Ryan White HIV/AIDS Treatment Modernization Act, 71

S

Sagarin, Edward, 38
Sally Jessy Raphael (talk show), 186
Sam, Michael, 49
San Francisco, California, 27
Sanchez, Diego, 96
Sandow (movie), 164
Sappho and Socrates (Hirschfeld), 12
Saroney, Gilbert, 165
Sarria, José, 52
"Save Our Children," 57
Scientific Humanitarian Committee, 12
Sergeant Matlovich vs. the U.S. Air Force (movie), 56
Sex and the Single Girl (Brown), 45
Sex environments,
  bathhouses, 75, 79–80
  internet, 81
  sex parties, 80–81
Sex identitiy, 93
Sexing the Body: Gender Politics and the Construction of Sexuality (Fausto-Sterling), 116
Sexology, 7
Sexual Behavior in the Human Female (Kinsey), 20
Sexual Behavior in the Human Male (Kinsey), 20
Sexual Inversion (Ellis), 9
Sexually transmitted infections (STIs), 74
Sexual orientation, 103
Sexual Orientation Disturbance (SOD), 24
Sexual Revolution, 45
Shamans, 5
Simpson, Amanda, 93
Simpsons, The (animated series), 182
Snowball sampling, 88

Society for Human Rights, 19, 38
Society for Individual Rights (SIR), 52
Socrates, 5
Sodomy laws, 36
"Song of Myself" (Whitman), 15, 135
Songs of Bilitis, The (Louÿs), 41
Sontag, Susan, 149
South Park (television), 183
Speakes, Larry, 68
St. Elsewhere (television), 180
Stalin, Josef, 33
Stanley v. Illinois (1972), 127
Star Spangled Rhythm, 169
Stein, Gertrude, 146
Stonewall riots, 53–54
Straight sexual orientation, 105
Strangers on a Train (Highsmith), 148, 170
Streetcar Named Desire, A (Williams), 137
Streitmatter, Rodger, 31
Stress theory, 195
Substance abuse of LGBT, 194
Suddenly Last Summer (Williams), 137
Survivor (reality show), 188
Survivor's guilt, 82
Susskind, David, 186

T

Talented Mr. Ripley, The (Highsmith), 148
Tales of the City (television series), 181
Tallmij, Billie, 29
Tavern Guild, 52
Taylor, William Desmond, 167
Television,
  animated series, 182–183
  comedies and dramas, 183–185
  Homosexuality issues on news programs, 177–179
  integration of homosexual characters, 179–181
  LGBT issues and characters, 177–188
  mainstreaming LGBT characters, 181–183
  talk shows and reality programs, 185–187

Testosterone Files, The My Hormonal and Social Transformation from Female to Male (Valerio), 160
These Three (movie), 170
Things As They Are, Q.E.D. (Stein), 146
This Day's Death (Rechy), 155
Three Essays on the Theory of Sexuality (Freud), 18
Three Lives (Stein), 146
Timmons, Stuart, 40
Tiny Alice (Albee), 141
Title VII, 122
Title IX, 122
Torch Song Trilogy (movie), 174
Tracheal shave, 119
Tracy, Spencer, 168
Trans-asterisk, 99
Transgender,
  insurance coverage, 123–124
  legal issues, 121–128
    access to public accommodations, 124–125
    employment protection, 121–122
    hate crimes, 128
    marriage equality, 125–126
    parental rights of, 126–127
  medical issues, 112–121
    aging, 120–121
    children and sex assignment of, 116
    gender dysmorphia, 112
    medical abuse of, 116
    standards of care, 114–115
    transitioning, 117–119
  social issues, 128–132
    etiquette with, 130–131
    living and working with transgender people, 129–130
    transitioning at work, 128–129
    transphobia in gay community, 131–132
  U.S. military and, 122
Transgender Day of Remembrance, 102
Transgender identity, 95
Transgender literary activism, 157–160
  Janet Mock, 161–162

Kate Bornstein, 158
Matt Kailey, 159
Max Wolf Valerio, 160
Transgender Nation, 112
Trans People of Color Coalition, 103
Transphobia, 106
Transsexual, 96
Transsexual Menace, 112
Transsexual.org., 114
Transvestite, 101
Troxel v. Granville (2000), 127
Turner Syndrome, 117
"Twinkie defense," 58
Two-Spirit, 101
Two spirited individuals, 5
Tylenol scare, 69

U

Ulrichs, Karl Heinrich, 10
Up In Arms (musical), 169

V

Valerio, Max Wolf, 160
Veterans Benevolent Association, 38
Vice Versa, 29–31
Victor/Victoria (movie), 172
Vidal, Gore, 138–139
Village People, 56
Voices of color: lesbian, gay and bisexual, 151–157
  Audre Lorde, 156
  Countee Cullen, 152
  Gloria Anzaldúa, 157
  James Baldwin, 154
  John Rechy, 155–156
  Langston Hughes, 152
  Paula Gunn Allen, 156

W

Wallace, Mike, 48
Weinberg, George, 55
Welker, Herman, 37
Well of Loneliness, The (Hall), 29, 31
We'wha, 102

White, Dan, 58
White gay and bisexual writers, 134–145
  Allen Ginsberg, 139–140
  Edward Albee, 140
  Edward Prime-Stevenson, 135–136
  Gore Vidal, 138–139
  Matt Crowley, 141-142
  Tennessee Williams, 137
  Walt Whitman, 134–135
White lesbian authors, 145–151
  Ann Bannon, 146–147
  Emily Dickinson, 145
  Gertrude Stein, 146
  Patricia Highsmith, 148–149
  Rita Mae Brown, 150–151
  Susan Sontag, 149–150
Whitman, Walt, 14, 134–135
Who's Afraid of Virginia Woolf? (Albee),
  141
Wilde, Oscar, 6, 12
Will and Grace (television), 184
William, Dan, 75
Wings (movie), 164
Woman of the Year (movie), 168

Women,
  advertisements with, 32
  depicted in movies, 32
  during the war years, 32
World Professional Association for Transgender Health (WPATH), 112
World War II,
  homosexual recruits, 27

Y

Ye Watchers and Ye Lonely Ones (Albee),
  140
Young and the Restless, The (television),
  185

Z

Zami: A New Spelling of My Name
  (Lorde), 156
Zamora, Pedro, 188
Zapata, Angie, 97
Zoo Story, The (Albee), 140